Can I Wear My Nose Ring to the Interview?

Can I Wear My Nose Ring to the Interview?

A Crash Course in Finding, Landing, and Keeping Your First Real Job

By Ellen Gordon Reeves

WORKMAN PUBLISHING • NEW YORK

Library of Congress Cataloging-in-Publication Data is available.

ISBN 978-0-7611-4145-7

Workman books are available at special discounts when purchased in bulk for premiums and sales promotions as well as for fund-raising or educational use. Special editions of book excerpts can also be created to specification. For details, contact the Special Sales Director at the address below or send an e-mail to specialmarkets@workman.com.

Workman Publishing Company, Inc.
225 Varick Street
New York, NY 10014-4381
www.workman.com

Printed in the United States of America
First printing March 2009

10 9 8 7 6 5 4 3

For my family and friends—and for everyone who asked the questions.

Contents

Acknowledgments

This book was Lindy Hess's idea and I want to thank her, the staff and students of the Columbia Publishing Course (formerly the Radcliffe Publishing Course) for their help and advice, Susan Caplan and Leslie Hendrickson in particular. Before she went on to become an agent, Jennifer Griffin signed up the book with the enthusiastic support of Peter Workman; she left me in the capable hands of Savannah Ashour and editor in chief Suzie Bolotin. The book couldn't have happened without Savannah's essential contributions on every level. Thanks to Katharine Cluverius who signed the book up at ICM and to Kate Lee who took over when Katharine left. Also at Workman, many thanks to David Matt and Janet Vicario for their expert design, Kristin Matthews and Oleg Lyubner for getting the word out, and everyone in sales and marketing for all of their hard work.

Many people read and edited chapters, including Sam Appleton, Michaela Daniel, Lori Goldstein, Jennifer Rappaport, Caroline Reeves, and Linda Saxl Minton. Emily Griffin, Sophie Rosenblum, and Bennett Singer took the time to read the entire manuscript and offered invaluable comments. Many friends provided advice, information, and anecdotes, including Asa Danes, Lisa Bernstein, Rose Bowen, Mih-Ho Cha, Simone Cooper, David Deschamps, Vicki Eastus, Melissa Ehlinger, Ted Janger, Marc Johnson, Lisa Gerson, Linda Heuman, Rona Leff, Michele Levin, Laura Meiselman, Andra Miletta, Maureen Miletta, Alice Naude, Thomas Neenan, Amy Remensnyder, Marika Rosen, Richard Rosen, Pam Rich, Stephen Saxl, Robert Schlesinger, Lizzie Seidlin-Bernstein, Bryan Simmons, Caroline Bliss Spencer, Lynn Turner Tennenbaum, Ann Vershbow, Ralph Vetters, Brenna Wilmott, Diane Wachtell, Peter Zachariah, and many others.

Nothing happens without family and I dedicate this to mine: Mom, Caroline, Jim Lee, Daniel, Andrew, Pamela, Jeffrey Goldberg, Talia, Elisheva, William, Edna Wharton, and the Ress/Reeves clan. Then there are family members who are no longer here, but I know they know: Dad, Annie and Joe, Rose, Ethel and Max, Jane, Bernie and Charlie, Grandma and Grandpa. Thanks to my other families and extended families: Billington, Cha, Gerson, Kaufman/Goldfine, Landes, Meiselman, Miletta, Mensch, Saxl, Silverman, Singer.

Nothing happens without community and I count myself lucky to have several: Harvard, Radcliffe, Buckingham Browne & Nichols (BB&N), The American School of Paris (ASP), Lincoln, The Lycée International de Saint Germain-en Laye, The New Press, Boston, Providence, Paris, NYC, and Martha's Vineyard.

Special thanks to Harriet Hoffheinz, my first and wisest career counselor at Radcliffe, and to Jim Billington, who is always there.

Introduction

This book isn't really about nose rings. Even the question itself—"Can I wear my nose ring to the interview?"—isn't really about nose rings. It's one I've been asked many times, by many job-seekers struggling with how to present themselves. My answer? Yes. If you wear one and intend to keep wearing it, don't take it out for the interview, get the job, and then wonder why you're never introduced to clients.

Of course, this book isn't just for job-seekers with nose rings, tongue studs, tattoos, blue hair, or pierced eyebrows. The nose ring is a metaphor for the complexities of the job hunt, which may involve more soul-searching than you imagine—and lots of questions about how to present yourself now that you're out in the real world. If the mere thought of looking for a job has your stomach in knots, you're not alone. I've dealt with enough college grads to know that the first job search can be a terrifying prospect.

As I write, a troubled economy makes that search appear even more terrifying than usual—but the key word here is *appear*. Here's what most new job hunters don't realize: An economic downturn will not destroy your chances of getting a job; indeed, it can actually offer opportunity, if you understand how to make the most of the situation. Entry-level jobs are often the least affected by recession. Why? You're relatively cheap, and you're probably willing to work hard to prove yourself. If you position yourself correctly, you'll also be perceived as highly adaptable and easily trainable. Yes, you'll need to be more innovative and assertive in your approach, and more patient and flexible—but stay optimistic and confident. The strategies I recommend are based on timeless principles.

When I began advising students at the Columbia Publishing Course on their résumés, I started collecting all the questions that came up. They weren't only about résumés; the concerns were all over the map. People wanted to know how to look for a job without wasting hours surfing the Web, what to wear to a job interview, and what they would be asked. They wanted to know what to put on a blank résumé page when they'd never had a job or even an internship in their lives. They wanted advice about how to look for a job if they had absolutely no idea what they wanted to do and then how to negotiate a job offer once they got one.

Over the years, the list of questions grew—and now they form the heart of this book.

When I graduated from college, I knew exactly what I wanted to do: teach, write, and edit. But I didn't have a clue how to turn those goals and interests into a job or career. While many of my friends became investment bankers, I got a part-time, minimum-wage job in a toy store called Henry Bear's Park. (Me: *I get 40 percent off all the toys!* My parents: *For this we sent you to Harvard?*) I wish I'd had this book, but I hadn't written it yet.

What I did have, it turns out, was a knack for helping people present themselves. I'd edit a résumé for a friend; then for a friend of a friend; then for colleagues wherever I worked. (One of the things my career path taught me is that if you follow your interests, a path will emerge.)

I have unearthed the inner résumés of a white rapper, a missionary from Mexico (*never use the word "crusade" on a résumé*), and a MacArthur "genius" grant winner. I have successfully advised people at all stages of their careers—CEOs, engineers, college professors, diplomats, investment bankers, lawyers, publishing professionals, and even an opera singer.

But there's nothing like your very first job search. I hope my years of experience can help make the process as easy as possible for you—who knows, maybe you'll even enjoy it.

What's the Big Deal?

Q. Can looking for a job really be all that complicated? Why do I need to read a whole book about it?

A. Looking for a job doesn't have to be complicated if you go about it the right way; that's why I wrote this book. I find that many people expend their job-hunting energies inefficiently. This book will help you find a job in the quickest, most efficient way, using resources right under your nose. It will help you figure out what you want to do and how to do it. Along the way you'll learn lifelong skills about presenting yourself on and off paper, and you'll create a personal and professional network that will serve you throughout your career.

Welcome to Job, Inc.

►►►►►►►►►►►►►►►►►►►►►►►►►►►►►►►►

SET YOURSELF UP FOR SUCCESS

Take a deep breath. Whether you've opened this book in optimism or despair, you can relax (a little); I'm going to tell you all the stuff nobody tells you about how people *really* get jobs—in any economy, boom or bust. I'm not talking about just any job, though. I'm talking about a good job, a job you like, a job that's right for you. It may take a little longer, but the results will be worth it.

First things first: Stop looking for a job. If you haven't started yet, good. I want you to stop looking for a job—and start looking for a person.

The right person will lead you to the right job.

In truth, you already have a job. As a job-hunter, you are now the official CEO (Chief Executive Officer) of your own company—a company I call Job, Inc. Think of yourself as a self-employed consultant, a one-person marketing and PR firm with a single thing to sell: YOU. You work for yourself now. You run a head-hunting firm with

DON'T LOOK FOR A JOB—LOOK FOR A PERSON

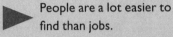 People are a lot easier to find than jobs.

Think about it. What is a job? Have you ever seen one walking down the street? Have you ever talked to one? Called one up on the phone? E-mailed one?

But you know where people are. They're everywhere. It's hard to escape them. They're in your classes, in your family, in your dorm, at the gym. They are at the supermarket, at the bar, waiting in line, sitting next to you on a bus or plane or train. People are everywhere (unless you live in a really sparsely populated area—and then you'll be more dependent on the telephone and Internet).

the most important client you could ever hope to place. You are a professional—a high-powered professional. Even if you don't feel like one, that's what you need to become—before you get your job. The more focused, directed, and organized you are as CEO, the quicker the process will be. And the more professional you appear, the more seriously you'll be taken as a job candidate.

You hold every position at Job, Inc. You are not just the CEO but also the CFO (Chief Financial Officer) and Human Resources director. You run the Marketing and Public Relations departments. This makes you indispensable. You might not be naturally adept at all the different positions you'll hold, and you don't have to be an expert in any of them. But I'll teach you how to master the basics.

The skills you'll pick up as CEO of Job, Inc. are highly transferable and will be valuable to any company, anywhere. You'll need to articulate a goal and vision; come up with a strategy and financial plan to achieve it; and implement that strategy, all the while publicizing and marketing Job, Inc.'s achievements.

But I'm an Artiste!

Q. I'm not interested in becoming a CEO-type—I'm looking for a job in graphic design! What's the point of acting like I'm going into business?

A. Don't get me wrong. I'm not suggesting you commit yourself to life in a suit. But all professions require a degree of organization and professionalism. These traits may be expressed differently across different industries, but when you're job-hunting, you must present your most professional self. Being professional means being well-dressed and well-groomed; being punctual, proactive, and efficient; presenting your experience and abilities articulately and with confidence; and making sure the documents that support your candidacy (your résumé, cover letter, and list of references) are impeccable.

The Organized Bird Gets the Worm

Even if you have never been organized in your life, you are going to have to get organized now. Undertaking a job search is a job in itself. Consider it training for the position you're going to get. In fact, if a prospective employer asks you about your organizational skills and you don't have much experience to draw from, you'll truthfully be able to say: **"Let me tell you how I organize myself. For this job search, for example, I set up a filing and tracking system. . . ."**

The first step? Set up a temporary office. It may be an entire room in a house or apartment, a desk at a library, some desk space in your bedroom, or even a chair in a dorm room.

While you don't need an executive suite, you do need good light. Don't suffer in the dark—you'll hurt your eyes and sink into depression. You'll need a good chair (or a bad chair plus a good pillow).

You'll need a filing system. Set up paper and electronic files for articles, contacts, and ideas related to each company that interests you and for each job you pursue. Every time you have an e-mail exchange about a particular job, print it out and file it. Every time you have a phone conversation about a job, make notes and date and file them.

Keep a small, professional-looking notebook with you at all times so that you can write down leads, contact information, and notes—you don't want to forget a valuable lead or lose a scrap of paper with an important number on it. Pulling out a notebook is much more professional than fumbling around for a napkin or matchbook—as long as that notebook isn't sparkly or covered in stickers. You'll need office supplies at the ready: pens

GETTING STARTED: SETTING UP JOB, INC.

▶ There are several things you need to do to find a job. Some are discussed in this chapter, others explained in the rest of the book.

1. Set up Job, Inc.'s offices, stat. Get organized—or you'll have to fire yourself. You'll be able to work much more productively once you've created a suitable work environment for your search.

2. Determine the timeline for your search. You'll be making a daily, weekly, and monthly plan.

3. Use the Rule of Three to determine how to organize your search and figure out whom to talk to. (You'll read about that on page 7.)

4. Create and refine your résumé and cover letter and prep your references. (See chapters 3, 4, and 5.)

5. Activate your network. (See chapter 2.)

and pencils, printer cartridges (if you have your own printer), thank-you notes, résumé paper, envelopes, stamps, a card file for all those cards you'll be collecting. I like big sorting baskets, Post-it Notes, small binder clips, staples and paper clips, clear plastic sleeves, and highlighters. Locate the nearest post office, along with a copy center with a fax and printer if you don't have access to these at home. If you're really strapped for space, buy inexpensive portable file totes— one for supplies and one for files—that you can carry with you to a library, park, or coffee shop.

At the end of each day at Job, Inc., take a few minutes to file or enter new information into a computer or electronic organizer. Every time someone mentions a person you should talk to, offers contact information, or suggests a book or article you should read, enter it in a place where you'll be able to find it again. Cut and paste information from e-mails—they have a way of disappearing when you most need them.

Clear some closet space to assess and organize your interview wardrobe; in chapter 6, Getting Through the Interview, we'll get into specifics about dress, but you should get a head start on evaluating the situation. You'll need two or three interview outfits, appropriately accessorized. You might need anything from new clothes to new shoelaces, stockings, an iron, or good hangers that don't leave odd protrusions in your clothes. (You don't want to wake up to a wardrobe crisis on the morning of an interview.)

All this takes time, but it's well worth the investment.

SET UP A PROFESSIONAL E-MAIL ADDRESS AND VOICE MAIL MESSAGE

▶ You might love the sassy moniker FoxyLady@ hotmail.com, but it is essential that you use a professional e-mail address during your job search. An employer won't want to hire dizzymissizzy@ gmail.com. Stick to first and last names, and avoid nicknames or private jokes. If you need to set up a new account for the job search, use a free Yahoo, Google, or Hotmail address. (Added bonus: You'll keep all your job-hunting e-mails together and won't be distracted by personal e-mail while you're online.)

If you don't already have one, you should also set up a cell phone account. An employer shouldn't have to leave messages with your mom to reach you. The greeting must be professional: "Hi, this is Sarah Smith. Please leave your name and number and I'll get back to you as soon as I can." No music, no noise or giggling in the background, no "Yo, what's up?"

Don't Just Hit "Send"

Here's how most people look for a job these days: They post their résumés on every website they can find, surf the Web looking for job postings, and e-mail their résumés to hundreds of anonymous addresses, barely expecting a response. I understand. You need a job. Why waste your time tracking down and calling a bunch of random people when you can send your résumé skyrocketing all over cyberspace at the touch of a button? You want to get the word out, and you hope the law of averages will take over. But I don't recommend blindly sending out resumes and cover letters. It might seem easier, but it's actually less efficient. And in the end, it's depressing. Weeks or months pass, and you end up saying yes to the first offer you get because the process seems so hopeless (never mind impersonal).

For better and more gratifying results, be strategic and intentional. Conduct a narrow and focused search, concentrating on quality over quantity. Decide what you would most like to do—at least for the moment.

You're going to avoid applying for jobs you don't really want or aren't qualified for. You will not waste your time (or an employer's time) on interviews for jobs you wouldn't take if they were offered to you. It happens more than you'd think. Job-hunters who apply for anything and every-thing call me in a quandary: "I got an offer, but I don't want it. I'm waiting to hear from a place where I really want to work. What do I do?"

You see?

There's nothing wrong with applying for jobs you find online—if you're truly interested—but even then you should be identifying and reaching out to someone inside the company so that your résumé gets looked at by the right person.

Getting Them Off Your Back and On Your Side

You are in charge of your job search. It's going to require a fair amount of self-discipline, which will be much easier to come by once you acknowledge that you are in the driver's seat. You may have friends and family on your back; part of managing the job-hunting process is learn-ing how to manage them. They mean well, but sometimes they show how much they care in really annoying ways.

If you're living with your parents or relatives to save money, you may find yourself besieged by a barrage of questions and comments: "Did you find anything yet? Did you call so-and-so? Maybe you should think about graduate school. You really should talk to my friend at the bank. . . . Haven't you watched enough television today? Your cousin Billy already has a job." But consider yourself lucky to have a roof over your head. (Oh, have you heard that line before?) Plus, you can't afford to blow up at the people clos-est to you; they're the ones you'll turn to for networking and outreach.

The trick is to get well-meaning friends and family members off your back and on your side. Instead of letting them get to you, engage them in your process. Get them to help you identify and connect to people throughout your search. If they can be objective enough, they may be help-ful in offering constructive criticism about your strengths and weaknesses and how you are presenting yourself. But don't let them boss you around. You are in charge.

Here's who's not in charge: some mythical employer you haven't even met yet. You do need to attempt to view things from the employer's perspective, but you also need to have a sense of your own worth. You should feel valuable, not vulnerable.

It's hard to feel in control when you're thinking, Look, I just need a job and I'll take anything. But I don't want you to end up dragging yourself out of bed to go to a job you hate. I want you to feel great about yourself, about the process, and about the outcome.

The Rule of Three

Maybe you're wondering how much time this process will take. It's partly up to you: How much time do you have? Often the answer will be determined by your budget: How long can you afford to be looking? Two weeks, a month, three months, six months, a year? In an economic downturn, when unemployment is high, there's more competition and job searches may take longer. Then more than ever, you'll need to be realistic about your goals. If in a particular industry, people are getting laid off left and right, don't expect to find your dream job in a month. You may need to expand the scope of your search or temporarily settle for a position you might not have considered in a better economy. Be pragmatic and flexible. No job has to last forever, and with the right attitude, you should be able to glean valuable skills and contacts from any position—skills and contacts that will prepare you for your *next* move (see chapter 9, The Art of Moving On). No matter what the economy looks like, though, the following strategies will get you going.

If you have a lot of lead time, you'll have more time to take advantage of your resources and target your search. But even if you need a job right away, you can still be strategic—you're just going to move faster.

> Three of anything shouldn't be daunting; it's finite, with a beginning, a middle, and an end.

Break down what might seem like an overwhelming project into small tasks and a daily, weekly, and monthly to-do list. What I call the Rule of Three works for many of the job-hunters I counsel. Three of anything shouldn't be daunting; it's finite, with a beginning, a middle, and an end. Here's how it works: Set a simple goal of making three job-related calls a day during a workweek—one in the morning, one at lunch, one at the end of the day. That's fifteen calls a week, or sixty in a month. If you also send three e-mails and three letters a day, at the end of the month you'll have contacted nearly two hundred people without realizing it.

When it comes to job-hunting, though, there's only so much you can do in a day. If you're not currently working, running Job, Inc. will be your number-one priority, but it can't be your sole focus or you'll go crazy. Balance is key.

Get Out of the House!

U nemployed job-hunters often retreat to their caves, eat a lot, watch a lot of reruns, and get depressed. "I have nothing to do and nowhere to go" is the common complaint. Well, to the rest of us, that actually sounds fantastic. An unstructured day with no meetings, no external demands, no deadlines? Bring it on! In my busy periods, I long to be bored. But the grass is always greener on the other side, so the jobless fantasize about being busy while the busy fantasize about doing nothing. You're not earning any or much money; it's not as if you're on vacation with money to burn. But still, there are many constructive and rewarding ways to fill your days.

Have a daily agenda. Set your alarm for the same time every day. Shower and get dressed—no lounging around in your sweats. Make appointments with yourself, scheduling downtime and fun time just the way you'd schedule a meeting. Play tourist in your own town. Do some community service. Explore your hobbies or find new ones (you never know where a good contact might lurk). Go to the post office, get the newspaper, visit the library. Go to the gym. Walk the dog, anyone's dog. Take a class. Do something, anything, so you have a routine. Make sure you get some exercise, get out of the house every day, and maintain your social life—you've got to see people and remain engaged in the world, even while you're in limbo.

Not only will all this help you survive what can be a difficult time, it will actually help you job-hunt. Picture this: An interviewer asks, "So what have you been doing with your time since you graduated?" Wouldn't you rather say, **"I've been temping in the industry, I have a part-time internship in the field, I'm taking a course, I started swimming every day at the Y, and I've finally had time to take advantage of all the great free events around town"** than "Nothing"? No one wants to hire a depressed, self-loathing slug, and if you're hanging around the house in your pajamas, you are less likely to convey an energetic, positive attitude.

Rise and Shine!

Q. I'm a night owl. Not setting an alarm and sleeping until noon are some of the things I really like about not having a job! I know that once I'm employed, I'll have to be up at dawn. Does it really matter what time I get up now?

A. There's nothing wrong with not wanting to set an alarm. But if you're serious about job-hunting, you should start changing your habits. First of all, it's often easier to catch people at their desks in the morning, before they plunge into their workdays. And changing your sleep cycle can take some time—you don't want to risk being late for work when you're new on the job. It all goes back to developing a professional mind-set and demeanor even *before* you think you need it.

IF YOU'RE STILL A STUDENT . . .

If you're currently in college or grad school, take advantage of your student status while you can.

The world loves a student. You are eligible for grants, internships, summer jobs, career advice from alumni, housing leads, and other perks (including travel, computer access, and other discounts). You may have access to free or reduced-fee career and psychological counseling; sports facilities; art, music, and dance classes; theater subscriptions and movie tickets; museum entrance; and perhaps even health care (annual checkups, inoculations, glasses). All these things might not sound so interesting now, but believe me, you'll miss them when you graduate and your student ID expires. So take advantage of all these perks while you can.

"But I Don't Know What I Want to Do . . ."

When people tell me they have no idea what they want to do, I don't believe them. With some probing, I can usually get them to articulate an interest in a field, if not a specific job.

DEAL-BREAKERS

▶ Some new job-hunters feel so much at the mercy of the process that they forget they are entitled to have deal-breakers. Determine yours. Are you willing, wanting or needing to relocate? What is your minimum salary requirement? (See page 172 for help figuring that out.) Are there things you will not or cannot do, for whatever reasons? Commute? Travel, work nights and weekends? It's important to understand what you won't or can't do so that you don't apply for jobs you don't actually want.

There must be things you like to do. What's stopping you from pursuing them? If you're unclear about how to translate your obsession with bee-keeping or Guitar Hero into the world of work, you just need to use your imagination and do a little research. Start talking to people, and you may find out about jobs you didn't even know existed! (Did you know companies hire video-game testers, for instance?)

Remember the old adage, "If you don't know where you're going, any road will take you there." Every journey begins with the first step, but I don't want you traveling down just any road. So start with three roads in which you're interested—it's the Rule of Three again. They could be general areas of interest *(sports, animals, food)*, professions *(sportscaster, vet, chef)*, places or companies *(ABC, the zoo, a hotel restaurant)*, people to talk to *(mom, dad, roommate)*, or fantasy jobs.

Let's say your first choice has to do with sports, but you have no idea what jobs you could have in the sports world. Choose three people to talk to: a coach you know; a friend or relative involved in sports in some way; and a sports reporter for the local newspaper (even if you've never met). You will contact each of these people and schedule an informational interview, either by phone or in person. You'll ask them a series of questions about their work, their paths, and the field in general. You'll also ask each of them to recommend someone else you might speak to. (Thus the cycle continues.)

Through these conversations, you'll learn more about options in the field. You'll use the Internet and/or library to build on what you learn. Eventually, you should be able to choose specific areas to pursue (fields or companies, such as *sports marketing* and *Nike*). You'll use your network to find people who work in these fields or companies.

But any time you find yourself at a loss as to how to proceed—you've hit a dead end or simply have no one else to call—you'll move on to the next of your three categories. You'll do this over and over, exhausting leads in each category and moving on.

This is just a strategy to get you moving, of course, but it's a strategy that works. Even if you find out that you're not interested in the three areas you set out to investigate, that's valuable information. Once you've jump-started the process, you can change your categories at any time.

If You're Really, Really Stumped . . .

IF NOTHING COMES TO MIND, TRY THIS EXERCISE. How do you spend your free time, or how would you spend your time if work or school were canceled for a week? List three things you'd do. The answers may offer a direction to pursue. Another method is to pretend there are no obstacles on the path to your dream job. Money is no object, and neither is location or your current skill set or experience. What do you want to do? Pick three things.

Beware: There is a difference between doing something as a job and doing something as a hobby. When I hear people say they'd like to own a country inn or run a restaurant, I always think, No, they don't. What they mean is: "I want to go stay in a country inn. I like to eat in restaurants." But if you think you are truly interested, talk to people in the business.

If you want to play tennis or swim or ski or fish or play an instrument or sculpt all day long and get paid for it—and you're not on the pro circuit or famous in your field yet—you could teach in the field or get involved with a magazine or organization dedicated to it. You'll soon discover whether you find it satisfying or frustrating.

Another way to focus is to identify what you like to do best and least. Write? Talk on the phone? Analyze data? Sell things? Interview people? What kind of day do you like? Busy? Slow? Varied? Are you a self-starter or do you prefer being managed? Do you enjoy managing others? What kind of environment do you like? Quiet? Bustling? Outdoors? Social? Would you prefer to work alone or on a team? From home, in an office, or on the road? Use your imagination. You must envision what you want to do and where you want to be—a job-hunter's visualization technique—in order to figure out how to move toward it.

Sometimes it's easier to come up with what you want to do and what you're good at by process of elimination: Focus on what you DON'T like to do and don't think you're good at. Back into your desires and talents this way if you have to.

For Big Dreamers

Q. I know exactly what I want to do: Be an astronaut. Seriously, it's what I've wanted my whole life! But I don't even like to fly and I have asthma, so it's just not going to happen. Now what?

A. Well, first you should figure out what appeals to you about being an astronaut. Do you really know what astronauts do? It's not just about floating weightlessly through a cabin in a big white suit, eating freeze-dried ice cream, and waving at the cameras as you plant the flag on a planet they'll name after you.

Are you interested in space exploration? NASA employs thousands of people who never go into orbit: scientists, photographers, communications and public relations people, and so on.

Is it the technology that appeals to you? Maybe you should look into engineering. If you can't stop thinking about the Big Bang theory, consider a degree in Astrophysics. The point is to figure out which concrete aspects of space travel really interest you, and to express those interests using skills and talents you already have or that you can realistically develop.

Do Your Research

Job, Inc. has a research department, and it's one of the best around. You guessed it: You're it. Once you've identified your top three industries or jobs or companies, begin to keep on top of any news about those fields and/or companies. Every news clip is a potential source of names (and great fodder for interview conversation). Subscribe to periodicals in your area of interest, read them online, or find a local library where you can access them.

Find out whether there are any conferences you can attend or industry associations you can join or visit.

Google everyone and everything related to your top three choices; print and file these notes as background for eventual interview preparation. Chance might favor the prepared mind, but employers favor the prepared candidate.

Explore the career center and alumni resources available at your college.

Read a local and national newspaper every day. You'll feel more connected to the work world, and you'll be better able to make conversation in an interview.

For specifics on the ins and outs of *pre-interview* research, see page 125.

Manage Your Time

I f you're having trouble self-motivating, use these tips from time-management guru Alan Lakein, whose book *How to Get Control of Your Time and Your Life* I read decades ago and still find relevant today.

1. Create running to-do lists prioritized into A, B, and C levels: A's are very important things that need to happen right away; B's are secondary—important but not crucial; and C's are nice for whenever you get around to them. Keep your A's, B's, and C's separate, and break large tasks into mini tasks. Don't write "Make résumé." Make a list of several discreet subtasks: "Buy résumé paper, spend twenty minutes brainstorming college activities, draft college activity entry, have Mom read and edit college entry."

2. Ask yourself what is really stopping you from doing a particular task. Assess, divide, and conquer. What steps will help you be ready to take this action? Do you really need to tear apart the apartment, or can you call someone else to get the number or information you need? Can someone talk you through this task or help you do it?

3. Try engaging in the task for five minutes. Use a timer. You can do anything for five minutes. If you get involved, you'll see that it might take less time than you actually thought. But if you can't get engaged, commit yourself for the five minutes and then walk away—you're not ready; your head and heart aren't in it. Try it again when you can engage.

4. If you really can't get started, try this: Sit alone in silence for a full five minutes. Usually doing nothing when there's so much to do makes people want to get up and do SOMETHING; then you can try those five minutes again.

Lakein had fewer technological distractions when he was writing his book, so I'll add a twenty-first-century warning: Watch out for black holes like endless channel surfing or obsessive online social networking. If you constantly find yourself getting sucked in, schedule time during which you are allowed to watch TV, play video games, or check your Facebook account.

Google Yourself

If you think you're the only one turning to the World Wide Web for information during this process, you are sorely mistaken. Discerning employers are doing their own research on you. Some companies even have employees whose sole job it is to research candidates online. Now how do you feel about those spring break photos you posted on MySpace?

Google yourself to make sure nothing negative comes up. If there's something unseemly attached to your name, try to get rid of it. Do you blog? Even if you post anonymously, an employer may be able to find you by plugging your e-mail address into a search engine. Password-protect your writing, unless it relates to the industry and it's something you want a prospective employer to see. If you belong to social networking sites, take down any inappropriate photos and set your privacy settings as securely as possible. Remember: It is illegal for employers to ask certain questions in an interview—but any information gathered online may be used to discriminate against you. Sounds unfair, but that's the reality.

If negative information about you (true or false) appears on a site you don't have control over—someone else's blog, for instance—do what you can to have it removed. Bloggers tend to be impervious to threats that they've engaged in libel, but some websites may be responsive. If you can't get rid of the information, be prepared to explain it (only if the employer brings it up, of course).

If you have a common name and are worried that you'll be held responsible for someone else's antics, don't worry—all is not lost. One job-hunter I know Googled herself and found a woman by the same name whose social networking profile was filled with unprofessional personal information; she knew it would be a deal-breaker for employers. My solution was to have her create a new page, using her middle name and the name of the professional course she had just completed. We decided that on her résumé, she would always include her middle name and list the course first under "Education." This way, she had a chance of controlling what would come up in a search. It's not an infallible technique, but it can work.

These are all warnings about virtual networking, but don't overlook its virtues. A discreet posting on Facebook ("I'm looking for someone to talk to about teaching jobs on the East Coast") or an active, focused involvement with a professional community like LinkedIn could be the ticket to scoring informational interviews from your virtual network.

"Looking for a Job Is the Pits"

I know that the job search can be an anxiety-provoking process. When you feel your fate is in the hands of some employer you haven't even met, it's easy to get depressed and immobilized, to doubt yourself and your experience, to sink into an existential crisis. It's scary not to know what lies ahead—unless you're sure it's something good.

Be open to the process. Embrace change and even rejection. The kind of job search I'm going to be leading you through can actually be a stimulating experience if you approach it with the right mind-set. You'll meet lots of different people, learn more about the industry or industries you're interested in (or find out what you're NOT interested in, which is just as important), and acquire professional experience along the way. You'll learn about yourself and the kind of job you actually want. And you'll do it all by using resources right under your nose.

If you're freaked out by your lack of focus, try to relax. These days, people change careers and direction at any age and stage, from their twenties through their eighties, reinventing themselves constantly. Some people will follow a track from the moment they're out of college until they retire, but that's just not right or in the cards for everyone. Especially when you're just starting out, it's fine to test out a variety of jobs. Follow your passions and be flexible—but have a plan. (A plan can be open-ended and subject to revision; it can be a plan for right now, and that's fine.)

Keep in mind that you're not hurting your career by not grabbing at the first thing that comes along. Not every job is worth taking just because it's available to you; not every opportunity is an opportunity if it's not right for you. Conversely, some jobs that might not appear desirable may be worth exploring if they fit into a long-term plan—or if the economy has tanked.

I'm going to be luring you away from impersonal job-search sites and out into the world. You're going to have to interact with real people, so it's especially important that you do everything you can to adopt a positive mind-set about your interim position at Job, Inc. You're embarking on an adventure. You don't know how it's going to turn out, but in actuality you have a lot of say in the outcome.

Another emotional obstacle new job-seekers often face is the feeling that they're somehow essentially unqualified. You are valuable, and so are your work and time. If you don't believe this, then you really need to stop looking for a job and start looking for some self-confidence. Being a novice is nothing to be ashamed of; everyone has to start somewhere.

A successful job hunt is the intersection of TWO searches: someone looking for the right job and someone looking for the right person to do a job. If you're having trouble seeing your value in this equation, remind yourself that you are not looking for a favor or handout. In fact, once you're in the right job, you'll be the one doing the employer a favor. Yes, you heard me. You're doing him a favor—even though he's paying you. Of course, you should never act that way in an interview or at the office, but still: The employer has a job to get done and a problem to solve, and if you're the right person for the job, you're solving it. In short, you're a hot commodity!

Value Your Inexperience

It is true that recent graduates and young job seekers without extensive track records in the work world pose a certain risk to employers—but, especially in a troubled economy, the benefits may outweigh the risks.

When you hear about widespread layoffs, keep in mind that many of the jobs cut are expensive, senior-level positions. At a difficult time when he's likely to be short-staffed, a smart employer may leap at the chance to hire an ambitious, reliable, and enthusiastic young person at an entry-level salary.

Even during flat-out hiring freezes, there are things you can do. Be proactive: Freelance, temporary, and part-time opportunities abound in bad economies. Be open-minded, too: You may have to consider options you wouldn't have thought about in better times, even as temporary measures—sharing housing, moving home, relocating for better opportunities.

Besides your youth, energy, and flexibility, you have another great asset: You're cheap. (But please don't tell your mother I said that . . .)

Act the Part

When I moved to France for a job, I knew I wouldn't understand everything, so I made an executive decision: I would say "yes" if asked a question to which I didn't know the answer. I wanted to be positive. When I was confused, I did not hesitate or panic; I replied with a resound-

DO YOU NEED FURTHER TRAINING?

▶ Do the jobs you're interested in require skills or credentials you wish you had? Worry not. Through the network you develop, you'll start getting them, or the equivalent—to the extent that it's possible—through mentorships, internships, or volunteer opportunities. I mean, if you can't sing, it's nice to have a fantasy about being a rock star, but it isn't going to happen. You can save it for karaoke night, start taking singing lessons, or decide to pursue a career on the business side of music.

List the top three skills you need to do your fantasy job. Which ones, if any, do you already have? What do you need to do to develop the others? Can you afford to take time to do an internship or volunteer to get some of the skills and experience you need? If you can't, figure out what you can do on nights and weekends: courses, seminars, volunteering.

ing "*OUI.*" True, I ended up with a savings account I didn't discover for years and had a few other minor mishaps, but having an answer made me feel better. A friend without a sense of direction has a "take a left" policy, chosen for her political leanings. Whenever she isn't sure whether to take a right or a left, she takes a left. Fifty percent of the time, she has to turn back, but she always feels in control and purposeful.

The lesson here is that no matter how unsure you feel, you're going to act confident and decisive. When someone asks you what kind of job you're looking for, you will not say, "I don't really know, do you have any ideas?" People can't help you if you don't give them any direction. But if you say, "I'm interested in fashion; do you know anyone in the field?" you'll be much more likely to get a name out of it. If they say no, prompt with more specifics: "I'm looking into sportswear marketing, children's clothes lines, and anything to do with accessories for women . . ." and see if that yields anything.

Keep in mind that once you have a job, you have it. You won't necessarily be able to stay up late, read a book just for fun, window-shop, run, or see a movie in the middle of the day.

So make the most of your hunting time—and your downtime, too.

Working Your Network

► ►

FINDING AND MAKING THE MOST OF YOUR CONNECTIONS

A man walks into a bar . . .

I know what you're thinking. "I need a job, and you're telling jokes?"

This is not a joke.

A man walks into a bar—an Irish bar, to be exact—and walks out with a job for his daughter.

This is a true story. I asked one hundred recent college grads to talk about how they had gotten their last jobs, internships, or job leads, and one of them said, "My dad was in an Irish bar and started talking to the bartender; his son worked in the field I wanted to get into. He told my dad to have me call him. I did, and I got a job."

You'll hear story after story like this if you start asking people. For good reason. You tell your parents you're thinking about exploring the real estate world in California and your mom says, "My hairdresser's son's mother-in-law works for an agency in L.A.; you should call her if you go out there." You might make a face and ignore her, but if you do, the joke is on you. The truth is, you need to get in touch with this woman—because this is how people get jobs, or at least learn about jobs. Certainly, many people do find work through traditional job-hunting channels like the "Help Wanted" or "Employment Opportunities" section of the newspaper, Internet job-hunting sites, company websites, recruitment sessions, job fairs, alumni career networks, or, for certain jobs and levels of experience, headhunters. These are all valid resources. But surveys estimate that 80 percent of all jobs fall into what's known as the "hidden job market"—an area in which jobs are not publicly advertised and are filled by word of mouth.

That hidden resource should be Job, Inc.'s focus. What you're going to be doing is finding people to talk to, people who can help get you inside a company or organization and steer you to these "hidden" jobs.

Looking for a Person

"**I** looked on the website of the company I'm interested in, and they don't have openings"—that's a line I've heard over and over in my job-counseling sessions.

The website may not list anything, but that doesn't worry me. Most websites do not have the real story about job openings. Ask someone inside a company what's really going on, and you'll be amazed at what you hear. Someone is pregnant and about to take maternity leave. Someone is about to get fired but doesn't know it. Someone is getting married and relocating. The company is being bought and reorganized. There is a posting but there are strong internal candidates for the job. A job is about to be posted but must first be advertised internally to conform to union or other regulations.

The possibilities are endless. So when you look at a corporate website and see few or no openings, don't write off a company you're interested in. Conversely, if you see an opening that looks good, apply for it—but realize that you must still try to connect with someone on the inside.

In our "six degrees of separation" world, tapping into a network is the most effective way to get a job. It will enable you to meet interesting people and to learn more about the industry or company to which you're applying.

You may make some friends in the process, and you may even meet someone who becomes a mentor or long-term professional resource. If you think you don't have a network, I'm going to show you how to create one.

What If They Hate Me?

Q. I hate failure and rejection. I don't want to call people and risk being rejected. I just want to curl up in a ball!

A. Nobody likes rejection, but I want you to learn to embrace it rather than fear it. If an employer rejects you, it's likely that her job wasn't the right one for you. You have been spared so you can move on to find the right situation.

Let's imagine the worst-case scenario. You call someone and he shouts, "WHAT? I can't believe you're calling to ask for my help. I'm busy, I don't even know you, and you're probably an idiot!" Okay, that would not feel good . . . Frankly, though, I've never, ever heard of such an outcome.

A more reasonable scenario: You e-mail someone to ask for advice and you get no answer. You try one more time, and then you forget about it. How terrible was that? Of course, you might start sabotaging yourself by inventing some special rejection scenario—your lack of experience sent the recipient into hysterics, and *that's* why you didn't get a response. Unlikely.

Don't waste your time trying to read other people's minds. If you don't hear back from someone after trying twice, move on! I once didn't hear back from someone I was sure would be willing to speak with a young job-hunter, and decided she had forgotten me or deemed my request inappropriate. Some months later, she apologized profusely: She had been grappling with a death in the family and a major health problem of her own. There was good reason for her silence.

"Where's My Network?"

Your network consists of a wide range of people, some of whom you know well, and others who are quite distant but with whom you have something in common: an interest, an experience, or a mutual acquaintance. Most of these people are right under your nose; you just haven't thought of them in relation to your search.

It's important to find people who work in or around the industry in which you're looking; but you never know who might be in someone else's network, so don't make hasty assumptions and dismiss people out of hand.

As you read through the following lists of likely networking sources, write down every name you can think of in each category, then begin to gather contact information.

Your network includes people from:

▶ **Places you've lived.** Your hometown and anywhere you've lived in the past, no matter how seemingly disconnected from where you live now. Even if you are looking within a specific geographical area, people outside of it may be able to unearth contacts where you are or want to be.

▶ **Schools you've attended.** Elementary, middle, and high school; college and grad school. Schools may have alumni networks, career advisory networks, class notes, career panels, and online resources. But also think about students and faculty you knew there; might any of them have connections in the field to which you're aspiring?

▶ **Workplaces.** Anywhere you, your friends, or members of your family have worked, interned, or volunteered. Think not only about former coworkers you knew well; it's never too late to reach out to someone you missed an opportunity to connect with—"I used to work in the PR Department and I'm interested in pursuing a career in your area; would you have time for a brief informational interview?" Same goes for people hired after your departure.

▶ **Religious and other community groups.** Places of worship are filled with people of all ages and professions.

▶ **Family members and friends.** Don't overlook your immediate and extended family and friends; sometimes the people right under your nose are the easiest to forget because you see them all the time. Include them in the process.

▶ **Activities and hobbies.** Think about the way you spend your time and the various activities, organized or more casual, with which you've been involved: the gym, yoga, sports, book clubs, theater, singing groups, and so on. Even if your career interests have little to do with your hobbies, you might find a connection there. (Perhaps the leader of your church choir is a lawyer in a firm you're applying to. . . .)

▶ **Your daily path.** Be open to talking to people you see regularly in everyday life—at the coffee shop, waiting for the bus or train, at your hair salon, dentist, or doctor's office. You have no idea who knows whom. Mention that you're looking for a job in such-and-such industry, and you'll be surprised at how often someone will say, "Oh, I have a friend who . . ."

▶ **Random acquaintances.** All of this also goes for strangers with whom you might strike up a conversation. The passenger sitting next to you on a bus, plane, or train; people waiting in line at the supermarket, the movie theater, or a restaurant.

▶ **Your references.** People often overlook their own list of references as a valuable networking resource. When you're asking for a reference (see chapter 5), why not add a line that says, "If you know of anyone I should speak with in this field, please let me know." Unless you ask explicitly, your recommender will remain in passive mode, waiting to be contacted by a prospective employer—not thinking about activating her network on your behalf. But if you ask, you may hear, "Oh, yes, my son-in-law is an engineer in Oklahoma; please feel free to give him a call."

Outside your existing connections, you can work to create a professional net-work by taking classes and seminars, joining professional organizations, and reading professional journals, websites, and periodicals related to your field of interest. Go to career fairs and networking events. You'll meet people inter-ested in what you're interested in, and you never know what might happen.

"But I Have No Connections, I Swear!"

O kay. You're a young job-hunter with few professional connections. How are you going to find that hidden job market? It's hidden, right? Well, it's visible to people on the inside—so that's where you need to be.

If possible—if it makes sense given your finances, schedule, and time frame—take internships, temp, or volunteer *while you're looking for a job.* You might be thinking, Yeah, right, I did that in college, or I don't have time for that—I need a job! But there's no substitute for being on-site in an industry. You have access to bulletin boards with all kinds of job postings, company newsletters, Listservs and annual reports, and industry periodi-cals. If you don't know a lot about the industry, you'll get the chance to identify what types of jobs you might like and to learn industry language and practices.

THE RULE OF THREE IN ACTION

▶ As you start your search, you should be trying to meet as many people as you can without going on overload. Organize the contacts you already have by creating a master document with contact info for each person, leaving room for notes: when you called, when you have an appointment, background info, questions you have, and so forth. Once you've done this, use the Rule of Three. Assign three names to each day of the week: one in the morning, one before or after lunch, one at the end of the day. (You get the weekend off, just like everyone else.) Transfer the names into your appointment book or electronic calendar—it doesn't matter what you use as long as you're diligent.

Reach out and offer to meet people at or near their workplace for breakfast, lunch, during the day, or after work—whatever works best for them. See if they'll schedule a phone call if they can't meet in person.

Keep in mind: You are simply looking for people to talk to in order to find out more about a field and about what kinds of positions might suit you. You are not looking for jobs. This should help take the pressure off. Because you'll be asking for new names from each person you talk with, you should always have another three to contact. But don't overdo it—don't meet with more than three people per day. You can't process that much information or do the right follow-up.

But most importantly, whether or not you're able to identify concrete job openings through your experience "on the inside," you'll get to meet people in the field.

Recognize that building your network is your most important task at this time. Make an effort to meet people. Invite people for lunch or coffee (yes, you should pay) for formal or informal informational interviews. If possible, spend a lunch hour in the company library (if there is one); ask if you can borrow and read office copies of industry newsletters and other periodicals; schedule an informational interview with HR; talk to everyone you can about what they do.

Most importantly: Work hard. Prove yourself, make yourself indispensable, and maybe you'll get hired when an opening appears. You'll certainly meet people who can steer you to other people and openings in the industry.

Set Up Informational Interviews

AN INFORMATIONAL INTERVIEW IS A MEETING, whether by phone or in person, at a company or in a department where there is no particular opening at stake. Not everyone will grant informational interviews, but try: They can be invaluable sources of insider data about an industry or company.

> An informational interview is a wonderful way to make a contact. Impress the person you meet, and you may find that she knows of other openings within the company—or maybe she's so taken with you that she tries to hire you.

They're also wonderful ways to make a contact. Impress the person you meet, and you may find that she knows of other openings within the company—or maybe she's so taken with you that she tries to hire you. Or perhaps she'll think of you when an opening does occur. She might even help you get a job elsewhere.

Think of the informational interview as a social encounter; it should be interesting, if not actually fun. For details on what you may be asked and how to prepare for this kind of interview, see pages 119–120.

Be an Intern

ONE OF THE BEST WAYS TO GET A JOB is by interning (often but not always for free) at a company or organization. Competent interns are among the first approached when entry-level positions open up; someone tried and true who knows how the office works and can hit the ground running is enormously valuable.

Internships range from formal to informal; if you are still in school, you can often even get course credit for the experience. Being an intern can give you a sense of the industry and company, allow you to meet people within the company or organization, and teach you concrete skills. Some internships actually rotate you through a company's departments to give you a sense of how the place works and where you would best be suited.

Don't be a slave to geography. If, for example, you want to work in a gallery in San Francisco but you don't live there yet, get whatever experience you can in your hometown. Be creative. Volunteer to be a docent at a local museum; get to know the museum staff and artists. After you've proven yourself, ask them if they know people you might get in touch with in San Francisco.

You should approach an internship the way you'd approach a paid job; see chapter 8, You've Got the Job, for tips on making the most of the experience.

How Old Is Too Old?

Q. I'm 22. Am I too old to intern? (I interned every summer in college.)

A. You're never too old to be an intern. Take it from me: At age 30, I took a summer internship at a new publishing company for $15 a day. I wasn't looking for a job; I was a teacher and I had the summer off. The internship turned into a fifteen-year book publishing career.

Volunteer

Most workplaces have many untackled projects waiting in the wings—there is almost always work for the willing. If you can't afford to take an internship (some require a full-time, semester-long commitment), see if you can volunteer, even in a place that doesn't usually take volunteers. But don't assume you have to work for free; first ask if the company hires freelancers or temps.

If you can't find a contact through your network, cold-call; you'll likely get a receptionist. Explain that you're hoping to find out the name of the person with whom you should speak regarding employment or internships. Once you reach the appropriate person, explain how you know about the organization and that you are looking for opportunities there.

You may be able to come in before or after work, on a weekend, or during a vacation. Though you might not have the full benefit of a formal internship, you'll still gain exposure to the field, you'll still be able to list the company on your résumé, and you'll still meet people and discover which aspects of the business look most interesting to you.

Shadow Someone

Another option is to find someone who will let you shadow him or her for a short period of time, from a half day to a day or more, like a college externship. This is basically an extended informational interview in which you speak with someone and then spend time observing him at work, in meetings, on the phone. Obviously all confidential content of the day must remain so, but shadowing someone allows you to get a feel for what a job is really like and to see the inside of an organization.

It is also something to mention in a cover letter and interview; even that half day can show your initiative and dedication to breaking into the field. A company name may ring bells you might otherwise not be ringing.

A word of caution: Don't try to pass off the experience as more than it is—be up front when describing it on a résumé, in a cover letter, or in an interview: "I had the opportunity to spend the day in court with Judge Marshall, a family friend, and he suggested I . . ." Or: "I met Mr. Singer through my choir, and was able to observe him in his classroom during my spring breaks; this experience confirmed my interest in teaching."

Networking Etiquette

The thing to remember when networking—or applying for a job, for that matter—is to make everything as easy as possible for the people who are helping you. *People help people who help them help them.* Try saying that three times fast. If someone is doing you a favor, you need to facilitate things for him as much as you can. Be easily reachable, make your intentions clear, and follow up. Don't hound or pester people, and don't abuse their good will. Above all, be respectful of people's time.

Read these nine simple networking rules, and you'll be well on your way.

1. Communicate Your Focus

WHEN YOU CONTACT PEOPLE FOR HELP, be specific about what you want.

You'll alienate a busy person who might be willing to help if you say, "I'm looking for a job and I'll do anything and am willing to live anywhere." He'll look at your e-mail or letter and have no idea where to start and no time to figure it out. Give him a lead. Identify a city, an area, an organization, even a job, and he'll be much more helpful. By the same token, you don't want to get too specific or limiting in your range. If you're on the phone with someone who says he doesn't know anyone practicing entertainment law in Nashville, have some alternate options at the tip of your tongue; maybe that person could introduce you to someone in a legal-justice nonprofit, for instance; or perhaps he'd be willing to review or pass on your résumé to someone in his contracts department.

GET A BUSINESS CARD

▶ Though it may seem premature, you should make yourself a business card to carry around with you during your job hunt. It's professional, and it makes it easier to take advantage of chance encounters with potential employers or connections. Rather than scrawling your contact information on scraps of paper, you just pull out your card.

You can easily get cards made at copy service centers, or you can print them yourself. You'll need card stock, templates, and access to a laser printer. Your cards must be professional, not cute. If you have one specific area you're looking into or have experience or training in, you might put that on the card—real estate, graphic design—but barring that, your name, address, and contact information are all you need. You'll also want a case to protect the cards.

2. Polish Your Elevator Pitch

SELF-PRESENTATION, ON AND OFF PAPER, IS A VITAL SKILL, but one that is rarely taught. Throughout your life, as you apply for jobs, fellowships, grants—or even as you formulate a brief introduction for yourself in a group meeting or answer the basic "What do you do?" question at a party— you will need to clearly and succinctly describe what you're involved in. Why don't we teach people to do this at an early age? Think about how much time we spend teaching children to identify animal sounds. "What does the cow do?" "What does the lion say?" If you live on a farm or in the Serengeti, I can see this being useful information. Indeed, the ability to moo and roar might serve you well now if you aim to work on a ranch or lead safaris. But at this point in your life, you'll be better off learning how to craft a brief but focused pitch about yourself and what you're looking for.

When you're job-hunting, you've got to have that spiel at the ready for a variety of media: by phone, in person, and via e-mail or snail mail. It's also known as the "elevator pitch" or "elevator speech"—what you'd say if you had only a minute in an elevator with someone in a hiring capacity.

Craft and rehearse your elevator pitch. You need to be able to confidently summarize who you are, what your background is, and what type of job you're looking for. Don't be afraid to be direct—communicate that focus: "Mr. Foster, my name is Florence Nightingale. I met your mother while volunteering at the hospital last week and she recommended I speak with you when I told her that I'm interested in getting into advertising. I just graduated from State U with a degree in communications, and I interned at *Adweek* last summer. I'm interested in new media and how companies like yours are using the Internet to reach young audiences. I'd like to ask you about this, and to talk to you about your job, your field, your path, and any job leads or career development opportunities you may know about."

The tough thing about elevator pitches is that, for many people, unemployment and job-hunting create or heighten insecurity. When someone asks you what you're doing, you can't flail about and mutter, "Well, nothing much . . . yet" or "When I'm not surfing Internet job sites, I'm catching up on lots of old TV shows." You've got to curb those self-defeating instincts and show off your best self, even if it's a theoretical self at this point. Remember times when you've been dynamic, efficient, and motivated, and focus on those as you work out your elevator pitch.

Quaking in My Boots!

Q. I'm shy. Talking to people I don't know is scary! Do I really have to do this?

A. Many people get anxious at the prospect of talking to someone they don't know, especially if they feel they're asking for a favor. But objectively, talking is not like bungee jumping or messing with large spiders. (Okay, those are things *I* wouldn't want to do.) No harm can come of networking. There's nothing to lose. If someone turns you down, he wasn't the right lead for you. You simply have to get over it. The more people you talk to, the easier it will get. No one is asking you to turn yourself into a social butterfly or accost people at bars or parties, but if you are going to launch an extended job search, you've got to talk to people. If you have a genuine interest in a company or industry, this kind of exploration should be a good experience. You'll meet interesting people and learn a lot along the way. If you're too paralyzed by shyness to get any enjoyment out of the networking process, I have two words for you: FAKE IT.

3. Be Prepared

IF YOU MEET SOMEONE THROUGH A CHANCE ENCOUNTER and find out that she works in a place or field you're interested in, be prepared to break out the pitch. Read her cues to determine how involved she wants to get. If

EASING YOUR WAY INTO NETWORKING

► If you're intimidated by the networking process and don't know where to begin, make it easy on yourself by starting small. Let's say you recently graduated or are about to graduate from college. Use the Rule of Three and start with three people closest to you: parents (if they won't hassle you), a roommate (she may have parents, relatives, neighbors, or family friends you should talk with), and other relatives (grandparents, aunts, uncles, cousins, siblings). Next, you'll move one layer out: a professor, an academic advisor, a boss at a summer job or somewhere you've volunteered. Once you see how easy it is, you'll be emboldened to broaden the scope of your networking efforts.

The good news? The more people you talk to, the more you'll have to say on your next call. Your questions will become more informed and specific. Without name-dropping or being indiscreet, you can use each informational interview to inform the next: "Last week I was talking with a dean at the Fashion Institute who's a friend of my aunt's, and he suggested I look into the Bloomingdale's training program. Do you know anything about it or perhaps know someone who does?"

she wants to keep talking, fine; if not, thank her and move on. If she asks to see a copy of your résumé, make sure you get her business card or contact information and determine her preferred mode of communication so you can follow up. Ask her directly: "Is a call or e-mail better for you?" Note her preference on her card right away, but not in front of her. Have your business card on hand to give to her, too (see box, page 27).

4. Foolproof Your E-mails

IF YOU'RE COMMUNICATING WITH A POTENTIAL HELPER BY E-MAIL— especially someone older who may not be as computer-savvy as you are—make everything as simple as possible.

Don't give busy people the opportunity to forward messages you don't intend for the recipient. If you attached your résumé to an e-mail that said

"Can you send my résumé to that cute guy I met at your party last night? His dad runs a contracting company I want to work for," wouldn't you die if I sent it on without editing it? Don't make me edit it. The same goes for your cover letter. It should be addressed and tailored to its intended recipient (see chapter 4 for more on this subject).

5. Don't Go Too High Up the Food Chain

CHOOSE THE RIGHT PEOPLE, AT THE RIGHT LEVEL. If one of your connections knows the head of a company you're interested in, sure, meet her if the opportunity is offered. But be aware that, depending on the size of the organization, the head may not be in touch with some of the more day-to-day aspects of the organization. If you get the sense that this might be the case, ask if the head of the company would be willing to put you in touch with someone in a specific department or with an HR person. Do enough research to know which people you should be talking to.

6. Follow Up

FOLLOW UP ON EVERY LEAD, and don't ask for leads if you're not going to pursue them. I don't like going out on a limb for people (especially people I don't know that well), asking others for favors and then finding out that the job-seeker never contacted the people I alerted on her behalf. If you don't want to talk to a person suggested by someone in your network or think you won't really follow up, just say so: **"I know I won't have time to contact everyone; of all the people you mentioned, the names, phone numbers, and e-mail addresses of X, Y, and Z would be most useful."** Also, make sure you know if *you* are supposed to contact a lead directly or if your intermediary is planning on doing it herself. Ask what the intermediary prefers; a heads-up call or e-mail from the intermediary to the lead is often best.

7. Don't Pretend You're Applying for Only One Job

WHEN YOU'RE LOOKING FOR A JOB, there's no sense in pretending you're applying to only one company; everyone knows you get jobs by talking to lots and lots of people and applying for more than one position. Monogamy is not expected until you accept an offer. If someone asks with whom you've been speaking, where else you've applied, or if you've already

WORKING IT: A MODEL OF EFFECTIVE NETWORKING

▶ Jonathan was moving from Boston to New York City and looking for a communications job. He e-mailed me his résumé; the first line of his cover letter read, "Dottie E. recommended I contact you." "Dottie" was the magic word—she was a colleague I had adored working with over the years, and anyone she referred to me got red-carpet treatment.

I invited him to my office, spoke with him about his career history, and sent him off with a list of the organizations I worked with to see if any of them sounded interesting. He did some research and identified three; I forwarded his résumé to people I knew there. While I knew he was looking for a job, I made my request as general as possible. I didn't ask my contacts to find him a job, I asked them if they knew anyone who would be willing to talk to him. Within twenty-four hours I heard from all three parties, all willing to provide a contact name or grant an informational interview.

As he pursued other job postings, Jonathan would contact me to find out if I knew anyone where he was interviewing. I was able to pass along more names: the sister of a colleague who worked at one organization, a college friend who knew someone who knew someone. All of this was done via e-mail, and within a month he had several interviews lined up.

What Jonathan did right: He gathered names before he moved to New York; he reached out to the names he was given with a résumé and an opening line that explained his personal connections; he focused his search; he followed up on the leads he was given; and he kept his contacts in the loop.

It helped that Jonathan was personable and ambitious, but you don't need to be Mr. Popular to network. The truth is, most people remember how they got their jobs, and they're willing to help a young candidate find his footing.

What's more, when Jonathan landed his job and proved himself as a valuable employee, it reflected well on all of us who had passed his name along.

had other interviews, be honest. He's only trying to help, and he may know people where you're interviewing; he may also be trying to get a sense of how much of a go-getter you are, in which case it won't hurt to show that you've been making the rounds.

8. Be Appreciative

BE SURE TO THANK THE PEOPLE WHO HELP YOU. Show them you're making progress and following up on their leads by keeping them in the loop. Acknowledge the efforts they make on your behalf; don't take their help for granted. When you get an interview or job—or even a rejection— through someone, let her know with a quick e-mail. **"Dear Ms. Lerner: I just found out that I didn't get the analyst job you told me about at Number-Crunch Company, but I wanted you to know how much I appreciated the introduction to the HR person there."** If you don't use a contact or take a job offered, be sure to let the intermediary know. This way she won't feel let down.

> Thank the people who help you . . . and once you get your job, be sure to share the wealth.

Toward the end of the process, think about whether you should send a handwritten thank-you note in addition to an e-mail, or, depending on how much trouble the person went to, a small gift like flowers, cookies, or a bottle of wine.

9. Return the Favor

WHAT GOES AROUND COMES AROUND. Once you get your job, share the wealth. Volunteer to be an alumni advisor for your high school or college or graduate school, or to talk with interns at your new company. Help friends and family in the situation you have recently been in.

"But How Do I Ask?"

How you approach people in your network depends on your relationship with them. Obviously, you can just call close friends and family and brainstorm possible leads on the phone. With more distant connections, though, you may want to reach out via post or e-mail.

If you're stuck on graceful ways to ask for help, try some variation of the following scripts.

A Casual Networking Query

To: sue123@cablestar.net

Cc:

Subject: A favor . . .

Dear Aunt Susan:

How are you? I hope you and Uncle Bob are well. I had such a great time hanging out with you guys last Thanksgiving; please send him my love.

So, as you know, I'm graduating in June. And I've decided (I think!) to explore a career in the fashion industry. I know most of your experience was in marketing, but I wondered if you might know anyone I could speak to about the fashion world. I'm planning to move to Los Angeles (can you believe it?), but I'm happy to speak with anyone working in fashion, anywhere!

I'm attaching a copy of my résumé so you can pass it along or talk me up. If you want to chat by phone, give me a call anytime. I would so appreciate any help you could give me—names, numbers, e-mail addresses, or just a little bit of wisdom!

Thanks and love,
Ann

A Formal Networking Query

Professor Ivan Cooper
The Professional Fashion Institute
100 Broadway
New York, NY 10001

August 14, 2008

Dear Professor Cooper:

My aunt Susan Reed recommended that I get in touch; she speaks very highly of you and still talks about the time the two of you spent as apprentices in Christian Lacroix's studio.

I'm graduating in June from Simon's College with a degree in American History. I've always been interested in clothing and fashion icons—but I decided to pursue fashion professionally after having the opportunity to write my thesis on design history. (I also worked at a local boutique last semester.) If your schedule allows, I would be so grateful if you would take the time to speak to me by phone or in person about your career path and any suggestions you might have for someone starting out.

Thanks in advance for your time. I'm attaching a copy of my résumé, and I look forward to hearing from you at your convenience.

Sincerely,

Ann Marshall

Ann Marshall

"But I'm Scared of Networking!"

I magine that a student from your hometown called or e-mailed and said, "Hi, you don't know me, but I went to your high school. I met your mom and she said you might be willing to tell me about your experience at City College because I'm thinking of going there." How would you react? I would hope you'd be willing to spend a little time in an e-mail or on the phone answering his questions and telling him about your experience. Networking doesn't have to be any more complicated than that.

Many people are shy about networking—or shy in general. But there's no place for shyness in this game. Most people's professional lives involve dealing with other people to some degree, so think of networking as training for the years to come. And realize that people are usually willing to help, if they're approached in the right way: professionally, with plenty of leeway built in so it's easy for them to say no if they're unable to help you, for whatever reason. Don't take it personally if you get turned down sometimes; people are busy and overcommitted, and if someone knows that he's not likely to be much help to you, he would rather tell you that at the outset than waste your time.

People often feel that getting a job through a connection is somehow "cheating," getting a free ride, or taking the easy way out. It's good to work hard for your accomplishments. But successfully using your network is not the same as being handed a job. If someone does hand you a job, consider yourself lucky. Get over any feelings of guilt, fast—and get to work. If you really feel guilty, turn that guilt into action on behalf of others. Help other job-seekers you know; make yourself available to mentor newcomers. What you need to understand is that you'll be expected to work plenty hard once you're on the inside; getting a job is only half the battle. (More on how to keep that job in chapter 8.)

What's in It for Them?

Q. People are so busy. Why should they waste their time talking to me? I'm in no position to help *them*.

A. Is that how low an opinion you have of yourself? Might it not be interesting for someone to meet you and talk with you, to relive highlights of her career, and to share her insights and tips with someone truly receptive? People who don't enjoy doing this will say no to your request. Let them. If they don't want to talk to you, you don't want to talk to them. Move on.

Isn't It Slimy?

Q. I've always felt there was something slimy about networking. I don't want to have to fake friendship or connection in order to get a job. That seems wrong to me.

A. "Networking" is only unseemly if done in an aggressive way with no regard for etiquette or respect for people's time. I once had a small gathering at which a guest terrorized all my friends by aggressively hounding them for leads for her new business. She was intrusive, and they told me they felt imposed upon. Yes, parties are good places to meet people; but what she might have done was ask if she could contact them later on to ask for help and advice, not monopolize their time and interrogate them at a social event.

There's a time and a place for networking. You must respect boundaries—those between social and professional spaces, or even those between religion and commerce. (While I do think that religious groups and leaders may yield networking leads, I would not suggest approaching clergy after a service; that would be highly inappropriate.) Be respectful of the other person's time by making a phone call or in-person appointment during office hours.

Isn't It Using People?

Q. Isn't networking the same thing as using people?

A. Exactly how are you "using" them? Part of being a professional, in my opinion, is sharing information about one's chosen field. Not everyone adopts this mentality, but in my experience, many do.

Again, though, it all depends on your approach. If you couch your networking attempts in other guises, you *are* using someone. Be honest and forthright about the purpose for your call or e-mail. Once, a young intern who, shall we say, was not my favorite, simply refused to respect my boundaries and lack of interest. He would call periodically, pretending he just wanted to say hello. Eventually he would get around to the purpose of his call: Could I recommend him for this or that job, or did I know of any openings? His approach wasn't genuine or direct.

Approach people politely, respect the possibility that they may not be available, thank them adequately, and offer to return the favor when you can, and no one will feel used. Sucking up to someone you don't know or like because his father runs a company you'd like to work for *is* "using" someone. Don't do it. If you really want to talk with his father, just be direct: "I have a favor to ask. I'm interested in telecommunications and would love the chance to speak with your father or someone in his company. Would you be willing to make the introduction?"

It's Awkward!

Q. I'm afraid that getting a job through connections will create an uncomfortable situation.

A. Many people share this fear. "Everyone will know I didn't get the job on my own," they say.

First of all, how do you think those other people got their jobs? Anyway, it's all in how you handle it. Be up front, without flaunting your connections or volunteering too much information. Let's say your family runs the business. Don't pull rank or insider tricks if you want to be liked and respected. Just be professional. You don't need to advertise how you got your job, but there's no need to hide it—I'd like to think you wouldn't have been hired if you couldn't do the job. That's when the most uncomfortable situations arise: when someone who isn't really qualified for a position gets one through connections and then does a bad job. If a colleague is having to cover for you because you really can't handle the work, that's a problem.

Reaching Out and Following Up

If you reach out to a contact and don't hear back within a week or two, phone the next week if you e-mailed the first time, or e-mail if you called—the person might be away. But if you don't hear back after a second attempt, forget it and move on down your list.

If you do reach a contact who's supplying you with a lead, be sure to ask for the lead's current title, phone, and e-mail information; also find out exactly how they know each other so you don't get it wrong and embarrass yourself. Then Google the person to find out as much as you can about him.

After you've done this, you'll reach out in much the same way you contacted the original party, but the opening line of your call or e-mail will refer to the intermediary: "Hello, Mr. Versace. My aunt Susan Reed suggested I call when I told her I was about to graduate from Simon's College and am exploring careers in fashion. Is this a good time to talk?"

Don't forget to log all calls and e-mail. You might remember the first few conversations you have, but after that, I guarantee that you won't be able to keep it all in your head. You need to know who referred you to whom, which e-mail/cover letter/résumé you sent, and when and how you thanked appropriate parties. Take good notes on all your conversations, and log all new contacts you receive. You don't want to do all this work only to forget or lose the information you gather.

FINDING A MENTOR

▶ As you make your way through your job hunt, it's helpful to have an official or unofficial mentor at your side.

A mentor is a more experienced person—usually someone who's quite a bit older than you, though not necessarily so—who takes an interest in your path and tries to lend you some of his hard-won wisdom. A good mentor is someone who knows more than you do and is willing to help. People often rely on mentors during their careers, but mentors can also be extremely helpful on the road to those careers.

A mentor-mentee relationship can be a close friendship or a more distant, professional relationship. You might have lunch or check in by phone or e-mail every few months, or you might have a couple of conversations at the beginning of your job search and then follow through with a thank-you at the end. A mentor might introduce you to key people or tell you about the inner workings of the industry you're interested in; even on a one-shot basis, a mentor could review your résumé and cover letter from a hiring perspective.

Many colleges and professional associations have programs in place to match newcomers or recent graduates with mentors. If such a program is not available to you, see if you can create your own mentorship. Talk to people you respect who work in or around your field of choice; think about professionals you've met through classes, informational interviews, or internships.

Mentorship relationships don't happen overnight, though, and you can't just run up to a stranger and ask, "Will you mentor me?" Institutionalized programs may help jump-start these relationships, but in general they emerge organically.

The Story in Your Résumé

▶▶ ▶▶ ▶▶ ▶▶ ▶▶ ▶▶ ▶▶ ▶▶ ▶▶ ▶▶ ▶▶ ▶▶ ▶▶ ▶▶ ▶▶

THE PIECE OF PAPER THAT SAYS IT ALL

People think it's hard to write a résumé, but it doesn't have to be. First of all, there's not that much to write. You have only one page to deal with. You can handle that. True, selecting what goes on that single page is extremely important, but the task is finite. I'll give you the format, you fill in the specifics within the structure.

Putting together your first résumé is hard because it's your first, but I promise you, it gets easier with time. Subsequent versions involve only refinement, reorganization, addition, and subtraction. Once you get the first one down, you'll never have to face that blank page again.

Maybe it's hard for you to write a résumé because selling yourself is not your style and runs counter to some cultural and societal norms. If you want a job, you're going to have to get over that. You must learn to present yourself with confidence.

Writing a résumé may be hard because you think you have no experience. But I can guarantee you that if you've been alive for more than eighteen years, you have experience. You have skills. You may not know how to talk about them, but you have them.

Maybe the process seems difficult because you can't imagine fitting all of your experience onto one page. Or not all of your experience has been positive. In fact, you were fired once. How do you deal with that on a résumé? Fortunately, there are easy answers to these questions. What's more, you may even find the writing process interesting. You might discover patterns in the choices you've made, or finally come to see that you picked up some valuable skills from a job you didn't really like.

Getting Started

How do you decide what goes on your résumé? First, look at a bunch of versions. See the models—good and bad—on pages 66–73 and read the résumés of friends who've successfully navigated the job search to get a feel for variations on the basic format.

Next, brainstorm a list of everything you've ever done: extracurricular activities, jobs, hobbies, volunteer work. Take that list and rewrite it in reverse chronological order (most recent first). This master document will be the basis of your résumé.

The first question I ask people after they make their preliminary brainstorming lists is, What did you leave out? Consider whether someone else might have a different perspective on this activity—perhaps it entailed a skill you never realized you had. If you can't remember what you've left off, try mapping out your schedule for a typical day or week to see how you really spend your time. If you find that you spend three afternoons a week in the garden, I'd say gardening is one of your "activities." Do you volunteer off and on for a particular organization? Incorporate those things into your list.

Now for the résumé itself. Here's all you need to put on the page: your name and contact information; your education, before or after your experience, depending on which is more impressive; and your experience, paid and volunteer, listed in reverse chronological order according to categories you will devise and tailor to each job. To convince the reader of your professional skills, you will add language and computer skills, if you have them; to hook the reader, you will add interests and activities.

UNDERSTANDING THE PURPOSE OF A RÉSUMÉ

At the base of it all, you've got to understand what a résumé is. It might seem to you like a brag sheet, but put yourself in the employer's shoes. What is a potential employer looking for? His main concern is to hire someone who can get the job done well, with as little supervision as possible—unless your boss is a control freak, and that's another story. The purpose of a résumé is to convince the prospective employer that you have the necessary skills and personality for the job—and that based on this document, you should be called in for an interview.

That's why when you present an experience, you should think not only about what you got out of a particular job but also about what the employer got out of you. Let's say you're applying for a job in a doctor's office. It may be important to you that you discovered your interest in ophthalmology during the week you filled in for your eye doctor's secretary, but "discovered interest in ophthalmology" is not something you write on a résumé. (It is, however, a great thing to note in a cover letter or interview.) The employer cares about the concrete skills you acquired through your experience. Here's how that would translate to a résumé entry: "Office of Dr. Carl Edwards, ophthalmologist. Temporary Assistant. Booked appointments; called patients to remind them about upcoming appointments; maintained confidential patient files; ordered office and medical supplies."

The Header: Name and Contact Information

The very first item at the top of your résumé should be your full name, which acts as the "header" and should not be preceded by any other text. (Translation: The words "Résumé" or "Contact Information" should not appear.) Nor should your name be preceded by an honorific ("Mr., Mrs., Ms., or Miss"). Convention stipulates that you use only your first and last name,

Seeing this piece of paper through a busy employer's eyes also helps to explain its length—one page, and no more. A résumé is a summary, a selection of highlights, not a list of every single thing you've ever done in your life. Every line, every word counts and should be code for "I can do *this*. . ." A successful résumé will make it appear as though all your life experiences have prepared you to apply for a particular job—no matter what the job.

There's an art to a one-page résumé; you need to be incredibly selective and prune your language carefully. Focus on what I call the four C's: Be Clear, Concrete, Concise, and Consistent. Avoid repetition and the use of most articles. Economy of language is key.

Every word should be essential, and as in a sonnet or haiku, there cannot be a syllable out of place. The one-page résumé is your calling card, the piece of paper that gets your foot in the door. If one page sounds too restrictive, keep in mind that it's just one part of your self-presentation package: You can say more in your cover letter, through references, and in an interview.

Within the standard framework, you are in control of the content. Computer templates should be used only for inspiration and guidance on matters of style. Question the conventions. Feel free to create your own categories to highlight your skills and talents as needed: Outdoor Experience, Athletic Experience, International Experience, Culinary Experience . . .

and middle name if you so choose. Do not list degrees or titles after your name—the "Education" section is the proper place for such information.

Though your name should appear in a large font, you don't want to overdo it. Names in enormous fonts might indicate a huge ego—giant capital letters are the equivalent of shouting. Yours should stand out without dominating or overwhelming the rest of the text.

Below your name, in a much smaller font (but not smaller than 10 or 11 point), insert your contact information: postal address, phone numbers, and e-mail address. List only one e-mail address; don't make the employer

The prospective employer must be able to reach you easily, and between cell phones and e-mail, that shouldn't be a problem.

guess which account you check regularly. Make sure your contact information is up to date.

If you do not have access to a cell phone, rent one or set up a message service. You don't want potential employers to call what they think is your number and end up having a long chat with your mom, who'll tell them how great you are—and then forget to give you the message.

Nickname Quandary

Q. I have a nickname. Do I use it on my résumé?

A. It's best to go formal and use your full name. On the other hand, you don't want an interviewer calling a reference who will deny knowing a "Catherine" if you were known only as "Kitty." So if you really don't ever use your given name, go with your nickname. You can also specify your nickname in parentheses between your first and last name: "Maribelle (Mari) Lowell."

If you currently use a childhood nickname, ask yourself if this may be a good time to switch to a more professional name—a new job can be a fresh start.

Out-of-State Résumés

Q. I currently live in Oklahoma and am applying for jobs in San Francisco. Do I stand a chance? Should I omit my permanent home address?

A. Some employers are wary of out-of-town résumés. If at all possible, use a temporary address in the city in which you are looking: ideally, a friend or relative's, or if that's not an option, a P.O. box.

I'm not asking you to lie, but an out-of-state address at the top of your résumé should not be the first thing an employer sees. Your cover letter is the place to indicate that you are an out-of-town candidate and are planning and/or willing to move.

Indicate that your contact number is a cell so people know they can always reach you there—before the phone number write "Cell Phone" or "(c)." You don't want interviewers to think you're in another time zone and unreachable at certain times of day.

CV'S, BIOS, AND SPECIALIZED RÉSUMÉS

▶ A "CV," or curriculum vitae, is a type of résumé used in academia. A CV typically goes on for pages, including publications, professional associations, talks given, and so on.

A "bio" or biographical statement is a document you may use later on in your professional life; it's composed of one or more paragraphs written in the third person, summarizing and highlighting accomplishments and experiences. You might be asked for one if you are giving a talk or speaking on a panel.

You may have heard of specific résumé styles, too: "functional," "chronological," "skill-based."

A chronological résumé orders your experience by date, with the most recent activities appearing first. A functional or skill-based résumé groups your experience by skill or type of experience. In my opinion, chronological résumés are far too rigid, allowing little room for you to control what to emphasize. I advocate organizing your résumé by experience and then ordering material within each category chronologically, starting with the most recent.

The "Education" Section

After your name and contact information, you'll list either your jobs or your education (see box, page 45, for guidance on making the choice). The main education entry should be the name of your school, with degree and year of graduation; if you have not yet graduated, write "B.A. in History, expected 2013" or "B.A. in History (2013)." You do not need to specify your graduation month and date unless you graduated midyear and want to keep the chronology clear.

Next, add any secondary areas of study and academic awards or distinctions: B.A., *cum laude,* Phi Beta Kappa. If you're short on material, list academic distinctions and scholarships in a separate category at the bottom of the page. You can also add and expand upon activities such as athletics or student government.

Organize the information in order of importance, using bullet points for clarity.

That's all the information that needs to appear, but if you're looking for filler, you can get more specific about your studies: "Course work in 18th-century English literature." Note the year or year plus semester. If possible, focus on areas related to the job for which you're applying. If you were applying for a chemical engineering job, you could include the header "Coursework in Chemical Engineering," then list a few specific courses. If your professor is famous in the field, include his name in parentheses next to the course name : "Introduction to Physics (Professor David Lee)."

While high school is a category that should usually be left out (and will be, the older you get), for a recent college grad it can be used to fill space and also to serve as a marker in a variety of ways. It may indicate where you grew up, or at least spent a few years. ("You grew up in Providence? Where? So did I! Did you know so-and-so?") It may indicate whether you went to a public school, private school, boarding school, all-girls, Quaker, Catholic, or other religious school. If the name doesn't indicate the type of school you attended and you think it's of interest, add your own description.

But think carefully about this choice and others like it. Listing public or private high schools may give an indication—not always correct—of your socioeconomic status. The name of an elite private school may attract the eye of an alum; but some readers may be biased against perceived privilege.

Honors + Awards

IF YOU RECEIVED ANY HONORS OR AWARDS IN COLLEGE, don't be shy about listing them; this information will definitely help characterize you as a desirable job candidate. List awards under the name of your school. The exact titles of your awards may not be sufficiently descriptive, so explain the award as succinctly as possible—"2008 John Smith Award for highest academic achievement." If you received a citation with the award, you might quote directly from it.

Scholarships, Financial Aid + Putting Yourself Through College

IF YOU'VE WON SCHOLARSHIPS OR FINANCED YOUR EDUCATION yourself, it's important to show that you've worked hard for your achievement. Do not rely on the names of scholarships to convey the message. Use parentheses and add descriptors as necessary: "Awarded $5,000 Trump Scholarship for Academic Promise" or "Worked 15 hours a week to defray tuition expenses."

Some counselors advise against noting the amount of a scholarship, but if it's over $1,000, it's worth sharing.

Oui, I Studied Abroad

Though Study Abroad programs are fairly common these days, it's still worth your while to mention that you took part in one. If you attended the Bucknell Spring Semester in Japan program, don't just write "Spent spring semester in Japan." Explain what you studied and did there: "Bucknell Study Abroad Program: Spring Semester in Japan. Lived with host family. Studied tea ceremonies. Course work included Intermediate Japanese, the Art of Watercolor, and Modern Japanese History."

Thesis Pride

Q. Should I list the title of my thesis or self-designed major?

A. Obviously you want to make it clear that you actually wrote a thesis or designed a major, but is the title necessary? It depends. A title can serve as a hook, but make sure it's the kind of hook you want. If you wrote a thesis on a provocative subject, include the title only if it's something you want to talk about in an interview. Make sure that the topic is clear to the reader: I once saw "Cry of Pain" listed as a thesis title. How could anyone know it was actually a history of flamenco dancing? Shorten and condense a long title unless you are applying for a position that relates specifically to the work you did.

Alpha Beta Phi!

Q. Should I mention that I was in a sorority, fraternity, or other social club?

A. People often assume that Greek societies are all about partying. If your organization was community-service oriented,

EDUCATION OR EXPERIENCE FIRST?

► If you are a recent graduate, the Education entry should probably be at the top of your résumé. The top entry creates the first impression, so lead with your most impressive material, whether that's your internship experience or your educational institution. Once you've been out of school for a couple of years, place the Education entry at the bottom of your résumé, but before your activities and interests or computer skills (unless you're applying for a job in the tech industry, in which case those skills would appear up front).

take the time to explain its work. If you're simply proud of your participation in what was a purely social organization, you've got a fifty-fifty chance of alienating someone by including that information—your interviewer may turn out to be a sorority sister or brother, or may be vehemently opposed to the Greek system.

Alternative Education

Q. I was home-schooled in high school. How do I indicate that?

A. Once you have a college degree, you don't have to include information about your high school; so there's no need to mention your home-schooling unless it's important to you and you want to talk about it in an interview. If you wish to mention it or don't have a college degree yet, write "High School Diploma" or "GED," then qualify with "Home-school program followed _____ curriculum," specifying whatever state or other curriculum was used.

Transfer Students

Q. How should I indicate that I transferred from one college to another? And should I? I'm worried that I'll come off as flaky.

A. Many college transfers seem to think their choice to switch might make an employer wonder. But in reality, there's nothing wrong with the fact that you were able to make a change in your life, whatever your motives.

One option is to list the college from which you graduated—or from which you will graduate—first, and then list the college from which you transferred. You will likely be asked about it in an interview, so rehearse a smooth, confident response: "I decided a larger school would make more sense given my academic and extracurricular interests." If you would rather not talk about the transfer, there's no need to list the first college.

In explaining the transfer, don't be too negative—you never know where your interviewer went to school. Choose objective criteria to explain your move: "While I liked Cool College, I found I really needed a bigger/smaller/ more urban/rural school so I transferred to Cooler U. . ."

I Dropped Out!

Q. I never graduated. What do I do?

A. You may still list the school you attended, along with the extracurriculars and course work you did, but you should indicate the years you attended: 2006–2008. Be prepared to explain matter-of-factly why you never got the degree and whether you have plans to finish it.

The "Experience" Section

Drawing a blank when it comes to the "experience" section of your résumé? This is normal, especially if you're just starting out in your professional life. I hear it all the time—"But I've never done anything." This is usually untrue. What people often mean is, "I don't think what I've done is meaningful or important," or they don't see how the experience they've had relates to the job they want.

Think carefully before omitting a seemingly unimportant activity. People typically leave off babysitting, dog-walking, or caring for the sick or elderly, whether these were paid, volunteer, or familial responsibilities. Some career counselors specifically recommend leaving off this kind of experience. I disagree. If you haven't had a great deal of other work experience, these positions indicate that people were willing to leave their most prized possessions in your care: their children, their dogs, their relatives.

You might be thinking, All I did during school was work at a fast-food restaurant and practice the piano—nothing that relates to a job I might want. Untrue. Working in fast-food restaurants indicates that you can handle pressure and deal with the general public. Practicing any instrument, sport, or hobby reveals commitment and discipline, even—especially—if you do it on your own. It's all about how you present what you've done. If it's true that in college all you did was take courses, flesh out your résumé by adding a "Course Work" section. Then, in an interview, you say that during college, you decided to focus exclusively on your studies.

For more guidance on describing your experience, see page 51.

How Much Detail?

Q. I was an intern. Do I list everything I did?

A. For administrative positions, give a sense of the range of your activities and emphasize the skills most relevant to the position for which you are applying.

Start with items that indicate the greatest responsibility: "Selected to orient new interns. Made travel arrangements for CEO." At the end of the entry, merge your most mundane duties into a single bullet: "Administrative duties included answering phones, assembling mailings, and filing." Make sure you list any task specifically mentioned in the description of the job for which you are applying. In an interview or cover letter, you might indicate that you can handle anything that's thrown at you and won't balk at the nitty-gritty stuff: "I did everything from setting up the coffee in the morning to revamping the company's billing process."

MARKETING YOUR SKILLS

▶ Sometimes it takes a little imagination to show a potential employer that your skills are relevant to his organization. Take the case of an experienced book editor who had decided to go back to graduate school in early-childhood education. "Milly is the ideal candidate for your program," her boss wrote in his recommendation. "If she can deal with temperamental authors all day long, she's obviously qualified to deal with very young children." All the skills you have—from internships, from course work, babysitting and other jobs—are relevant, if you can learn to repackage and present them correctly.

Volunteer vs. Paid

Q. How do I indicate paid versus volunteer experience?

A. Recent graduates and people returning to the workplace often have a great deal of volunteer experience, which is totally valid—the skills you gained are transferable, so don't leave something valuable off your résumé just because you weren't paid for your work.

You do need to differentiate between paid and volunteer positions, however. Depending on how things break down, you can choose to have a section entitled "Volunteer Positions/ Internships." But stratifying your experience this way is not always the best option: If you have done volunteer work that relates directly to a job for which you're applying, that experience may wind up getting lost in the Volunteer section. In that case, present all of your related work under one heading ("Communications Experience" or "Customer Service Experience," depending on the job), noting "volunteer" or "unpaid internship" in parentheses beside your titles as needed. A note: If your volunteer work entailed a good amount of responsibility, I think it's fine to invent a title such as "Intern Coordinator" for yourself (obviously, without going overboard, and also checking with a former supervisor first if possible, especially if you are asking him to serve as a reference).

Location, Location

Q. Do I need to list the location of each job and school on my résumé?

A. You should list the city and state (and country, if out of the U.S.) once, but don't repeat it if all your entries are in the same place or if the location is obvious: "University of Chicago." The location of your jobs should be consistently listed either after the name of the company or in the right-hand margin. Use standard postal abbreviations for state names if you don't have the room to spell them out.

Title vs. Company Name

Q. Should I feature the name of the place I worked or my title?

A. You'll need to make a global decision and be consistent throughout your résumé, but you should choose to feature whatever is more impressive. If you've worked or interned for well-known companies, you want to draw attention to that; if you've had good titles at lesser-known companies, start with the titles. (See the models on pages 66–73.)

The Bonus Section: Skills & Interests

The "Skills and Interests/Activities and Affiliations" section at the bottom of your résumé is not just optional filler. It provides handles—digestible bits of information about your personality—and conversational openers, distinguishing you and rounding you out as a job candidate and potential colleague.

The category itself, along with its content, will differ for each person. How do you spend your time out of the office? Are you a sports enthusiast? Do you volunteer for a not-for-profit organization or charity?

Choose at least four activities, ideally in four domains: one that shows teamwork (perhaps theater or sports), one that shows long-term dedication (you run daily or have studied an instrument for years), one that reveals a cultural interest (you're a film buff and go to film festivals), and one that illustrates your commitment to volunteerism (tutoring, working in a shelter or soup kitchen, raising money for charity through your sorority or fraternity, and so on).

Foreign Languages

As everywhere else on your résumé, be truthful about your foreign language abilities. Don't put yourself in the shoes of the candidate who claimed to speak Russian, hoping to impress an interviewer; it turned out the interviewer was fluent and tried to continue the interview in Russian, only to find out that the candidate had exaggerated his proficiency.

Indicate your real level of reading, writing, and speaking. Don't say you've had six years of French if those years were third through ninth grade and you don't remember it anymore. The employer wants to know what you can do in that language. Can you continue the interview in the language? Make a phone call? Write letters, faxes, and e-mails? Read a novel? Here are the keywords you can use to indicate your language level:

▶ Beginning: Beginning/Rudimentary/Basic/Tourist Spanish

▶ Comfortable but rusty: Conversational/Fluent Conversational/Basic Written Spanish

▶ Advanced: Fluent Reading, Writing, and Speaking Knowledge of Spanish; Bilingual English/Spanish (Mother Tongue: English).

What do language skills mean to an employer? If the employer deals with foreign clients or has work that needs to be executed in a foreign language, a specific language skill may be useful to him. But even if he doesn't, he may still be impressed by your mastery of a language. Why? Because a smart employer understands that mastery indicates a flexibility of mind; a bi- or trilingual job candidate may be better able to pick up industry-specific lingo and technical terms, and may even have an easier time communicating in general.

Always include your foreign languages, no matter how unlikely it seems to you that you'll use them in a particular job.

Computer Skills— Useful or Humdrum?

Basic computer skills (Word, the Internet) are assumed these days, so there's no need to list them if you're having trouble fitting all of your experience on a page.

If you need filler or have knowledge of specialized programs, though, the "Computer Skills" section will come in handy. Since résumé readers may do no more than skim a skills section filled with technical terms, you may choose to add detail under your job entries: "Designed flyers using QuarkXPress." "Managed ticket sales using Access database." If a job description lists specific programs you have worked with, definitely feature them somewhere on your résumé.

The Minefield of Résumé Wording

There's a Gary Larson cartoon I love in which one panel is titled "What We Say to Dogs" and the other, "What They Hear." In the first panel, a man is scolding a dog: "Okay, Ginger! I've had it! You stay out of the garbage! Understand, Ginger?"; in the second, you see what the dog hears: "Blah blah GINGER blah blah blah blah blah blah blah blah GINGER."

That's exactly how people read résumés. They scan the page in a matter of seconds, picking up only a few details: proper names (i.e., the names of places you've worked); positions (if they're looking for a financial analyst and your résumé lists "financial analyst," this is good); and other keywords. Some résumés are actually scanned for keywords by computers. But whether it's a human or a computer taking the first look at that piece of paper, the same principle applies: The words that stand out relate to what we're looking for.

That's where the discriminating use of jargon comes into play: "Insider terms" let the reader know that you've had exposure to her field. A legal résumé might have phrases like "took depositions, filed motions"; a teaching résumé might read "designed and implemented curricula."

How do you come up with that jargon if you've had limited exposure to the field in which you're applying? First, read the job description carefully. The language on your résumé should be an answer to that description. You don't want to mimic the exact wording—too obvious—but use it as a starting point. Then, research the duties associated with the position you're applying for; interview people in the field about what tasks they perform and the industry terms they would use to describe them. Once you've accrued a good vocabulary list, use it to frame the experience you've already had. Be careful not to overdo it or misuse terms, though. Have one of your industry contacts read your résumé to make sure it sounds authentic.

Building in Hooks

It's important to add a few "hooks" to your résumé but don't fake interests or include outlandish or overly provocative information. Hooks come in many forms. An "Activities and Interests" section is an obvious place for them, but there are others.

RÉSUMÉ WORDING: A CHEAT SHEET

▶ There is no special set of grammatical rules when it comes to résumé writing, but make sure you are consistent and aren't violating the basic tenets. Beyond that, I've assembled some pointers to help you make the best possible use of the limited space—one page!—you've got.

■ Résumés are generally composed of sentence fragments. You don't need to include articles ("managed $10,000 budget" as opposed to "managed *a* budget *of* $10,000").

■ Be consistent in your use of punctuation. Even though it's technically incorrect, you may use periods at the end of sentence fragments—or not. Just decide on what you are doing and do it throughout. If you are stringing together a row of sentence fragments, you may separate them with commas, semicolons, or even periods.

■ Do not use the first-person pronoun. A résumé is an objective recounting of your experience, as opposed to a cover letter, which should be written in the first person.

■ Verbs should be cast in the past tense, except in entries about jobs or positions you currently hold.

■ Avoid repetition. Group experiences and consolidate entries when you've had many jobs at one place. Don't repeat words or phrases. Avoid redundant adjectives and phrases: "Restocked shelves

One candidate included the fact that she had worked at her father's regionally famous reptile zoo. Although her work there had nothing to do with the job she was applying for, the interviewer was intrigued, they had a great conversation, and she was hired. Think about it: How many résumés have you seen containing the word "reptile"?

Expressing Who You Are

While a "hook" is designed to grab the reader's attention, a "marker" is an item or word that intentionally or unintentionally gives away as necessary." Why would you be restocking the shelves if you didn't need to? "Kept orderly files." We assume so—we wouldn't want you keeping "disorderly" files.

■ Avoid the overuse of italics, bold, underlining, asterisks, and so on.

■ Don't turn nouns into verbs! Words like "liaised," "impacted," and "referenced" may have crept into the dictionary, but they look silly. Don't verb nouns, even if everyone else does it! (See how ridiculous it sounds?)

■ Don't assume readers will know the name of the company where you worked or what it does unless it's known in the field. Use parentheses to add explanatory information as necessary— "Pyrotechnics, Inc. (largest U.S. fireworks display company)"—or make sure the nature of the company comes through in your bullet points.

■ Dates and prices aside, spell out numbers under ten and use numerals after that: "Organized three fund-raisers, each attended by more than 1,000 invitees."

■ Draw attention to your use of any specialized tools of the trade. Instead of "Copyedited manuscript" try "Copyedited manuscript using *Chicago Manual of Style*. Familiar with typesetting and copyediting symbols."

some aspect of your background and identity. You need to understand how every word on your résumé comes across—I don't want you to include any unintentional markers.

You may want to use markers intentionally, for a particular purpose. I'm frequently asked if—and how—one should indicate things like race, socioeconomic status, religion, sense of humor, sexual or political orientation, health, and marital status. If you wish to define yourself in some particular way, it's easiest to do it in the Activities and Interests section of your résumé: Gay Students' Association, Church Choir, Campus Hillel, African-American Students' Association, Young Republicans Club, and so on. Markers can work for or against you, depending on your reader's

SOMETIMES YOU NEED TO SPELL IT OUT

▶ In some cases, information that may seem obvious or complete to you will need to be contextualized for the reader. One candidate I worked with wrote "Classical Course Graduate" on his résumé. Although I had grown up in his hometown and was familiar with Classical High School, I had no idea what the Classical Course was. He explained that it was a specialized, intensive four-year study of Latin—and we added that to his résumé. Why? Because although Latin is a "dead" language, this entry revealed that he was smart and had been chosen for a selective program; since he knew Latin, he might more easily learn new grammatical systems, and perhaps languages, and by extension other systems and technical languages. His four-year commitment in high school told me a lot about his work ethic. Same goes for acronyms or obscure company names: Spell them out.

personality and politics. Usually it's worth the risk: By showing your true colors, you can find like-minded colleagues, increasing the chances of a comfortable work environment.

Beware of marking yourself incorrectly. When I saw a résumé featuring the Democratic National Convention, I assumed the candidate was a Democrat. I asked her about it, and it turned out that she was a staunch Republican but had worked on a nonpartisan welcoming committee. We added the nonpartisan line. Whatever your personal or political beliefs, be aware of how the items on your résumé might stereotype you in the mind of the reader.

People often ask about expressing their sense of humor. The best way to introduce the subject is by including markers that allude to your sense of humor—you might mention that you wrote for the campus satire magazine, or list comedy or improv in the Interests and Activities section. The real thing is best left for an interview or thank-you note, or for your references to address. If you're really funny, an original turn of phrase or tone may attract a reader—but humor that falls flat will absolutely work against you.

So will overembellishing your hooks. I've seen people write "Extensive travel" under Activities and Interests. This means different things to different people. If you include Sweden on your travel list and it turns out the interviewer is Swedish, a barrage of questions might follow. What did you like best about Sweden? How long were you there? When did you go? If you spent a couple of weeks there and can't even remember where you were, you're in trouble. If you lived there or have relatives there, visit frequently, and know the culture, then you have something to talk about. (If the job relates to travel, or to that particular region, you'll have a lot to talk about.)

Conveying a Timeline

Conveying a sense of time on a résumé can be tricky. If you've taken breaks between jobs or held a particular job for only a brief amount of time, you may feel that specifying dates will work against you.

Don't worry. No matter what your track record, dates should be as discreet as possible. Set them in a smaller font than the rest of the text and/or in italics and parentheses. Consolidate. Instead of writing "Summers, 2001, 2002, 2003, 2004," try "Summers 2001–2004." You never need to note specific days ("January 28, 2004, to March 4, 2005"); bracket your time using months or seasons, as in "January 2003" or "spring semester, 2001." (Using seasons is a great way to get around a short stay at a job—though you can't lie if you're asked exactly how long you stuck it out.)

If you're still at a position, the copy should read "2007–present." What's more, any job you currently hold should be described in the present tense. Past jobs should be described in the past tense.

Put Your Best Foot Forward, but Don't Lie

Yes, you want every item on your résumé to help you stand out. But keep in mind that you own your résumé and thus are responsible for everything on it. Sometimes the line between self-promotion and dishonesty can be a fine one, so ask yourself: Is there anyone from whom you would wish to hide your résumé because you've exaggerated your responsibilities, inflated your title, or lengthened your stay at a job?

Assume that everyone you've ever known and everyone you've ever worked with will see your résumé. Let's say you send it to the head of a company. It turns out her assistant is someone you went to school with. You don't want the assistant telling her boss, "I can't believe he said he ran the tutoring program on campus—because I did that, and he was one of my tutors!" The world is very small. You never know who will see your résumé, so put your best foot forward, but don't make things up!

Bumming Around

Q. I spent my post-graduation summer traveling in Europe. How do I indicate that?

A. I would advise you to leave it off, unless you're applying for a job that requires language skills or an interest in travel. In spite of what you may have heard elsewhere, you don't have to be a slave to chronology. If someone asks you about that time period in an interview, feel free to tell him. If you earned the money for this trip yourself or were awarded a traveling fellowship, by all means mention it. But if you didn't, be careful how you present the subject. It is not a college graduate's inherent right to travel the world—although the tone of many privileged students would lead you to believe otherwise.

Abbr. O.K.?

Q. Is it all right to use abbreviations?

A. With the exception of state names, try to avoid abbreviations. Rather than saying you worked somewhere "Jan–Feb 2002," just say "Winter 2002." If you must abbreviate, do so consistently and correctly—though if you're that short on space, you may not be adequately consolidating your information.

Abbreviations may be necessary to avoid orphans—a publishing term that refers to a single word left dangling on a line at the end of a paragraph. Never, ever leave a word or part of a word alone on a line of your résumé. Every line is sacred. Cut or rewrite to fill as much of each line as possible.

The Visa Issue

Q. I am not an American citizen. Do I need to indicate that somewhere on my résumé?

A. Yes. Don't get an employer all excited about hiring you and then tell him at the last minute that you're not legally able to work in this country—or that you can only work if the company procures your visa. I've been on the hiring end of what I consider a bait-and-switch situation and I didn't like it.

So that you can't be accused of pulling any punches, I recommend centering your status on the bottom of your résumé in italics. For example: "French National. J-1 Visa Pending" or "Irish Citizen; Eligible for Company-Sponsored Visa." Not sure whether you have the proper documentation? It's your responsibility, not the employer's, to investigate your employment status. Save yourself some time and disappointment by applying only to companies that you know sponsor foreign nationals.

The All-Important Format

You want your résumé to look professional and neat; you also want it to be legible. It's supposed to be about your accomplishments and experience, so you don't want to be remembered as "the one who sent in her résumé on purple paper." Likewise, avoid all seals, embossing, logos, designs, drawings, and postage-stamp-size photographs (unless you are an actor or performer of some kind). Note: If you are looking at jobs in a design realm, different rules apply, as your résumé doubles as a showcase for your work.

Separate your entries (Education, Experience, and so on) and give your résumé visual clarity by using horizontal lines or space breaks. Category headings should be left-justified or centered.

Use a hierarchy of fonts and styles throughout: bold capitals for your name, capital letters for your categories, bold for company names, italics for job titles, and so on. Dates should be right-justified on the company name line.

These basic guidelines should have you covered:

▶ **Paper size:** 8½ by 11 inches

▶ **Paper quality:** The paper should be good-quality, sturdy stock that's not flimsy or see-through; neither should it be as thick as cardboard. If you can see a watermark (the seal or pattern on good-quality paper identifying the manufacturer) when you hold the paper up to the light, make sure you print so that the mark is upright and reads in the right direction. Use envelopes from the same paper stock. (Buy them with the paper to make sure they're a true match.)

▶ **Paper color:** Use a conservative white, off-white, cream, or ivory.

▶ **Ink color:** Black

▶ **Font:** Times New Roman, Palatino, Garamond, or similar—go for something clean and professional.

▶ **Font size:** 12-point font is preferable; you may use 11 or 10 if absolutely necessary, but don't go smaller.

▶ **Margin:** One inch on all sides. Beyond setting the margins, you also want to make sure you don't end up with too much white space. Trace around the written portions of your résumé; if you end up with odd amoebalike patches, rewrite so that entries don't vary so much in length.

Template Shortcut

Q. What about the templates that came with my computer?

A. Most computers come with résumé templates, but they're not necessarily always formatted in the most intelligent way. Just make sure you're deciding what to emphasize. A template might look nice, but does it prevent you from tailoring your experience to suit a particular job?

Make It Job- and Industry-Specific

Though people would have you believe that a résumé is a static, objective summation of experience, it can and should be a constantly evolving entity. You are in control of what it conveys, no matter what your job experience has been.

It's easy enough to tailor your basic résumé to each job for which you apply, rearranging entries and language to highlight particular skills and experience. If you are applying for positions in several fields, it's especially important that you have a variety of résumés.

Let's say you were a dancer in college and gave ballet lessons. You waitressed during the summers, you've walked dogs, and you've volunteered at various animal shelters.

There are three résumés here, waiting to be written: a dance résumé, an animal-care résumé, and a waitressing/customer service/hospitality résumé. If you were applying for a job at a restaurant, you would expand the entries in the "Restaurant/Waitressing Experience" section and move it to the top of the résumé. If you were applying to work in a dance program, you would use your "Dance" résumé, leading off with "Dance Experience." Ideally you should have more than one entry in each category; don't be afraid to link categories to achieve this. You might create a section called Dance and Teaching

SUPPLEMENTARY MATERIALS

Depending on what type of job you're in the market for, you may need to create additional materials beyond the standard résumé. Generally, you wouldn't want to mail these out with your résumé; just bring them along to an interview so you can pull them out if you need to.

By the way: Never bring your only copy of any document; assume you'll be leaving materials behind for good. Your name and contact information should appear on every piece of paper. (Time- and production-intensive art portfolios are a different story.)

Items you may want to include:

■ A list of nonfiction clips (published articles from newspapers, magazines, and websites) and writing samples. Don't include fiction or poetry unless requested.

■ Course summaries, tailored to the job for which you are applying.

■ Portfolio of work: sample pitch letters, brochures you've designed.

■ List of references: See model, page 113.

Note: Don't send a transcript unless the job announcement specifically calls for it. Do have several sealed copies ready to go just in case. Call your college or university registrar's office in advance; you can usually receive copies by mail for a minimal fee.

Experience, for instance. And you might leave certain realms of experience out of one résumé only to highlight them in another.

Multiple résumés are a great way to diversify your search, especially if you're undecided about what you want and are using the Rule of Three to explore several realms of interest.

Don't Get Tossed

In order to understand why the seemingly minute details of résumé writing are so important, it's helpful to consider things—again—from an employer's perspective.

After a job is posted, the first cut is often made by the HR (Human Resources) department or an assistant. Since the sorter might be faced with a stack of several hundred résumés, she is as invested in finding reasons to reject people as she is in finding qualified candidates. Don't give her a reason to eliminate you.

So what would make someone toss a résumé?

First, there are easy physical criteria: The paper is not standard size (8½ by 11 inches) or a neutral color, or is dirty, stained, or ripped; the ink is not black, the text is handwritten, there are pictures, quotations, or any other decoration (though again, this doesn't apply if you're going for a job in an art, design, PR, or advertising milieu, in which case the résumé can serve as a sample of your work); there is something handwritten as an addition to the typed résumé—meaning that you did not take the time to correct or update it adequately; the font is too small or too big, the margins are too wide or nonexistent. If you use a confusing or messy format, you might be weeded out. That means no résumés with splits down the middle or boxes. Stick to the classic models on pages 66–67 and 70–71.

Stick to one page at this phase. If you go over a page, assume the second page will not be read. Some readers literally rip off and toss away the second page of a two-page résumé. (Later on in your career, though, a longer résumé may be appropriate.) If your potential employer needs more information, he will ask for it.

Why is the look so important? The reader may instinctively assume that, if you can't be bothered to figure out the conventional résumé format, she can't count on you to master the conventions of her field. In general, employers want the candidate with the most experience for the job, one who will, as they say, hit the ground running. They want evidence that you have been in the field or have been exposed to the field through internships or volunteer experience—and they want evidence that you can learn quickly.

Typos

IF I SEE A TYPO, I tell candidates their résumés might be rejected right off the bat. What's so bad about one tiny mistake? It's really not so tiny. A typo is actually a huge red flag that says, "I cannot be trusted to proofread my own work. I am likely to send out error-ridden letters with your name on them—you'll have to check everything I write." Now, as an employer, do I want to take on this responsibility? NO! I want someone who will catch MY errors, not make his own.

HOW *NOT* TO DEAL WITH TYPOS . . .

▶ Once, a colleague with whom I was jointly hiring an assistant convinced me to interview a candidate she found promising, even though there was a typo on his résumé. She had let the candidate know she had noticed the typo, and he was appropriately embarrassed. I said nothing in my interview with him, waiting for him to bring it up—and this is how he did it: "Your colleague said there was a typo on my résumé. Where was it?" At that moment, I knew I couldn't hire him. He had shown incredibly bad judgment. What he should have done was to go home, correct the mistake, and resend his résumé by fax or e-mail with a thank-you note for the interview—something along the lines of "I was mortified to discover that I had sent my résumé with a typo. I hope my interview assured you that this was an aberration. Enclosed is a new version with my apologies." Instead, he revealed that he hadn't even bothered to give his résumé a second look after the mistake was pointed out!

Some people are better proofreaders than others—but no matter how good you are, you should always have a second and even third reader take a look at your résumé. (See pages 64–65 for more on proofreading.)

Occasionally, you'll need to make a last-minute change to your résumé and won't have time to proofread carefully. In the event that you do make a mistake, apologize and do what you can to redress the situation.

Intentional "Typos"

Q. I worked as an assistant brand-manager for a product whose name looks like a typo—Dr Pepper. I know perfectly well that there's a period after "Dr" but in the brand name they don't use the period. I can't change the name of the product, but I don't want it to look as if I have a typo on my résumé. What do I do?

A. Here's where Latin comes in handy. Insert the italicized word "sic" (meaning "thus") in parentheses after the offending word. This convention indicates that the phrasing or spelling is intentional and not a mistake on your part. Another option is to punctuate "Dr." correctly for jobs outside the soft-drink world, and spell it "Dr Pepper" for positions within the industry.

The Stuff You Can't Help . . .

THE LAST ELEMENT OF THE FIRST CUT isn't something you can control, at least at this stage: Where you have worked, and for how long. The reader will choose candidates with what he considers the best and most relevant experience. The only way you can protect yourself from being tossed on the basis of lack of experience is by doing as much research as possible before you apply.

One of the top mistakes job-seekers make is applying for jobs for which they are unqualified. Make sure you're in the right bracket for the job; don't waste your valuable time applying for positions well beyond your experience level. Of course, you don't have to play by the book. If you express serious interest and show how your skills pertain, perhaps you'll be considered for a position you don't even know exists. You certainly won't get a job you don't apply for.

But be realistic. If you're a recent grad or haven't worked in a given field, you are not going to be hired as CEO. If the ad says MBA and you don't have one but you ran your own business, apply. If it says PhD and you're ABD (All But Dissertation), you might apply, but you have to figure out why they're asking. To teach in some universities, a PhD is simply the minimum requirement. Outside of academia, though, the request for a PhD may simply indicate that the organization is looking for someone with a certain level of knowledge.

Many ads state a minimum number of years of experience. You can still apply if you're shy of the stated mark, but not if you have no experience whatsoever. Here's a guideline: If an ad says "two to three years experience required" and you have one year, apply. If it says "three to five years" and you have two, okay—the ads are trying to weed out people with no experience in the field.

Sometimes the ad is designed to recruit candidates of a certain age and maturity. If you can prove that you have enough experience and you present yourself professionally, you may be considered. If your family is in the business or industry, find a way to slip that in. Even though you had only summer internships in the business, you may have more concrete and practical knowledge than someone with two years of low-level experience.

The Skeletons in Your Closet

For many people, a major stumbling block to résumé writing is a fear of skeletons in the closet. First of all, don't obsess about gaps in chronology and jobs that didn't work out. Those happen to everyone. What matters is how you deal with your skeletons. A skillfully organized résumé can minimize them. Inevitably, though, someone will ask a question you don't want to answer: why you left a job you were fired from, how you spent that unaccounted-for year between college and grad school.

The only solution is to practice answering questions about gaps and skeletons out loud. Try rehearsing in front of a mirror, and then practice with a friend. Though you'll see a list of probable interview questions in chapter 6, here's a preliminary look at three skeletons that typically create a great deal of anxiety for résumé writers.

1. You Were Fired

Do you list the job or not?

If the job was short-term or not relevant to the position you're applying for, you may simply be able to leave it off your résumé and list other activities—such as volunteer work or community service—you were engaged in during that time. A long-term job should appear on your résumé, though.

In an interview, you don't need to advertise the fact that you were fired, but if asked, you should be direct. Were you fired as part of a general layoff or downsizing? If so, try to offer a plausible explanation for why you were let go—you were the most recently hired, most junior person, and so on. A personality conflict? Be careful not to criticize your previous employer, sound like you carry a grudge, or appear vindictive—even if these things are all true.

Focus on the transferable skills you acquired, and discuss the issue of your firing calmly, matter-of-factly, and practically. While it was a difficult situation for you, you quickly picked yourself back up, polished your résumé, and began a new job search. You consider yourself stronger for the experience, and you realize firing someone can be as unpleasant as being fired.

2. You Worked in a Family Business

You worked in a family business or for a relative? So do thousands of people. Some job-seekers feel that listing a family job on a résumé smacks of nepotism. Don't worry about it. Nepotism rules! If you're lucky enough to have a family business to go into or a relative to hire you, great! Acknowledge the uniqueness of the situation in a way that reflects positively on you. Prepare some anecdotes about the pleasures and perils of working with and for relatives. If your direct boss was a relative, list a coworker or client as a reference. I don't want to call a reference you've listed with a different last name than yours and find out I'm actually talking to your dad—I'll feel you tried to dupe me.

3. You Have a Major Chronological Gap, for a Complicated or Personal Reason

YOU HAD A NERVOUS BREAKDOWN. You were depressed. You were sick, or someone in your family was sick or died. You were recovering from an addiction. You were hanging out with a boyfriend. You were bumming around Europe or surfing in Hawaii.

You are not alone. All of these scenarios—and many others—are more common than you think. The key is in how you present them. Some résumé readers are highly focused on chronology, so you must be able to matter-of-factly explain gaps; others won't even notice, but you should be prepared.

If you were dealing with a chronic illness or death in the family and chose to make this a priority, people generally understand. If you were dealing with something like substance abuse or a nervous breakdown, be discreet—you don't want to raise red flags: "I took time off from an unsatisfying job to rethink my options." "I spent time with my family, reconsidering my priorities and researching career options." (More on these situations in chapter 6, Getting Through the Interview.)

Proofreading Your Résumé

Once you've got your résumé drafted, proofread it. Use spell-check, then read it through again. Then, have it read and proofread by someone meticulous; if possible, get someone in a hiring position to look at it as well—it doesn't have to be someone in your field.

Do not trust spell-check alone. The program doesn't truly understand grammar, and it sometimes creates errors—a reference to the book *Madame Ovary* was one memorable example. Don't take this risk. You can't afford to have a single typo, spelling, grammatical, or punctuation mistake on your résumé.

Proofread every time you make a change, no matter how minor. Cutting and pasting often leads to formatting errors.

If you must proofread your résumé on your own, read it through at least three times, with a night of sleep in between readings for good measure—you'll be better able to look at things with a fresh eye after a certain amount of time has passed. Techniques used by professional proofreaders include reading each word aloud, and sliding an index card or ruler along in order to focus on each letter individually.

Printing and Sending Your Résumé

Once you've polished your résumé to within an inch of its life, don't just hit Send or Print quite yet. If you're e-mailing, open and print your document to make sure there aren't any formatting issues. (One way to get around that is to save your Word file as a PDF.) If you're sending a hard copy, make sure it's clean; no stains or ink smears. If you do not have a letter-quality or laser printer, have it printed at a service bureau.

If you're applying for a job online, you may encounter Web-based forms requiring you to fill in résumé information in specific fields. Be just as careful about typos when you're filling these out, and save and print a version for your files. Be selective: If space is a consideration, make sure you are listing the most important information possible.

Digital or Hard Copy?

Q. What's the best way to send my résumé?

A. If the job posting indicates a specific way in which the employer would like to receive your résumé—fax, mail, or e-mail—send it as directed.

Title your résumé document file clearly, with your first and last names and the word "résumé." I can't tell you how often I've seen job-seekers sabotage their applications by titling their documents "ProfessionalResume.doc" or "GoodVersionWithDan'sEdits." It's all in the details. The subject line of your e-mail should read, "YourLastName Résumé for X Position." If someone specific has recommended you send the résumé, add that information: "per Professor Y."

(continued on page 76)

The Samples

The résumé samples on the following pages represent the best—and the worst—of what I've seen over the course of my career. (Names have been changed.) Good résumés are identified by a check mark; undesirables by an X. On right-hand pages, résumés are "decoded" in depth.

Clear and Organized

The format below is clear and readable. Titles, employers, locations, and dates are presented in an easy-to-follow and logical hierarchy. Bolding, italics, bullets, and varying font sizes are used to maximum efffect.

KATHERINE PEARSON
19 Barclay Street
New York New York 10011
917-288-1234 (cell) • pearson@post.washington.edu

EDUCATION

WASHINGTON POST UNIVERSITY, College of Arts & Sciences, St. Louis, MO   *Class of 2008*
- B.A. in History with College Honors; Legal Studies/ Classics Minor
- Recipient of the Geller Prize, awarded annually by the History Department
  for best sophomore essay in an advanced seminar
- Deejay, world music show on KWUR, college radio station; literacy tutor for Spanish-speaking
  immigrant students; peer-elected residential college representative to student government;
  captain of a nationally recognized debate team

PONTIFICIA UNIVERSIDAD (Junior Year Abroad Program), Santiago, Chile   *Spring Semester, 2007*
- Lived with Chilean family; traveled in Peru, Bolivia, Argentina, Chile, and Brazil
- Course work in Spanish; South American culture and history; human rights
- Taught English in a local elementary school one morning per week

MAYVILLE SCHOOL, Los Angeles, CA   *Class of 2004*
Valedictorian; Captain of award-winning debate team

LEGAL EXPERIENCE

GOLD BANK, New York, NY   *Summer 2006*
Legal Department Assistant
- Compiled market data used as basis for transactions with domestic clients
- Reviewed corporate policies for compliance with local and federal finance regulations

NATIONAL ORGANIZATION FOR LEGAL JUSTICE, San Francisco, CA   *Summer 2005*
Legal Research Intern
- Answered phones, copied and filed contracts

LOS ANGELES PUBLIC DEFENDER'S OFFICE, Los Angeles, CA   *Summer 2003*
Intern
- Organized one murder defendant's 25-year medical and criminal histories;
  created materials used as part of a successful defense

COMPUTER AND LANGUAGE SKILLS

Computers: Power Point, LexisNexis, and Excel
Languages: Fluent Spanish; basic conversational French; Latin

INTERESTS

Jamaican, Latin, and African music; black-and-white photography; modern dance

KATHERINE PEARSON

19 Barclay Street
New York New York 10011
917-288-1234 (cell) • pearson@post.washington.edu

EDUCATION

WASHINGTON POST UNIVERSITY, College of Arts & Sciences, St. Louis, MO   *Class of 2008*

- B.A. in History with College Honors; Legal Studies/ Classics Minor
- Recipient of the Geller Prize, awarded annually by the History Department for best sophomore essay in an advanced seminar
- Deejay, world music show on KWUR, college radio station; literacy tutor for Spanish-speaking immigrant students; peer-elected residential college representative to student government; captain of a nationally recognized debate team

PONTIFICIA UNIVERSIDAD (Junior Year Abroad Program), Santiago, Chile   *Spring Semester, 2007*

- Lived with Chilean family; traveled in Peru, Bolivia, Argentina, Chile, and Brazil
- Course work in Spanish; South American culture and history; human rights
- Taught English in a local elementary school one morning per week

MAYVILLE SCHOOL, Los Angeles, CA   *Class of 2004*
Valedictorian; Captain of award-winning debate team

LEGAL EXPERIENCE

GOLD BANK, New York, NY   *Summer 2006*
Legal Department Assistant

- Compiled market data used as basis for transactions with domestic clients
- Reviewed corporate policies for compliance with local and federal finance regulations

NATIONAL ORGANIZATION FOR LEGAL JUSTICE, San Francisco, CA   *Summer 2005*
Legal Research Intern

- Answered phones, copied and filed contracts

LOS ANGELES PUBLIC DEFENDER'S OFFICE, Los Angeles, CA   *Summer 2003*
Intern

- Organized one murder defendant's 25-year medical and criminal histories; created materials used as part of a successful defense

COMPUTER AND LANGUAGE SKILLS

Computers: Power Point, LexisNexis, and Excel
Languages: Fluent Spanish; basic conversational French; Latin

INTERESTS

Jamaican, Latin, and African music; black-and-white photography; modern dance

Category Problems

This résumé is in dire need of revamping. Every piece of information is equally weighted; the result is that the reader's eye skims over the whole document, landing on nothing in particular.

J. Farrell

734 Plymouth Road
Ann Arbor, MI 48103
313-345-1279
hotgirl@hotmail.com

EXPERIENCE
Assistant Manager at Pizzeria Fresca
Ann Arbor, MI
Summers 1999, 2000, 2001, 2002
Serve as Assistant manager at gourmet Italian pizzeria/restaurant
Oversee staff; worked my way up from dishwasher then waitress
• Reference: Mario, 902-123-1234

Fundamentals of Bread Baking
Norwich, VT
June 2003
Completed course with master baker (uncle)
• Reference: Joseph Reilly, 901-222-2222

Time Out Guide
New York, NY
Reviewed restaurants briefly in 2001*
• Reference: Sue Fredericks, 212-666-3333

Internship at the International Herald Tribune, Daily Supplement
Rome, Italy
2001 Academic Year
Lived in Trastevere district
Travel writer

SKILLS
Excellent verbal and written skills/well-versed in all major
software packages and internet applications/striving
creative-fiction writer/longtime musician and music-lover.

STRENGTHS
High personal standards of honesty, loyalty, integrity

* Additionally I have worked on a freelance basis starting in 2002.

A huge font screams huge ego; and unless "J." is actually your first name, it should be spelled out so a reader knows what to call you.

J. Farrell

734 Plymouth Road
Ann Arbor, MI 48103
313-345-1279
hotgirl@hotmail.com

Don't waste an opportunity for detail; in this case, "Culinary Experience" would make sense.

This is far from an appropriate, professional e-mail address! See page 5.

Avoid using strings of numbers. "Summers 1999–2002" would be a much more efficient way to present this information.

EXPERIENCE

"Serve as" is redundant here.

Assistant Manager at Pizzeria Fresca
Ann Arbor, MI
Summers 1999, 2000, 2001, 2002
Serve as Assistant manager at gourmet Italian pizzeria/restaurant
Oversee staff; worked my way up from dishwasher then waitress
+ Reference: Mario, 902-123-1234

No narrative language or first person pronouns on a résumé. Save the story for the interview or cover letter.

No,no, no! No need to share this information here.

Fundamentals of Bread Baking
Norwich, VT
June 2003
Completed course with master baker (uncle)
+ Reference: Joseph Reilly, 901-222-2222

This résumé-writer probably thought she was being efficient by merging her résumé and references—but in fact it looks as though she's jumping the gun.

Time Out Guide
New York, NY
Reviewed restaurants briefly in 2001*
+ Reference: Sue Fredericks, 212-666-3333

Qualifiers like "briefly" don't belong on a résumé.

Where's the Education section? I'm guessing this candidate had some reason to leave it off—perhaps she didn't finish college, or maybe she never went. . . . In any case, her "Education" section could easily have been filled out with that breadbaking course.

This is not for you to assess, and strengths and weaknesses don't belong on a résumé anyway.

Internship at the International Herald Tribune, Daily Supplement
Rome, Italy
2001 Academic Year
Lived in Trastevere district
Travel writer

Though this kind of experience is great, the real world doesn't operate on an academic calendar; and the neighborhood reference is irrelevant.

SKILLS

Excellent verbal and written skills/well-versed in all major software packages and internet applications/striving creative-fiction writer/longtime musician and music-lover.

STRENGTHS

High personal standards of honesty, loyalty, integrity

Everything about this section is off-base. Skills should appear in concrete categories like "Computer Skills" and "Language Skills." "Striving"sounds juvenile, and now an employer is going to worry that you'll be writing your novel on the job. As for the love of music, appreciation is not a skill but an interest.

* Additionally I have worked on a freelance basis starting in 2002.

Whether typed or handwritten, notes should never appear on the bottom of your résumé; you'll look forgetful, as though you rushed to throw things together and stuck some last-minute information at the bottom of the page.

Solid and Businesslike

Though this kind of format isn't a good fit for applicants with an overabundance of material, it's clear and navigable. In this case, high visibility in the left-hand "category" column serves to emphasize the candidate's unique mix of experience.

JOHN WINTERS

61 Armory Road, Manchester, NH 06873 • j23winters@jmail.com · (603) 123-4567

EDUCATION

CANTER COLLEGE, Winterville, ME   2004–2008
- B.A. in Biology, magna cum laude, Chemistry Minor, 2008
- Honors thesis on the role of the Wnk-4 gene in developing Drosophila embryos
- Captain, Canter Woodsmen; events included timed wood chopping and sawing, log-rolling
- Member, Canter Crew

UNIVERSITY OF ONSWAIN, Dunedin, NZ   Spring 2007
- Studied native plant and marine biology; explored the North and South islands

RESEARCH EXPERIENCE

ST. YORK UNIVERSITY DEPARTMENT OF GENETICS, Darien, CT   Summer 2007
Intern
- Searched for genetic factors linked to intracranial aneurysm;
  assisted head researcher in lab screening; created weekly status reports

UNIVERSITY OF ONSWAIN DEPARTMENT OF GENETICS, Dunedin, NZ   Summer 2006
Intern
- Searched for genes connected with autism and Tourette syndrome;
  sequenced and screened thousands of patient samples;
  results were published in *Science* magazine article

OUTDOOR EXPERIENCE

MAINE OUTDOOR EDUCATION SOCIETY (*volunteer*)   Summer 2008
- Led high-school seniors on four-day backpacking trips on the Appalachian
  and Grafton Loop trails

LONGSHORE SAILING SCHOOL, Westport, CT   Summer 2006
- Taught kayaking classes for ages 9-11 and 12-16 on the Long Island Sound

HABITAT FOR HUMANITY (*volunteer*), New Haven, CT   Summer 2003
- Gutted and constructed homes, improved property

STUDENT CONSERVATION ASSOCIATION (*volunteer*)   Summers 2002, 2003
- Dinosaur National Monument, UT: Expanded the park's backcountry by creating fresh trails
- River of No Return Wilderness Preserve, ID: Surveyed for invasive species of plants in the backcountry

CERTIFICATIONS

Infant/child/adult CPR; Wilderness First Aid; First Aid

JOHN WINTERS

61 Armory Road, Manchester, NH 06873 • j23winters@jmail.com · (603) 123-4567

EDUCATION

CANTER COLLEGE, Winterville, ME   2004–2008
- B.A. in Biology, magna cum laude, Chemistry Minor, 2008
- Honors thesis on the role of the Wnk-4 gene in developing Drosophila embryos
- Captain, Canter Woodsmen; events included timed wood chopping and sawing, log-rolling
- Member, Canter Crew

Note the explanation of obscure associations or terminology.

UNIVERSITY OF ONSWAIN, Dunedin, NZ   Spring 2007
- Studied native plant and marine biology; explored the North and South islands

RESEARCH EXPERIENCE

ST. YORK UNIVERSITY DEPARTMENT OF GENETICS, Darien, CT   Summer 2007
Intern
- Searched for genetic factors linked to intracranial aneurysm;
  assisted head researcher in lab screening; created weekly status reports

Separating these two categories was a great move—this résumé might have seemed disjointed otherwise.

UNIVERSITY OF ONSWAIN DEPARTMENT OF GENETICS, Dunedin, NZ   Summer 2006
Intern
- Searched for genes connected with autism and Tourette syndrome;
  sequenced and screened thousands of patient samples;
  results were published in *Science* magazine article

Another great example of the use of concrete detail to link your work to a greater purpose . . .

OUTDOOR EXPERIENCE

MAINE OUTDOOR EDUCATION SOCIETY *(volunteer)*   Summer 2008
- Led high-school seniors on four-day backpacking trips on the Appalachian
  and Grafton Loop trails

A simple way to differentiate volunteer from paid work . . .

LONGSHORE SAILING SCHOOL, Westport, CT   Summer 2006
- Taught kayaking classes for ages 9-11 and 12-16 on the Long Island Sound

HABITAT FOR HUMANITY *(volunteer)*, New Haven, CT   Summer 2003
- Gutted and constructed homes, improved property

STUDENT CONSERVATION ASSOCIATION *(volunteer)*   Summers 2002, 2003
- Dinosaur National Monument, UT: Expanded the park's backcountry by creating fresh trails
- River of No Return Wilderness Preserve, ID: Surveyed for invasive species of plants in the backcountry

CERTIFICATIONS

Infant/child/adult CPR; Wilderness First Aid; First Aid

Don't omit this kind of information from your résumé; first-aid and CPR are extremely valuable in any workplace.

Column Craziness

This résumé suffers from a case of over-formatting. Instead of adding clarity, the columns create chaos and confusion. To boot, the more complicated you make your format, the more difficult it will be for you to reorganize your résumé so that it suits each job for which you're applying.

RÉSUMÉ

Ms. Jane Smith
42 Huntington Avenue, Boston, MA 02115
Telephone: (617) 262-3210 • Mobile: (617) 448-8792 • jsmith@myemailaddress.com

---

EDUCATION

St. Elmo's University	**Associations**	St. Elmo, NC
Graduated 2010	Member of Pi Beta Pi Sorority	September 2006-present
Bachelor of Arts	Member, Special Advisory	
Major:English	Committee to Admissions	
Minor in History	Peer Tutor, UWC	Florence, Italy
Studio Arts Center International	Student (abroad)	August-December 2008
	Activities	
	Varsity Field Hockey (New England	St. Elmo, NC
	Championship Participant),	May-September 2008
	Varsity Squash, Lacrosse,	
	Softball, Photography program	

GENERAL WORK EXPERIENCE

University of St. Elmo Press	**Publicity Intern**	
	As intern, duties included proofreading	Newton, MA
	copy, assembling Press kits, drafting	2004-2006
	press releases	
	Updating computer databases,	
	Market researching, selecting	
	Pull quotes from reviews. Contributed	
	original ideas	
Vino e Mare Restaurant	**Hostess**	
	Tasks included greeting and Seating	St. Elmo, NC
	patrons in a timely manner	Summer 2008
	Food Running, Garnishing Food,	
	answering phones	

INTERPERSONAL EXPERIENCE

Summer Fun Day Camp	**Counselor**	
	Tasks included leading small and Large	
	groups, coordinating Schedules,	
	organizing Activities	
Canterbury Hospital	**Clinical Volunteer:**	
	Tasks included providing information to	Canterbury, MA
	patients and visitors; basic filing, open-	June 2008-August 2008
	ing and sorting documents; photocopy-	
	ing and general office assistance	

PERSONAL INTERESTS

	Working with people	Sustainability
	Writing/Reading	Volunteering
	Avid photographer www.jdoephoto.com	Exploring and contributing
	Passion for cooking	to new communities
	Athlete	Travel

EXCELLENT REFERENCES WILL BE FURBISHED UPON REQUEST

*A résumé is a résumé—
we know what it is . . .
Your name and contact
info are all you need.*

RÉSUMÉ

Name only! No titles. **Ms. Jane Smith**
42 Huntington Avenue, Boston, MA 02115
Telephone: (617) 262-3210 • Mobile: (617) 448-8792 • jsmith@myemailaddress.com

---

EDUCATION
St. Elmo's University
Graduated 2010
Bachelor of Arts
Major:English
Minor in History
Studio Arts Center International

*A more professional way to convey
this information: "St. Elmo's
University, BA 2010. English Major,
History Minor"*

GENERAL WORK EXPERIENCE
University of St. Elmo Press

*Don't waste space with such a
general heading. Tailor it to the
job for which you're applying.*

*We got it the
first time . . .*

Vino e Mare Restaurant

INTERPERSONAL EXPERIENCE
Summer Fun Day Camp

*Not a viable category.
Try Teaching Experience.*

Canterbury Hospital

PERSONAL INTERESTS

*If they're yours, they're yours . . .
"Personal" is redundant.*

Associations
Member of Pi Beta Pi Sorority
Member, Special Advisory
    Committee to Admissions
Peer Tutor, UWC
Student (abroad)
Activities
Varsity Field Hockey (New England
    Championship Participant),
Varsity Squash, Lacrosse,
Softball, Photography program

Publicity Intern
As intern, duties included proofreading
    copy, assembling Press kits, drafting
    press releases
Updating computer databases,
Market researching, selecting
Pull quotes from reviews. Contributed
    original ideas

Hostess
Tasks included greeting and Seating
    patrons in a timely manner
Food Running, Garnishing Food,
    answering phones

Counselor
Tasks included leading small and Large
    groups, coordinating Schedules,
    organizing Activities

Clinical Volunteer:
Tasks included providing information to
    patients and visitors; basic filing, open-
    ing and sorting documents; photocopy-
    ing and general office assistance

Working with people
Writing/Reading
Avid photographer www.jdoephoto.com
Passion for cooking
Athlete

St. Elmo, NC
September 2006-present

Florence, Italy
August-December 2008

St. Elmo, NC
May-September 2008

*How is an employer supposed to know what
this stands for?*

Newton, MA
2004-2006

*This candidate had some strange ideas
about the use of capital letters. . . .*

As opposed to what? Unoriginal ideas?

St. Elmo, NC
Summer 2008

*Nice concept, poor execution:
just say "promptly"*

*Don't waste even one precious
line of a resume with this kind of
useless convention. And the proper
word is "furnished."*

Canterbury, MA
June 2008-August 2008

*Do you really think an employer
has the time?*

Sustainability
Volunteering
Exploring and contributing
    to new communities
Travel

EXCELLENT REFERENCES WILL BE FURBISHED UPON REQUEST

RÉSUMÉ DON'TS

▶ Let me offer a few words of advice about what to avoid—despite what the Office of Career Services at your school tells you.

■ **Never offer an "objective."** Your objective is to get the job you're applying for, or a job you didn't even know existed at that company. If you state that your objective is to "obtain an entry-level job in the marketing industry" and I have a job beyond entry level for which you might be qualified, I have every right to toss your résumé. Save the space for listing your experiences and achievements.

■ **Do not include your GPA or SAT score.** If someone wants to know, let him ask—then look for another job. What does your GPA really say about you? If you were a high academic achiever, you have probably won awards; if your GPA is low or middle-of-the-road, it will only diminish your other achievements. A focus on grades will reveal only that you're stuck in a high

school mentality. One exception: for an academic job or a graduate school application, a GPA is meaningful and may even be required.

■ **Do not say "references available upon request."** Is there really another option? References *not* available upon request?

■ **Do not include "leadership" as a category.** Though employers always look for self-starters, for many entry-level jobs the ability to follow and take direction is just as important. The term "leadership" may also appear juvenile; your position as captain of the squash team or chair of the student affairs committee will speak for itself.

■ **Do not abuse the "action verb."** Don't use "performed" unless what you were performing was a play. You don't need to "perform research" or "perform light office duties." Just do them. Don't write "served as assistant to the director." Just be the assistant! Sure, you should try to use the most precise and active language you can, but not to the point of absurdity.

■ **Do not quantify if you don't really have enough to quantify.** If you have a specific number for an amount of money you helped raise or subscriptions you sold, fine—use the numbers. But don't write "published one poem in school literary magazine." "Poetry published in school literary magazine" is fine—or better yet, add a publications section and list the name of the poem and the date of publication.

■ **Do not reveal height, weight, date of birth, health, or marital status.** Do not attach a photograph unless you're applying for a modeling or acting job and need to submit a headshot.

■ **Do not use acronyms unless they are well-known.** Explain all insider terms. Avoid abbreviations (with the exception of state names) if possible.

■ **Show, don't tell.** Do not use adjectives describing your own achievements (dynamic, efficient). The employer (and your references) will be the judge of that! If you "increased circulation from 10,000 to 100,000 subscriptions," we assume you're dynamic and efficient. If you "proofread copy to meet weekly deadlines," we understand that you can work under pressure. If you were a "waitress in a 500-seat seaside tourist restaurant at high season," this tells us more than if you write "efficient server at busy restaurant."

■ **Do not list Web addresses on your résumé.** I'm not looking—unless you're a Web designer or wrote content and are applying for a job where that's relevant.

■ **Don't leave too much white space.** Add and reorganize material or use a slightly larger font and wider margin to make sure the page looks filled.

(continued from page 65)

Attach your résumé and your cover letter (see chapter 4), and also paste the cover letter into the body of the e-mail, replacing paragraph tabs with line spaces and correcting any formatting problems. In the closing paragraph of the e-mail, add: "My résumé and a copy of this letter are attached."

MyWebsite.com

Q. My résumé is posted on my website. I have writing samples posted there, too. Can't I just send a cover letter that directs employers to my site?

A. Are you kidding me? You think employers have the time to go to people's websites to read their résumés? Think again.

Farming It Out

Q. What about professional résumé services?

A. What about them? You've read this chapter, so you don't need them. Better to set up an informational interview with someone in a hiring position in a field you're interested in. During the session, ask if he'd be willing to review your résumé and make suggestions. Free, and more effective!

The Must-Read Cover Letter

►►►►►►►►►►►►►►►►►►►►►►►►►►►►►►►►►►

ALLOW ME TO INTRODUCE MYSELF

S o now you have the perfect résumé. You stick it in an envelope and send it to your dream company, right?

Wrong.

Now you write your cover letter.

The problem is, many people don't know what a cover letter is, why you need one, or what goes in it. Here's what a good cover letter can do, besides introduce you and your résumé:

► Serve as a sample of your writing and communication skills. Can you write well and vividly? Does the letter conform to standard business format? Does it contain typos, misspellings, or grammatical errors? (In other words, how meticulous are you?)

► Convey a sense of what you're like as a person and potential colleague. Do you sound smart? Fun? Boring? Pompous? Negative? Driven? The cover letter is a personal ad of sorts—you want the reader to want to meet you.

▶ Serve as a road map for an eventual interview. The cover letter can highlight the things on your résumé that you'd like to talk more about.

▶ Show that you know where you're applying and aren't just blindly and randomly submitting résumés. A great cover letter is tailored to the particular job for which you're applying.

Cover letters should be concise and informative, radiating competence and confidence; professional, but with enough personality to intrigue without ringing alarm bells. A good cover letter should not inspire me to call over a colleague and say, "Hey, get a load of this."

Keep your letter short and to the point, never more than a page. The information should be objective—stick to facts, not your judgments and estimations of your own talents and worth. Your goal is to show why you, among hundreds of applicants, should be selected for an interview and why you are the right person for this job.

What's the Point?

Q. I see what you're saying, but do I really need to write a cover letter? Can't I just send my résumé alone or write "see attached"? I mean, they'll figure it out—I want the job!

A. If you send your résumé without a cover letter, here's what you're saying: I am so egocentric that I think you, the employer, have been waiting around for my résumé. There is only one job open at your company and you know I want it. In short: Sending a résumé without a cover letter is a great way to look arrogant and sloppy.

They Asked for It!

Q. What if I called the person to whom I'm sending my résumé and he's expecting it? Do I still need a cover letter?

A. Yes. The cover letter is the formal and written reminder of whatever was said in the phone call—especially if the call revealed useful information about the job. Perhaps the employer said that although the ad didn't mention it, the job may involve some fund-raising. The cover letter is your chance to highlight that you helped your former boss with grant proposals and served as fund-raising chair for a college theatrical production.

Does Anyone Really Read Cover Letters?

Q. Aren't people so busy that they'll just throw away the cover

letter and go straight for the résumé?

A. Sure—if your cover letter says so little it's garbage-worthy, in which case your résumé might end up in the trash as well. Yes, people are busy—and if they're looking to hire a new person, they're probably even busier than usual. But your letter will stand out because it's short, to the point, well-written, well-presented, and appears to offer a solution to their problem.

It's true that some people won't bother looking at cover letters, but it's also true that some people pay more attention to the cover letter than they do to the résumé. A cover letter can't hurt (unless it's poorly written and typo-laden), but it can help.

No Letters, Please!

Q. What if the ad says "no cover letter"?

A. If the ad says no cover letter, don't send one. But prepare one anyway, and make it your business to find someone, anyone, who works at that company and can put your résumé—with a cover letter—directly into the hands of the person doing the hiring.

THE FORMAT

▶ Like a résumé, a cover letter should never be longer than a page. It should be double-spaced, with only three to five paragraphs, in 12-point type.

Follow the format of a standard business letter by including the following components, in order of their appearance:

- The date
- The full name and address of the person to whom you are writing
- The salutation ("Dear Mr. So-and-So")
- The body of the letter
- The sign-off
- Your name, both typed and signed
- Your contact info.

See the sample on pages 90–91 for a visual.

Anatomy of a Cover Letter

The cover letter is not to be taken lightly—especially after you've worked so hard on your résumé. The cover letter can—and should—do things your résumé can't. It covers your résumé, both literally and figuratively. It's the first impression an employer or Human Resources (HR) manager has of you, or the way to convey who recommended that you apply—the information that can make the difference between your application being read or dead. This is not information found on your résumé; if your cover letter simply rehashes your experience, you need to go back to the drawing board.

You've probably heard that your résumé is what gets your foot in the door. But a résumé without a cover letter is barefoot. Who walks around barefoot in an office? (Actually, my boss used to pad around in his socks. But he was the boss.) Don't go barefoot.

First, the cover letter needs to explain why you're sending your résumé. Which job or internship are you applying for? Don't make the mistake of thinking that the job you're applying for is the only position an employer has open. Did someone tell you to send it? If so, the most important piece of information you can include is that person's name. (More on that later.) Are you answering an ad for a specific job posting, or hoping to secure an informational interview? Did you hear from a friend that there was an opening? Have you identified this company as somewhere you want to work and are hoping there's a job open?

The next crucial piece of information: Who are you? Are you someone who just graduated from college? Who interned at the company several years ago and now wants a full-time job? Who just spent a year working in a related industry? Who has many years of experience in the field? Let the reader know up front. Don't bury your lead!

Organize your information in order of importance. Don't follow a paragraph about what you did in college with one about a job you had in the industry—that's the more important experience, even if you've just graduated. Don't be a slave to chronology. Yes, perhaps getting your degree is the most recent thing you've done—but that doesn't mean it's the most significant to the employer. He may only be looking at candidates with college degrees—which means that if you have relevant industry experience from an internship or part-time or summer job, he will be intrigued.

Next: Why should the company be interested in you? In the "Ask Not" tradition, ask not what the employer can do for you, but what you can do for the employer. The employer doesn't care whether or not this is your dream job—he's looking for a dream employee.

Keep in mind that the cover letter is a brief introduction to who you are, not your chance to tell the story of your life. No one has time to read your autobiography. I remember reading one cover letter that was essentially a two-page personal statement with a Hemingway quote at the bottom.

Unprofessional and a big turnoff. (On the other hand, don't go to the other extreme with a cursory "See enclosed.")

The structure is simple: All you'll need is an introduction, one to three body paragraphs, and a conclusion.

Last, the cover letter should contain clear contact info and a suggestion for the next course of action. Your contact info will appear on the top of your résumé, of course, but an employer may also glance at the last paragraph of your cover letter to see what your plan is. Will you call to follow up? Are you an out-of-town applicant who'll be coming in at the beginning of the month? Will you wait to hear back?

"Dear Prospective Employer"

Don't take the risk of appearing presumptuous by using the addressee's first name only. Address your letter using both first and last names, i.e., "Dear Sally Williams." Make sure you have spelled the addressee's name correctly and gotten the title right (Mr. versus Dr., for example) by checking the company's website and calling the receptionist. (Tell him that you are calling to check the spelling of so-and-so's name; it's a common request that won't come as a surprise.) Why bother to call when the information is available online? Because the Web is notoriously full of typos, errors, and out-of-date information. Do not mix title and full name. Write either "Dear Sally Williams" if the full name is given or "Dear Ms. Williams" if not, but not "Dear Ms. Sally Williams. (When you're writing thank-you notes or any correspondence after a call or interview, you may use first names as appropriate, especially if you were encouraged to do so during the meeting.)

Can't Get a Name?

Q. I don't know anyone where I'm applying. May I address my cover letter "To Whom This May Concern"?

A. Others may tell you differently, but I think you absolutely need to find someone to whom to address your letter. I'm guessing you know someone—you just don't know it. I'll bet your mother's cousin's daughter's boyfriend works for that company—or in the industry—and can find you a name. But you've got to spend time doing research. Once you come up with someone at the company— in any department—get in touch, introduce yourself, and find out to whom you might send your résumé. Look back at chapter 2 for more on networking.

If you've truly exhausted every resource and can't find a name, then you must rely on whatever information you do have: Dear Human Resource Department. Dear Sir or Madam. To: The Smith Corporation Re: Analyst Position. Being accurate will help to ensure that your cover letter and résumé end up in the right hands. Please don't use terms like "Dear Associates" or "Dear Colleagues." I've seen it done, and it's a big no-no. They're not your colleagues yet!

Grabbing Their Interest

Good cover letters start with a hook, like the lead of any good news story. "Dear Crocodile Dundee: I've just returned from a semester in the Amazon and was thrilled to see you're hiring tour guides." A caveat: Though you want to grab the reader's attention from the very beginning of your letter, you need to be professional. (That's why the best way to get someone's attention is by using a name he'll recognize.) Throughout your letter you need to reveal as much voice and personality as you can while maintaining a professional and confident tone. In their quest for immediate attention, people sometimes go very, very wrong in their openings.

"Look no further!" (Gimmicky, juvenile.)

"How are you?" (Fawning, ridiculous. This is not a letter to a friend.)

Something written in a bubble on the top of the page as if it's a cartoon.

Yes, these are all from real cover letters. See box, opposite, and page 85 for more examples of tragic cover-letter diction.

You want the reader to want to meet you, but remember, this is not a social encounter; the employer has a job he needs to get done. Even when e-mailing, make sure to use a proper greeting. No "Hey" or "Hi." You are not writing a casual e-mail to a friend. Make sure to use proper spelling, grammar, and punctuation; no IM language or abbreviations, emoticons, or text-message spelling or shorthand.

Isn't It a Stretch?

Q. My father's friend recommended I use his name when applying to a company where he has a personal connection. I've met him only once. Isn't it stretching it for me to mention him?

A. A recognizable proper name in the opening of a cover letter is a real attention-grabber, and there's no shame in using a contact, no matter how

TERRIBLE OPENINGS . . .

▶ Hold on to your armrests—the atrocious cover-letter openings you'll see below were actually used by unwitting job-seekers. Needless to say, you should file these as DON'TS.

- Dear Associates . . .
- Look no further!
- My name is . . .
- Greetings!
- HELLO!
- How are you?
- Ms. Simmons, fellow book lover . . .
- I hope this letter finds you well . . .
- I hope you're having a fantastic week . . .
- After scanning the options available to me . . .
- A company needs to run smoothly for creativity and efficiency to flourish, and it is the position of the assistant to facilitate this ease of operations.
- Allow me to introduce a seasoned administrative professional who has been exposed to the office environment on many levels.
- This letter is an application for the position of . . .
- Recently, I have been exploring potential employers that deal with my experience, education, talents and skills. Today, I am in search of employment and have taken this opportunity to introduce myself.
- The ad immediately appealed to me and I recommend myself for this position because I have the skills you specified.
- I posted my résumé on the Careers Website a few months ago hoping perchance that a position I may qualify for will open up soon and I would like to express that I am very much interested should you have the time to go over my updated résumé.

distant—so long as you've been given permission to use it. Just make sure you explain the connection clearly and honestly: "When I met John McBride at a family wedding last week, he suggested . . ." Don't imply that you know someone better than you do.

Using Effective Language

Have you ever heard people talk as if every statement is a question? You know what I mean? They inflect up with every sentence? Even if it's a statement? Aargh. You've got to exorcise your inner Valley Girl. Inflecting up out loud is bad enough . . . Don't do it on paper.

Get rid of all tentative diction right off the bat. Women are guiltier of this than men, but it's not just women. "I hope that my experience in developing digital media products may make it possible for me to be considered for this position." WHAT? "I hope that"? "May make it possible"? "To be considered"? How much lack of confidence can a person reveal in one sentence? NO, NO, NO! Let's try again: "I have extensive experience in developing digital media products, including X, Y, and Z."

Immerse yourself in newspapers, general-interest and industry magazines, and trade periodicals so that you'll have access to industry keywords (and things to talk about in an interview). Apart from that, stick to simple but precise language. Use a dictionary and thesaurus to vary and refine your language if need be, but don't use words or phrases you don't completely understand—you risk misusing them.

The greatest rule of thumb in cover-letter writing is one that works for any kind of writing: Show, don't tell. As Mark Twain wrote, "Don't say 'The old lady screamed.' Bring her out and let her scream." Amplify your assertions through anecdotes, but be brief and to the point. Ambition and drive should be shown through action, not adjectives: **"As a waitress, I had extensive contact with the public. The job required patience under pressure, physical strength, and the ability to multitask and prioritize."** No need to add ". . . all skills I think would be useful as your assistant." The employer will be the judge of that. Lead him to the conclusion through unassailable facts, evidence, and anecdotes. You might describe the time six tour buses pulled up and you had forty-five minutes to serve three hundred people who didn't speak English.

Many cover letters include the phrase "I am interested in . . ." But in fact, what you are interested in doing is not an employer's first concern. Remember, the cover letter is about what you can do for the employer. An employer definitely doesn't care if the job meets the criteria you are looking for in a place of employment, as many naive job-hunters explain. Instead, you need to make the link between what you've been doing, what you are capable of doing, and the job.

DON'T TELL THEM WHAT THE
JOB WILL DO FOR YOU . . .

▶ . . . tell them what *you* will do for the company. It can't be overstressed: An employer is interested in what you can bring to the table, not in what you would get out of the job. So don't fall into the word-traps used by these self-interested job-hunters:

■ The job is well suited to my interests and qualifications.

■ The job advertised is one which seems very beneficial to my learning and development.

■ This position is a natural extension of my experience and offers me the opportunity to relocate to New York City, a transition I see as a necessary step toward achieving my career goals.

On the other hand, even when you're focused on what makes you useful and hirable, you need to let your experience speak for itself. The following bad cover-letter language makes the mistake of *telling* rather than *showing:*

■ I am a motivated college graduate who would love to gain experience in the film industry. Although I am young and inexperienced, I know I would be an asset to any company. I am bright, hardworking and have lots of enthusiasm.

■ I am sure my services would be useful to you.

■ I believe if given the chance, I could make a significant contribution to your accounting department.

■ I have confidence in my ability to succeed in your organization.

■ I am confident that I could both contribute to and benefit from a position at your company.

I'm the Best!

Q. How do I blow my own horn without sounding conceited?

A. It's a question of tone and, once again, of showing, not telling. Don't write, "You will never find a more diligent worker." Instead, cite concrete experiences that reveal you are qualified for the job. Stick to facts, rather than your judgment of your own talents and worth. Best is to use things other people have said about you: Quote someone or use a line from a written evaluation, review, or letter of recommendation. "In my final review, the intern coordinator told me I was the most responsible intern he'd ever seen." Much better than "I am highly responsible." Offer anecdotal evidence: "After setting up an event for sixty people in just a few days, I was voted assistant of the week."

Industry Terms

Q. I have worked in the industry. How much insider's lingo am I allowed to use in my cover letter?

A. Use enough to appear to be an insider, but don't overdo it. If you sling around too many terms, you'll sound like you're just showing off. Refer to skills you gained and tasks you did that show you will be able to hit the ground running with minimal training. "At my most recent position as an intern at Law Inc., I researched historical antecedents, prepared case summaries, and proofread briefs."

Bringing Your Résumé to Life

E ven the most expressive résumé is no more than a bulleted list of accomplishments; the job of the cover letter is to make that list come alive—and in some cases, even to alter the way the reader perceives it. You must make the connections between your résumé and the job at hand. If you haven't had direct experience in the field of magazine circulation, for instance, you might draw the link to your résumé by saying, **"My experience working in the box office of our college theater offered me insight into the importance of seeking annual subscribers."**

Sometimes a job will call on less-than-obvious skills you picked up in a variety of jobs or internships; the cover letter is a great place to bring those skills together so they paint a picture of a well-rounded candidate. **"As a competitive runner, I've always understood the importance of discipline. During my internship at Rogers and Sons, I was able to add to that an appreciation for detail."**

If your résumé is sparse, work concrete experiences into your cover letter. I'm convinced that unless you've been living in a cave doing nothing your whole life, you have useful skills—for something. If, in fact, you have been living in a cave, I could write you a great cover letter touting your survival skills, your ingenuity and initiative, and your ability to work on your own.

If it's truly the case that you did very little except go to classes in high school and college (and maybe party, if that's what you were doing), you've got to turn vice into virtue. Instead of thinking of yourself as a loser, how about presenting yourself as someone who is highly focused and can follow instructions and dedicate yourself fully to any single task at hand? **"I am a recent graduate of Smithson College. While at Smithson, I concentrated exclusively on my studies. Now I am ready to apply the rigor and discipline that marked my college career to the workplace. My longstanding interest in history led me to (your organization)."** Then mention a few courses and projects you feel are relevant to the job.

Or let's say you've done "nothing" but babysit for your younger siblings. How about presenting yourself as the caretaker of the three younger children in your family, as someone with endless energy, enthusiasm, and the ability to react quickly to changing situations?

Ideally, though, what you emphasize in your cover letter should be determined by the job for which you're applying.

Spinning Your Experience

Q. I've never worked in this industry before. Do I stand a chance? What do I write in my cover letter to convince them to at least interview me?

A. Okay. The first thing to think about is getting an internship—paid or volunteer—or a temp position in a related company. If you're serious about pursuing a job in this area, volunteer for an hour a week. Then you can truthfully say, "I am currently volunteering at . . ." or "As a temporary assistant at the Rutledge Company, I learned the basics of . . ." At the very least, find someone to shadow even for a day or half a day. For more on identifying this kind of opportunity, review chapter 1, Welcome to Job, Inc.

Employers understand that people switch careers, but since hiring someone from outside their field is risky, you have to convince them that you bring valuable skills or perspectives to the table. Be enthusiastic and confident about your prior experience—bashing the industry you're leaving will just make you look like a whiner. And again, emphasize your transferable skills. Let's say you're applying to be a school-group docent in a museum and are a former camp counselor who just graduated with a B.A. in Art History. You might write: "My work as a camp counselor over the last four summers has given me extensive experience with eight- to fourteen-year-olds. On rainy days I led them in arts and crafts activities, drawing on my course work as an art-history

(continued on page 96)

GREAT COVER-LETTER SAMPLES

▶ Suffering from a lack of cover-letter inspiration? Take a look at some of the following sample paragraphs, taken from real letters, to help you communicate your experience.

While these are obviously not to be plagiarized, note the basic structures and the way concrete examples are used to convey skills.

Revealing Your Skills Through Your Experience

"While interning at Pacific Pictures, I read submissions and digitally archived thousands of scripts, developing my instincts about what made for a salable project. As part of a working team, I became familiar with the day-to-day operations of a large company. At my next internship, at the County Public Defenders Office, I organized one man's scattered medical and criminal records, which came to over a thousand pages; though it wasn't part of my assignment, in the process I stumbled upon behavioral patterns that the public defender said helped save the defendant's life. This year I worked as a researcher for a professor of constitutional law, independently using the offices and archives of the American Liberties Union and the Charles Law Library. I synthesized weeks of reading into a few pages on the twenty-year history of one Supreme Court case."

Showing Ingenuity and Adaptability

"I recently completed a semester as a student-teacher at the Moses School in Nashville, an experience that honed my managerial and communication skills. As a Spanish, French, and English teacher, I brought enthusiasm and rigor to a results-oriented approach. Working with high school students taught me flexibility and calm in the face of pressure. When a lesson fell flat, I had to quickly and seamlessly readjust my plan to engage my students. I became an adaptive, improvisatory communicator—no simple task when your audience is a group of twenty restless adolescents. My approach paid off: My French and Spanish students broke into the top rankings on national exams, and each of my eleventh graders wrote and presented a fifteen-page research paper. Now I am eager to apply that drive, discipline, and creativity to a position in a fast-paced marketing department."

Applying College and Internship Experience

"I know what a difference education can make in a person's perception of the world, and I respect your mission. I'm a recent graduate of Greenville University, where I interned at the university press and completed an independent study in Web design. I also studied abroad in Asia, teaching English in local immigrant communities.

Of course, I understand that while missions are important, marketing is a concrete art. My internships with a literary agency, two publishing houses, and a web communications department have provided me with a diverse set of skills including:

- Knowledge of targeted marketing techniques—I worked directly with the Marketing Director at Weinberg Media.

- Writing experience—I drafted pitch and rejection letters, posted web articles, and wrote editorial notes and reader reports.

- Administrative experience—I've conducted interviews and answered phones.

- Familiarity with the adult-trade book market—I researched potential markets at Borders and Barnes & Noble."

If You're Entering a New Field . . .

"As you can see from my résumé, I graduated from Yorktown University in May of 2009, after which I jumped into the working world in Boston as an office assistant at Wholespring International, a European investment firm. While this is not the long-term professional setting I envision for myself, it has allowed me to work on challenging, detail-oriented projects in a multi-lingual environment. As the sole assistant to all members of the investment team, I have done everything from setting up meetings for senior associates to editing and formatting a PowerPoint presentation for the CEO's keynote address to investors."

Cover-Letter Samples

Experiencing a bit of cover-letter-writer's block? Read the following for inspiration—and some worst-case cautionary tales to keep you on the right track.

An Exemplary Cover Letter

By now, I hope it's sunk in: The cover letter is an ever-evolving entity, tailored to its recipient and to the job description. So obviously there's no such thing as the perfect cover letter—but this one is close. It's got specificity, clarity, appropriate tone, and solid structure.

ELIZABETH ROWLEY | 455 MAIN STREET | LEDGEWOOD, NJ 07852

Jane Brandt
News Magazine
6400 Chalkstone Avenue
Dayton, New Jersey 08810   June 6, 2009

Dear Ms. Brandt:

I am writing at the suggestion of David Mitchell to apply for the Advertising Assistant position at *News* magazine. David was my supervisor at the campus Box Office at the University of Michigan. As a long-time admirer of *News* magazine, I was excited to learn about this opening.

I'm a recent graduate of the University of Michigan, where I served as Advertising Manager for the Michigan *Independent*, a weekly student-run magazine with a circulation of 50,000. I was responsible not only for supervising a team that sold over $5,000 of ads weekly, but also for the layout, copy-editing, and proofreading of the ads themselves. The position required flexibility and responsibility, and allowed me to experience the wide range of tasks involved in an advertising department—from trafficking art files to logging income.

Working at the Michigan Campus Box Office provided hands-on training in professional client relations, both in person and over the phone. A typical shift entailed browsing Filemaker for new events, addressing questions about concerts, handling ticket exchanges, and managing group sales. As a box office staffer, I needed to respond quickly and politely to all requests, while learning the rudiments of both sales and publicity. These are all skills I hope to use in the service of *News* magazine.

I look forward to hearing from you at your earliest convenience.

Sincerely,

Elizabeth Rowley

Elizabeth Rowley
erowley@inbox.com/201-334-4728

ELIZABETH ROWLEY | 455 MAIN STREET | LEDGEWOOD, NJ 07852

Jane Brandt
News Magazine
6400 Chalkstone Avenue
Dayton, New Jersey 08810

Nice use of a personal introduction in the opening line, with additional detail in the following sentence.

June 6, 2009

Dear Ms. Brandt:

Express your interest without fawning or selling the company back to itself.

I am writing at the suggestion of David Mitchell to apply for the Advertising Assistant position at *News* magazine. David was my supervisor at the campus Box Office at the University of Michigan. As a long-time admirer of *News* magazine, I was excited to learn about this opening.

More specific examples to show insider knowledge of the field and an attention to detail . . .

I'm a recent graduate of the University of Michigan, where I served as Advertising Manager for the Michigan *Independent*, a weekly student-run magazine with a circulation of 50,000. I was responsible not only for supervising a team that sold over $5,000 of ads weekly, but also for the layout, copy-editing, and proofreading of the ads themselves. The position required flexibility and responsibility, and allowed me to experience the wide range of tasks involved in an advertising department—from trafficking art files to logging income.

Contextualize information for your readers.

Excellent use of numbers and specifics! That's the kind of thing that grabs a reader's attention.

Savvy link from one type of job to another.

Make that Computer Skills section come alive!

Working at the Michigan Campus Box Office provided hands-on training in professional client relations, both in person and over the phone. A typical shift entailed browsing Filemaker for new events, addressing questions about concerts, handling ticket exchanges, and managing group sales. As a box office staffer, I needed to respond quickly and politely to all requests, while learning the rudiments of both sales and publicity. These are all skills I hope to use in the service of *News* magazine.

A better way of implying these attributes than saying "I am flexible and responsible" . . .

I look forward to hearing from you at your earliest convenience.

Sincerely,

Elizabeth Rowley

Elizabeth Rowley
erowley@inbox.com/201-334-4728

The "Funny" Cover Letter: Dangerous Territory

Humor is such an iffy thing. If it works, it works, but if it doesn't, disaster! What may work for one reader won't for another. Here's an example of a letter in which some of the humor falls flat and some doesn't. Still, my overall advice is to stay serious. You're applying for a job, not a spot on *SNL* (aspiring comics aside).

SAMUEL TAYLOR
439 Harbor Street • Portland, Maine, 04104

Ms. Monica Jones, Executive Director
The McGuire Group
1001 Executive Drive
Kansas City, MO 66101

July 11, 2009

Dear Ms. Jones

Look no further!

So you need an Assistant to the Executive Director and you'd like him to perform administrative duties while multitasking without appearing to be a chicken with his head cut off?

Show me the filing pile and I'll bring the label-maker after grabbing folders from the supply room I just reorganized. Useful skills include but are not limited to scanning, graphic design, un-jamming photo copiers, translating inner-departmental memos, expense reporting, and delivering piping hot cappuccinos for meetings.

My résumé is included for your consideration. My salary is negotiable, starting at $28K with health, dental, and 401K. Contact me today to learn what more I have to offer at (910) 234-5678.

Best,

Samuel Taylor

Samuel Taylor
T: (207) 654-3210
staylor@cox.net

Encl.

SAMUEL TAYLOR
439 Harbor Street ♦ Portland, Maine, 04104

Ms. Monica Jones, Executive Director
The McGuire Group
1001 Executive Drive
Kansas City, MO 66101

This lapse in tone might be read as an indicator of poor judgment.

July 11, 2009

Okay, I'll admit, I cracked a smile when I read this paragraph. But I frankly don't think it's worth the risk. Even if an employer thinks you're funny, he might be wary—someone who's brazen enough to joke around in a cover letter might use inappropriate humor in a front of a client.

Dear Ms. Jones

Look no further!

So you need an Assistant to the Executive Director and you'd like him to perform administrative duties while multitasking without appearing to be a chicken with his head cut off?

This paragraph actually works well. The examples are concrete and convincing, and the wit is somewhat subdued. Still risky, but here he pulls it off.

Show me the filing pile and I'll bring the label-maker after grabbing folders from the supply room I just reorganized. Useful skills include but are not limited to scanning, graphic design, un-jamming photo copiers, translating inner-departmental memos, expense reporting, and delivering piping hot cappuccinos for meetings.

My résumé is included for your consideration. My salary is negotiable, starting at $28K with health, dental, and 401K. Contact me today to learn what more I have to offer at (910) 234-5678.

Never volunteer your salary requirements unless you have to! And don't make demands in a cover letter.

Best,

Samuel Taylor

Tone problem again. This sounds like a line from a bad personal ad!

Samuel Taylor
T: (207) 654-3210
staylor@cox.net

Encl.

There's a paragraph missing here; the applicant should explain where he acquired these skills, highlighting and contextualizing jobs from his résumé.

Misplaced Pizzazz:
A Classic Cover-Letter DON'T

I've seen many cover-letter blunders in my time. So much wasted effort, so many missed opportunities . . . This letter is a good example of how a lack of detail and an even unintentionally arrogant turn-of-phrase can destroy an applicant's chances.

FAX

To: HR   **From:** James Carter

Fax: (222) 456-2222   **Pages:** 2

Phone: (222) 456-2225   **Date:** April 2009

Re:

To Whom It May Concern:

Recently, I have been exploring careers that might suit me experience, education, talents and skills. I am in search of employment and have taken this opportunity to introduce myself.

Allow me to introduce a seasoned administrative professional who has been exposed to the office environment on many levels.

I am a motivated self-starter with drive and determination to get a job done. In addition, my skills range from general office responsibilities to overseeing the needs of staff. I am an organized yet a flexible team player and I continue to grow and learn within my profession.

Would you consider my request for a personal interview? I can be reached at the below number and or address. I am ready!

Sincerely,
James Carter
535 Jackson Street
Sioux City, Iowa 51111
Cell: 712-329-4307
E-mail: jcarter@mymail.com

Clearly, this job-hunter didn't read chapter 2 carefully enough. If you don't have a name, and you're sending your materials in by fax, you certainly need to indicate which job you're applying for.

FAX

To: HR	**From:** James Carter
Fax: (222) 456-2222	**Pages:** 2
Phone: (222) 456-2225	**Date:** April 2009
Re:	

To Whom It May Concern:

It's unclear what level this applicant is aiming for—or even what industry! Details, please.

Recently, I have been exploring careers that might suit me experience, education, talents and skills. I am in search of employment and have taken this opportunity to introduce myself.

I believe you meant "my" experience. A typo in the first line means game over.

Allow me to introduce a seasoned administrative professional who has been exposed to the office environment on many levels.

Thanks, nice to meet you!

I am a motivated self-starter with drive and determination to get a job done. In addition, my skills range from general office responsibilities to overseeing the needs of staff. I am an organized yet a flexible team player and I continue to grow and learn within my profession.

Sorry to break it to you, but "general office responsibilities" is not a "skill."

Would you consider my request for a personal interview? I can be reached at the below number and or address. I am ready!

Stock phrases like "my profession" convey no information and add no interest.

Sincerely,
James Carter
535 Jackson Street
Sioux City, Iowa 51111
Cell: 712-329-4307
E-mail: jcarter@mymail.com

Yikes!!! I know this is supposed to show initiative and attract attention, but it's just bizarre.

(continued from page 87)

major to come up with projects from copying Picasso's pottery to making Jackson Pollock–like splatter paintings. I especially loved squeezing in mini-lessons on these artists. Creating curriculum and leading museum tours for middle-school groups would be a natural extension of this experience."

If you are a recent graduate, you must convince prospective employers that you are a quick learner. You already have the advantage of being a cheaper hire, and an employer naturally wants to get the most bang for his buck.

Show You've Done the Research

Take the time to show your reader that you know something about his company. But don't waste precious space in a cover letter selling the company back to itself. "Best Hotels has always stood for excellence in the field. With 50 properties around the world, Best Hotels has been a leader in international resort development . . ."

No. The people hiring at Best Hotels know all about what makes it a great company. They want to know who you are and what you can do for them. But you still need to communicate that you have done your research and aren't just randomly applying to jobs. Better would be to say, **"I just spent a study-abroad semester in Dubai through an exchange program. I was enrolled at the university and got to travel extensively across the Middle East. When I learned recently that Best Hotels was opening several world-class properties in the Arab Emirates, I was eager to find out how my knowledge of the area and my degree in hospitality could contribute to the development of this exciting new venture."** Make sure, too, to vary your pronouns, balancing the number of "I"s and "you"s.

Flattery Will Get You Everywhere

Q. How do I communicate that I have always wanted to be in the industry without sounding naive?

A. A simple "I have long admired" in some form will do. "As a lifelong subscriber to *The New York Times,* I would welcome the opportunity to work in the advertising department." "I have long admired Nordstrom's customer service ethic." But don't go into an "Ever since I was a child" routine—that sounds young and self-involved.

Here's the deal with entry-level jobs. When an employer is hiring an assistant, she essentially needs someone who can handle phones and photocopy correctly and cheerfully. Of course she wants someone with a brain, someone who can write, who sees the big picture, who is committed enough to the industry—perhaps, yes, because of a childhood passion—to put in the years of grunt work. So she will care about your passion, but only in the sense that it's a motivating factor to you. First and foremost, she cares that you know how to use a database, and that you are able to answer the phone professionally. While you want to sound enthusiastic, an interview is a more appropriate place to give background detail about your various interests, though you should still avoid talking too extensively about your childhood.

NO SPILLING YOUR GUTS

▶ The cover letter is not the place for true confessions. I'm asked all the time, "How do I de-emphasize that I took a year off, that I was fired, that I'm recovering from a drug problem?"

Here's how you de-emphasize it: by not mentioning it!

People are so highly sensitive about what they perceive as their faults and deficits that they tend to wear them on their sleeves. Tuck them back in! You don't have to worry about these things in a cover letter, because that's exactly what it is: a COVER letter. As well as covering a lot of ground, a cover letter can cover a multitude of sins and flaws.

Comedians Need Not Apply

Q. Can I be funny?

A. I don't know, can you?

I know you mean "may I?" The answer here is, only if you truly are. Like comedians, cover letters that try to be funny but aren't are the worst. Why bias people against you right off the bat with corny jokes and putrid puns? Save the humor, unless you're applying to be a comedy writer.

Your humor can come out in the interview or in a thank-you note, once you've established a rapport with the interviewer.

Jazzing It Up

Q. Every time I write a cover letter it turns out totally generic: here's how I heard about the job, here's my background, attached is my résumé. How do I jazz up my cover letter and make it stand out, without opening myself to ridicule?

A. I'm not a fan of artificially "jazzed up" letters—better to sound highly competent and professional. The most important ways to make a cover letter stand out are a) to include the name of someone who has recommended or referred you to the organization; b) to include the names of places you've worked or where you've been trained; c) to use language from the job description or highlight skills that will ring a bell with the reader; d) to make sure your letter is well written and has a voice, using anecdotes to sustain a reader's interest and prove your points. Read it out loud to yourself as a test—it should sound as though it's coming from a human being.

Using the Want Ads

Q. I am answering an ad. Should I address its points directly in my cover letter?

A. Yes, the ad should be your road map for both your cover letter and résumé. Customize them to reflect everything in the ad or job description. Address stated job requirements with evidence and anecdotes. Again, don't be slavish to the point of parroting language or addressing every last little detail. Keep the big picture in mind.

Too Qualified?

Q. Because I took time off, I am older than the average candidate at my level, and I'm worried that I'll be dismissed as overqualified. Is there any way for me to address that in my cover letter?

A. This is another "turning vice into virtue" situation. Your cover letter needs to show how your previous skills are relevant and explain why you're looking at jobs that appear to be beneath your level of experience. Older candidates have years of professionalism, expertise, and wisdom that younger candidates haven't had time to acquire. Career-switchers bring a new perspective and new contacts to a field. If you're afraid your résumé will close doors, this is where "Selected Experience" comes in—don't list everything you've done.

Closing and Signing Off

In the very last sentences of the letter, indicate your intentions without issuing any ultimatums. Closing with "I will need to hear from you within the week" is not a good idea. You shouldn't call the shots—you are the supplicant. Instead, try this: "Thank you for your consideration. I look forward to meeting with you at your earliest convenience." (Realize this could be never if they do not deem you a worthy candidate.)

Many people write: "I will contact you next week to follow up." Some readers feel this shows initiative, but I think it can appear pushy. Perhaps soften this to "in the next few weeks." You can say what you like, but remember: The employer is in the driver's seat at this stage.

Don't agonize about how to end your letter. Use a standard, conventional closing: "With thanks," "Sincerely," or "Best." Stay away from overly casual or touchy-feely phrases like "Peace" or "Have a Great Day."

Out-of-State Blues

Q. What do I say in my cover letter if I live out of state? It seems like the place to explain my whereabouts and situation, but I don't want to set off any alarms or complicate things.

A. One way to get around the issue is to propose a time frame for interviewing: "I will be in New York City the week of January 3. I'd be happy to come in for an interview that week if it's convenient for you." If you are moving to this new town regardless of whether or not you get a particular job, make that clear; when it comes to entry-level jobs, many companies shy away from the responsibility of bringing on someone who doesn't live locally. (Some employers are willing to pay for some or all moving expenses, but most do not.) Also, an employee just moving to an area will likely need time to get settled—the company knows it won't have your full attention if you're apartment hunting, having your Internet and cable installed, and so on.

There's no need to go into detail about the reasons for your move. Do not volunteer that you're moving for your boyfriend or that you just broke up with your fiancé of five years and need a change. Too much information.

Enclosing References

Q. Should I enclose writing or other samples? References?

A. Only if they are specifically requested. As for references, you should wait until asked, with one exception. If someone definitely known to the potential employer has offered to serve as a reference, include his or her name in the cover letter: "Bill Smith has offered to serve as a reference; he may be reached at (contact info)."

Color Shock

Q. One of my friends sent her résumé and cover letter on neon paper. Should I do that?

A. Is neon what you want to be noticed for? That's the paper equivalent of a woman going to an interview in a tight dress or miniskirt. Not recommended!

Get some good white, off-white, or cream stock to match your résumé paper, with matching envelopes and conservative stamps. No personal stationery or overdone letterhead, and no cartoon-character or "LOVE" stamps. Not that anyone is really looking—the envelopes will be tossed—but why not err on the side of caution?

Send!

Q. Okay, I'm ready to send my cover letter. Now what?

A. No, you're not, unless someone has read it one last time for tone and to check for errors. (See pages 64–65.)

Then make sure you have all the contact information: a correct e-mail or street address with all names spelled properly. Double-check names and titles through Web searches and calls to the company.

Make sure you are sending the right résumé and cover letter! (Yes, I've heard of people sending the wrong letter—a total waste after all that hard work.)

Last, make sure you have copies of both résumé and cover letter for your files—whether paper or electronic—and that each one is dated (i.e., Sent September 3, 2009).

To Attach or Not

Q. If I send my cover letter and résumé electronically, should the cover letter be an attachment, or the body of the e-mail?

A. Let's put it this way. If you include the letter as an attachment only, the recipient opens a blank e-mail and has to take the trouble to download the document. While this may not seem like a big deal, you have delayed the process and added a step. I would send the cover letter both ways; your résumé should be an attachment only. As with your résumé, print out the letter to make sure it's formatted correctly or PDF it before you send it.

Faxing Etiquette

Q. If I'm asked to fax my résumé, do I use my cover letter as my fax cover sheet?

A. To avoid confusion, include a cover sheet with the appropriate information—

a very brief cover letter. Use a simple, businesslike template from your computer's office suite. In the subject line, give as much information as you have: "Re: Assistant Opening in Data Department." In the body of the cover sheet, type up a brief note explaining what you're sending and why. "Dear Mr. Williams: My mother, Anne Jones, let me know she had spoken with you about an opening as a gallery assistant. I am faxing a cover letter and résumé, and would be happy to come in for an interview at your earliest convenience. Best, Sarah Jones." Be sure to specify the number of pages you're sending. Including the cover sheet, that should be three.

Repurposing Your Cover Letter

Q. **Can I use one cover letter for multiple jobs?**

A. You might use the same framework, but you should be tailoring your cover letters to each position for which you apply. Another good reason to do this: Sloppy candidates who use form letters often end up sending them addressed to the wrong person. That kind of carelessness is an obvious ticket to the wastebasket.

Typo Turmoil

Q. **I sent a cover letter, and then I found a typo—and not a little one. Help! What do I do!?**

A. Here's my question: WHY DID YOUR LETTER HAVE A TYPO??? You shouldn't have sent it without having someone proofread it. Okay, I'm calming down . . . So first, correct the mistake on your computer so it doesn't happen again. Now, you have two choices: If the typo wasn't too egregious, do nothing and hope the employer won't notice, but bring a corrected copy to the interview. Either wait for the interviewer to bring it up or be proactive and say: "With great embarrassment, I realize that I sent an old version of my cover letter with an uncorrected error; here's a new copy for your files."

Or you can send a new version with a simple note: "Dear Mr. Powell: On January 15 I sent a résumé for the accounting opening. Please accept this updated version as a replacement." It's a fifty-fifty proposition. If the employer hadn't noticed, you have now called attention to the fact that you made a mistake. But if he has noticed and hasn't rejected you out of hand, at least you're offering a correction. You might think it's not fair for you to be rejected just because of one little mistake. Yes, it is! With hundreds of candidates vying for a single job, why shouldn't an employer eliminate anyone who's made a typo, something that's one hundred percent under a candidate's control? We all make mistakes, but a résumé or cover letter is not the place to use your allotment.

Rallying Your References

▶▶▶▶▶▶▶▶▶▶▶▶▶▶▶▶▶▶▶▶▶▶▶▶▶▶▶▶▶▶▶

SETTING UP YOUR FAN CLUB

As a teenager, I took a Red Cross babysitting certification course. We smooched and smacked baby dolls for CPR training and learned how to change cloth diapers in the pre-Pampers era. (If you stick a safety pin into a baby, it will cry.) We learned what to say to the Operator if we had a child in crisis (911 was still new) and how to reach parents in the pre-cell phone era. This was useful: On my first paid job, the baby started power-puking (the medical term, I now know, is projectile vomiting), but I had insisted the parents give me the number at the restaurant where they'd be. They came rushing home, grateful that I'd called right away. The last time this had happened, they told me, the baby ended up in the hospital.

In addition to a lot of other useful advice, the Red Cross trainers provided this lifelong gem: They suggested we create a running list of references to give to prospective employers. Although I can't say I've ever gotten over the sight and smell of the regurgitated peas and carrots that marked my first certified babysitting job, I knew the parents would give me a glowing reference since they felt I had saved their baby's life. Any babysitting job I wanted in Providence—no, dare I say, the entire Ocean State—would be mine. This was my welcome to the world of references and recommendations.

References, both formal and informal, play a critical role in the job search. You have to know how to get them, and eventually, how to give them.

In other realms, references are casually tossed around. Friends ask you for the best place to eat in your neighborhood, the best movie you've seen lately; you ask for the

WHY CAN'T THEY JUST TAKE MY WORD FOR IT?

▶ On a basic level, employers need to verify the information you've provided in your résumé and cover letter (you'd be amazed at how many résumés contain false or embellished information). So they want to know that you have actually worked where you said you did, acquired the education you've described, and mastered the skills you're touting.

They also want to hire someone they can trust, possibly to represent the company in their absence. For that, they may be looking for social qualities too subtle to discern over the course of several interviews; this is another way in which a reference comes in handy.

name of their dentist or vet. These are casual, harmless recommendations. No one is going to sue you over them (you hope); they shouldn't change the course of anyone's life; nor will they put your reputation on the line. Sure, they might not ask you again if they don't like your picks, but it's not a big deal.

Job references are a bigger deal. After you've been interviewed, if an employer is seriously considering hiring you, you will be asked for the names and contact information of people willing to speak on your behalf—generally three to five, though I've heard of candidates being asked for six to eight. Why? Because as impressive as you may sound during an interview, an employer needs to take what you have to say about yourself with a grain of salt. You're a biased source of information. Yes, employers are interested in what you think about yourself, how much confidence, energy, and enthusiasm you exude, and how you present yourself and your set of skills. But they also want input from people who have worked with you in some capacity: in an academic, professional, or volunteer setting. Your references will be quizzed about your performance, skills, capacity for growth, ability to work with others, efficiency, productivity, punctuality, honesty, reliability, and general attitude.

You'll provide your references on a prepared list, not on your résumé. You'll choose the names very carefully, and you'll prepare your recommenders for a call, providing them with as much information as possible.

Choosing Your References Wisely

Be strategic in deciding whom to ask for a recommendation: Don't just reflexively go after your three most recent supervisors. If possible, your first choices should be people who have openly admired you and your work. Also consider your recommenders' personalities. Ideally, they speak and write well and have the ability to be enthusiastic, positive, and responsive. If you know a particular supervisor is notoriously bad about responding to calls and e-mails, try to choose someone else; after a few attempts, your prospective employer may give up.

Whatever their qualifications, the best references are those who know you well; even better are those who work in fields relevant to the jobs for which you are applying. Appropriate parties include:

▶ Previous employers or internship supervisors

▶ Colleagues

▶ Clients

▶ Volunteer supervisors.

If you have no employment directly relevant to the job you're pursuing, that's okay. If you've had a minimum-wage job or walked dogs or babysat, your managers and employers can speak to your maturity, responsibility, trustworthiness, punctuality, and other good qualities.

If you don't have professional references, consider using a coach, piano, dance, theater, art, or voice teacher—someone who can attest to the fact that you are diligent, disciplined, and self-motivated, that you ask questions when you don't understand things, give 200 percent to the task at hand, and work well with others.

If you've just graduated from college and have never had a job or internship, you may also use professors; the key is to prepare them adequately. (For tips on helping a professor through the reference process, see pages 107–109.)

Who's That on Your Reference Sheet?

I'VE SEEN REFERENCES SO INAPPROPRIATE they cast doubt on the candidate's judgment. Here's a short list of people who shouldn't appear on your reference sheet:

▶ The senior in charge of the school paper for which you wrote some articles. Employers don't want to talk to college kids—with rare exceptions, they won't have had the real-world experience necessary to evaluate a candidate.

▶ Your roommate. I know what you're thinking—"But we lived together for four years; she knows me better than anyone!" Even if that former roommate is now working in the field you're trying to get into, forget it. If a friend or roommate works at a company you're applying to, include her name as the lead in your cover letter—she's probably how you heard about the job in the first place.

▶ A best friend from childhood or a family friend. ("But she's really objective and can be critical of me because she's known me my whole life.") Nope. The one exception: an adult who knows someone at the company where you're applying. If you have worked with him directly, by all means use him as an official reference; if not, mention him in a cover letter and have him put in a good word.

▶ Your family physician. Sounds outrageous, but I've actually seen it done (once). This one confused me. If the candidate had been applying for a job in medicine or to med school, I *might* have considered it valid. (His explanation: "But he knows me inside and out.") Same goes for your priest or rabbi—inappropriate unless you're applying for a religious position or he supervised volunteer work you did in the community.

To sum it all up: I'm talking about *professional* references. There *are* character and personal references, but they are less commonly called for.

The No-Reference Blues

Q. What if I truly have *no* references, never mind a choice of references?

A. I think you may be exaggerating, but I'll take your question at face value and assume that you've never had a positive relationship with a professor or volunteered or had an internship. If you really feel you have no one to ask, you have to go out and seek experiences through which you'll acquire references. This might seem backward, but it's not a bad strategy. Let's say you're interested in getting into television. Take an internship, temp job, and/or a course in that area, and soon you'll have references. But make sure the experience is substantial enough to talk about—an employer won't want a reference from someone you temped with for one day.

Once you've gotten to know some of the people at that internship, job, or course, think about whom you might ask for a letter or verbal recommendation. Express your interest in the field up front—if a supervisor knows you want to learn more, you might get the chance to participate in a wider range of activities.

After you've mastered the basics of your new job, take initiative and volunteer to do things outside your job description—with the blessing of your supervisor, of course. He will probably be happy to delegate work to a competent and enthusiastic new employee. And that will translate into kudos for you.

Contacts from Abroad
Q. May I use references from overseas?

A. You may use an international reference, but make sure it's easy for the employer to contact him or her. E-mail is usually the simplest medium, but provide phone numbers with explicit dialing instructions and time differences. An employer doesn't want to have to look up country codes and try to figure out what time it is in Zimbabwe. He'll move on to the next résumé if you make his life too difficult.

All in the Family
Q. What if I work in a family business?

A. I don't want to talk to your father or your mother or your sister or brother or aunt or uncle—unless you worked in a family business and there truly is no one else who could speak with me on your behalf. But this is unlikely. Even if the business is run by your mom and dad, you presumably have clients who could serve as references. Don't try to fake me out if you happen to have a different last name from your parents or other relatives. If I find out what the real connection is, you'll look like you were trying to hide this information—which you probably were. That was sneaky. Now I don't trust you.

Asking for a Recommendation

F irst things first: Yes, you do need to ask. You can't just list people as references, not warn them, and expect them to remember you and give you a glowing recommendation. If a prospective employer calls or e-mails a reference listed on your contact sheet and the person says, "Oh, Suzie Q . . . the name sounds familiar but I don't really remember her," you've just dug your own grave.

Reintroduce yourself to your potential references if necessary, and ask if they're willing to have you use their names. Give them a chance to say no if they're busy or don't feel they can speak well on your behalf. **"I am applying for a job in the energy department of Green Company. Would you be comfortable writing me a recommendation?"** Unless you know your recommender well, you may be better off asking by e-mail rather than over the phone. (Less awkward for everyone if he needs to turn you down.) The process may be a bit nerve-racking, but better to be rejected by a prospective reference than a prospective employer.

Ask as early as you can—as soon as you start your job search. Especially in the case of written references, don't leave it to the last minute and then demand a rush answer—"I need this by tomorrow." Busy people will need time to process your request. Years ago when I was teaching high school, a student ran into my office during lunch. It seemed urgent, so I let him interrupt. "Ms. Reeves, I want to ask you for a letter of recommendation for college, and it's due really soon!" I told him not to worry; we could talk about it in class later that afternoon. "But that's the thing; it's Senior Skip Day, so I won't be there—that's why I need to ask you now!" I liked him enough to write him a positive recommendation anyway—but I would *not* recommend this approach.

You also need to give yourself time to reach out to other potential recommenders should you find that your first choices are unavailable or unresponsive—too busy, away on sabbatical, sick, or on vacation. Have backup names ready to go.

If your contact with your former employer or professor was minimal, asking for a reference may seem daunting. It may be too late to cultivate a relationship—so vow that from this point on, you will start off on the right foot. Whenever you begin a new course, internship, job, or volunteer position, make a concerted effort to get to know the people in charge, to ask for a written reference *before* you leave—it can be updated periodically

WILL YOU BE MY REFERENCE?

▶ Here's how you would ask someone to be your reference over the phone:

"Hi, Professor Carter? This is Sandy Richards from your Introduction to Legal Theory Class last year. How are you?"

"I'm applying for jobs at law firms in the area and I wondered if I might use you as a reference."

"You would? Thank you so much! They're looking for someone to research law-case precedents, and I hoped you would be able to speak to the research skills I honed through my thesis on *Brown v. Board of Ed,* my writing skills (my thesis won the department prize) and my reliability, since I met all the department deadlines."

"They don't require a written reference: They would like to call or e-mail you. Which is better? What contact information should I give them?"

"I appreciate this very much. I thought I would send you a copy of my résumé, the job description, and my thesis overview so you'd have them before they call. Also, if you know anyone at local law firms you would suggest I speak with, I'd appreciate the introduction."

Whether you're asking by phone, e-mail, or post, be descriptive but succinct and appropriately grateful. Request all of the information you require in that one approach. It's far less burdensome to the other party to receive one complete, thorough e-mail than to receive several communications—"Oh, I forgot to mention that I would really appreciate it if you would pass on my résumé to anyone you might know who practices law. Thanks!"

with the input and approval of the writer—and to keep in touch after you've left. If you were a student in a large lecture course, though, you might ask your section leader to write a recommendation letter at the end of the semester—and then see if the big-name professor will cosign it. The same goes for former employers; you might have had a direct supervisor who knew you well and can write about your work.

Once you've gotten the okay from a reference, don't expect that you'll be able to call on his services in perpetuity. I was once told I had written a recommendation for someone applying to the company where I worked. I said I hadn't. It turned out the candidate had reused an old recommendation without alerting me. (I knew him from a different context and didn't make the connection.) I could have been helpful, had he bothered to give me a call in advance. Some employers assume—and don't mind—that they will be contacted for several years after agreeing to recommend a former employee, but even if this is the case, the more the recommender knows about what you're doing and what you're applying for, the better he can talk specifically to how your strengths apply to the new position.

You don't have to ask and await an answer each time you use a reference. Just send an e-mail saying, **"I'm applying for a job at Cisco and have taken the liberty of giving your name as a reference again. Thanks."** This is also a good way to make sure the contact info and title you have for this person are still valid.

Been Forgotten?

Q. What do I need to do if I want a recommendation from a professor I had a few years ago? She'll never remember me.

A. Include copies of a paper or two you wrote in her class with the grades and comments to jog her memory. If you need to explain a bad grade or you weren't a top student but still think the person is the right reference for you, explain why: *While I realize I wasn't a phenomenal student, I got more out of your class than many I took, and the project we did on toads was one of the highlights of my college career. I only got a B-, but you may not realize how much time and effort I put into catching those toads, and I thought you might speak to my diligence and persistence.* Sometimes absent-minded professors need coaching!

Prepping Your References

When you e-mail a recommender to ask for assistance, include a current résumé. Provide as much information as possible about what you've been doing and the jobs for which you're applying—if there's a job description online, paste it into your e-mail.

I always ask interns and assistants to keep a running list of all their tasks and copies of everything they create; if I'm asked for a reference, I use those documents to jog my memory and provide concrete material for a phone call or letter. You should be doing this at every job you hold.

WRITING YOUR OWN RECOMMENDATION

▶ Don't be surprised if you're asked to write your own recommendation. It's increasingly common for busy supervisors to have their employees draft letters for them to review, edit, and sign. Don't assume, though, that they're simply going to sign and send. They may just be prompting you for a reminder about all your good qualities.

Ask if the recommender would like you to go ahead and draft the letter or just make a list of highlights. Do not heap praise on yourself. Focus on solid evidence, drafting answers to the questions often asked of recommenders:

■ **Context.** What dates did you work there? What was your role and title? How does the recommender know you?

■ **Competence and skills.** What were your responsibilities? Add information about how well you handled them, using concrete detail and data, not adjectives. Describe things you did that went above and beyond the call of duty (special projects you volunteered for or initiated).

■ **Comments.** If possible, include comments from colleagues about how you work with others, your work ethic, and so on.

If you want to micromanage the inevitable weaknesses question—"If you could pinpoint a weakness in this candidate, what would it be?"—add a subtle note to that effect: "Public speaking is an area I'm working on." (See pages 149–150 for more on handling the question.)

Make It Easy for Them

IF YOUR RECOMMENDER NEEDS TO PROVIDE A WRITTEN REFERENCE, make the physical aspects of the chore as easy as possible. Enclose the original advertisement, job description, and your application. If a check sheet or form is required, fill out all that you can. Include a self-addressed, stamped envelope or an envelope addressed to the employer. These small courtesies mean a lot.

Praise on Paper

Q. Do I need written recommendations?

A. These days, formal recommendations are fading fast, replaced by e-mails, phone calls, and even checklists. But I still suggest asking for a written recommendation letter at the end of a course, job, or internship—it gives you a record to send back to the recommender as a prompt for a verbal or e-mail recommendation.

Once you have the letter, make copies or save it electronically. If the reference is generic, don't just keep reusing it—ask first.

What They'll Be Asked

Your references will be asked the same kinds of questions you will be asked in an interview. Familiarize yourself with them so you may prepare your recommender with at-the-ready anecdotes.

There will be factual questions, checking up on what appears on your résumé: How do you know the candidate? For how long and in what context have you known him? When did he work with you? What was his role and title? What were his responsibilities? How long did he stay? Was he promoted? Why did he leave? What was his starting and ending salary? Who was his direct supervisor?

There will be specific questions about your competence and skills. A reference may be asked about your writing, telephone manner, foreign language proficiency, computer and organizational skills, and so on.

There will be questions about your work ethic: Did he regularly meet deadlines? Was he on time? Did he miss work frequently? Stay late and come in early as necessary? Was he honest and reliable?

There will be questions about how you fit into a team: How did he respond to direction? Did he take initiative? Behave professionally? How did he respond to constructive criticism? Did he get along well with his supervisor? Colleagues? Clients? Was he pleasant, enthusiastic, easy to work with?

Language Barrier

Q. What if my former supervisor speaks little or poor English?

A. You may need to ask a colleague to serve as a "translator" or have the supervisor compose a written reference and edit it with him if he is open to it. Let the employer know what the situation is.

FORMATTING YOUR REFERENCE SHEET

▶ Unlike a résumé, a reference sheet requires just basic formatting (see model, opposite). Since you're listing only three or four names, you won't fill up a whole page—and that's fine. The most important thing is that all of the information you list be accurate. Double- and triple-check phone numbers and e-mail addresses for typos, and follow these simple guidelines:

- Use the same font and paper as you do for your résumé and cover letter. Lead with a centered heading: "References for FirstName LastName." Below that, center your contact information in case the page gets separated from your résumé.

- Left-justify the recommenders' names, titles, addresses, phone numbers, and e-mail addresses. Again, make sure all information is up-to-date and free of typos. Verify contact information when you first call or e-mail your references.

- List references either in reverse chronological order (most recent first) or most to least relevant.

- Find a way to make your references correspond to something on your résumé so the employer understands the professional connection. If a reference has left the company at which you met, indicate his former position: "CEO, Nature Incorporated; former Manager, Walden Pond."

The Fame Game

Q. Will employers be impressed if I list a celebrity as a reference?

A. Famous names are fine—if the person really knows you, and knows you in a professional context. Otherwise this can backfire big-time. Don't list the President as a reference unless you worked closely with him in the White House. (He's not going to reply directly to a request for a reference anyway.)

Saying "Thanks"

Q. How do I thank my references?

A. You definitely need to thank them, but *how* depends on your relationship. For one person, a note might suffice, while for another, a gift (flowers, a plant) or a meal might be in order. It's nice to keep in touch with the person throughout the process, alerting him when you've been offered and accepted (or declined) the job. Even if you don't get the position, you should write a thank-you note. You might say, "I was disappointed that despite your help, I was not offered the job. If you have any other leads or contacts in this field, they'd be much appreciated." You never know.

References: Clean and Simple

The format of a reference sheet isn't complicated. Just be consistent and use the same font styles as you do on your résumé.

CYNTHIA MAY

1001 Broadway #3G New York, New York 10027-6903
212-725-6789 cynthiamay@mymail.com

REFERENCES

James Mason
Myconcierge.com
Associate Manager
jmason@myconcierge.com
(212) 480-1234

Margot Burnham
Seattle Marketing Group
Intern Supervisor
mburnham@smg.com
(206) 729-4300

Jeffrey Toewes
University of Washington
Professor, American History
jefftoewes@universityofwashington.edu
(206) 328-6297

When and How?

Q. How and when will employers contact my references?

A. Employers will check references at various times in the hiring process: often when they've narrowed the field down to a few top candidates and sometimes right before they offer you a job. In some cases they may wait until after they have offered you a job and tell you the offer depends on how your references check out (not a great practice). Some never check references, but don't count on that.

No Longer There

Q. What if my reference has moved to another company?

A. You can still use that person as a reference. Specify his current place of employment as well as where he worked with you. Format should be simple: "Diane Jones, Metropolitan Savings, Director, Communications Department (former supervisor as Associate Director of Communications at Powers)."

Multiples

Q. Can I have more than one reference from the same place?

A. Yes, but make sure titles and responsibilities are clear. An employer won't want to waste time figuring out whom to call or what the pecking order really is.

Employer Confidentiality

Q. My current boss doesn't know I'm looking for a new job. Is it a problem not to use her as a reference?

A. During an interview, you may very well be asked whether your current employer will recommend you. Be honest. First, you may need to say, "In fact, my current employer does not know I'm looking, so I need to ask you to keep my search confidential." This is a perfectly valid and normal request.

But be aware that a prospective employer may check you out informally by calling people she knows at your company. Any item on your résumé opens you up to an unasked-for reference check.

Boss Drama!

Q. My supervisor at my last job hated me, but I had positive relationships with other people in the company. Can I use one of them as a reference, or will that raise the issue of why I didn't use my boss? Should I just leave that job off my résumé entirely?

A. If you were at that job for any significant length of time—over three months or so—you should leave it on your résumé. If you're asked why your boss can't speak for you, be honest but neutral. Cite a difference of opinion: "My former boss and I did not have the same working style and he would not necessarily be my best reference. My colleague Eric knows my work just as well."

References + Résumé?

Q. Should I put references on my résumé or just say "references available upon request"?

A. Please see chapter 3, but the bottom line here is: NEITHER. NEVER.

Everyone Is Fair Game

Though you've carefully thought out your official references, you should know that informal references have also become important. As the work world has grown increasingly litigious, employers have become wary of negative references, and ever more cautious and tight-lipped. Some corporations even prohibit official references; they may only acknowledge that a particular employee worked there, stipulating position and dates of employment. Many employees will offer verbal or "off the record" recommendations but won't commit negative comments to paper.

All of which goes to show the importance of the informal reference. Rather than going down your official list, an employer may choose to pick up the phone and call someone she happens to know. How can you prepare for that? The best strategy is to maintain professionalism across all of your various jobs or job-related activities. No one's perfect, and personality conflicts are just a part of life—but if you do a good job, no one will really be able to take you to task.

Gender Dilemma

Q. My best reference is having a sex change operation. How should I list him/her?

A. This was one of the more unusual question I've been asked. A student applying for a job wanted to use a famous former teacher who was about to undergo a sex change. His old name would certainly have been recognized, but his—well, her—new name would not. He had been a mentor to the student, and it was an important reference. I suggested she use a dated but effective marker for women's maiden names and write, "Joan Smith, née John Smith."

Getting Through the Interview

► ►

PREPARATION IS EVERYTHING

You've used your network. You've sent out your cover letter and résumé. Now you get the call. "Can you come in for an interview tomorrow at ten?"

That's good news, but don't just say yes and hang up! There are several things you need to take care of before you get off the phone—and even before you answer it.

In the cell phone era, the first thing to determine is whether or not you're able to have a professional conversation at that particular moment. If you're alone and somewhere quiet—where you can sit, take notes, and possibly be interviewed—yes, you may be able to take the call. If not, let the phone go to voice mail and return the call as soon as you can. In short: While you're job-hunting, don't reflexively answer your cell phone when you see an unknown number.

If you're on the road or in a store and you do answer a call when you shouldn't have, be brief and polite: "Thank you so much for calling! May I call you right back in a few minutes? At what number?" (Don't just assume the number that shows up on your cell phone is the number to call.) If the phone wakes you up, don't answer it! Believe me, you are not at your best when you first wake up. Let it go to voice mail, take a shower, have a cup of coffee, and then call back.

Handling the Call

W hen you do pick up the phone for an interview request, how should you respond? Be positive but not gushy. No squealing, no jumping up and down, no yelling, "Oh wow, I can't believe you called! When I didn't hear anything I figured you didn't want me. . . ." Say nothing but, "Thank you so much for calling. I'm available tomorrow and Friday—what times work best for you?" Be available. Juggle appointments if you need to, accommodating the employer's schedule as much as possible. Write down the date, time, and place of the interview and make sure you find out:

▶ With whom you'll be interviewing. It may be the hiring party, an assistant, an HR person, or some combination thereof. Get names, titles, and positions so you'll be able to look people up before the interview and thank them afterward.

▶ Whether there's anything in particular you should bring. Would they like references or writing samples? (Even if they say no, bring them and have them ready just in case.)

Make sure you get the name of the person who calls you to schedule the interview. That way you can thank her personally when you meet at the interview, and you'll have a contact if anything comes up before then. If you need directions or parking information, do some research following the phone call. Asking, "So how do I get there?" during an initial call may send the message that you're not that resourceful.

A Screening Interview

WHEN YOU ANSWER YOUR PHONE to schedule your interview, you may find yourself in the middle of an impromptu "screening session." A screening session is the preliminary phone conversation you have with a potential employer after your résumé has been received. It may be scheduled or spontaneous.

Whether or not a phone call actually qualifies as a screening session, it's essential that you take it seriously. Your answers to seemingly offhand questions are significant. Prompts like "How did you hear about us?" or "What made you decide to apply for this job?" are opportunities for you to break out your spiel (see pages 27–28).

Types of Interviews

Interviews with HR and Hiring Managers

THE HUMAN RESOURCES OR PERSONNEL DEPARTMENT of a company is technically in charge of recruiting and hiring; it also deals with internal personnel issues such as employee benefits and relations. Large companies are likely to have HR departments, small companies and nonprofits less so; an employee may function as an unofficial recruiter and personnel manager.

The degree of influence an HR department has on the hiring process varies greatly from company to company. In some places, HR interviews are pro forma routing sessions in which you'll fill out basic informational forms outlining your job history, contact information, and salary requirements (see page 172 for guidance on how to handle the latter). For other companies, the process may be much more involved.

An HR interview is essentially a screening interview. An HR person's main goal is to narrow the pool, selecting a short list of candidates for the boss-to-be to see. HR interviews also tend to run shorter than staff interviews. If your interview is a success, your "callback" may be immediate; it's not unusual for candidates to be shepherded directly from HR to the hiring party's office when all goes well.

If you've followed my advice, you'll have found someone on the inside with whom to interview; either a person who's in a position to hire or someone in a department in which you're interested. Even if that's the case, you should still read this section, as you may be required to go through an HR interview per company policy.

Depending on whom you ask (and, of course, on the HR interviewer), HR interviews can be easy, useful, useless, boring, or difficult. A good HR person will be a perceptive people person who has a real sense of the job and the culture of the organization as a whole. You can learn a lot from a good HR person, especially if you're meeting for an informational interview and trying to get your name on the company's roster. A less skilled or experienced HR person will do the interview by the book, robotically running through a list of prepared questions. Whichever one you get, it's important that you remain composed. Some HR people try to "throw" you, asking questions to catch you off guard. Keep your cool, and know that if you are qualified for the job and manage to maintain your professionalism throughout the interview, odds are you will make it to the next round. Essentially, HR's job is to weed out inappropriate candidates. So if you do get weeded out, perhaps the job wasn't right for you.

What are HR interviewers looking for? How interested you are in the company and what you know about it; whether or not you appear to "fit" the company culture; and how presentable, professional, and articulate you are (qualities any employer will look for). In a general way, they want to see if you're suited for the job. If they feel you aren't, they may turn you away or suggest other departments or openings for you to investigate.

Informational Interviews

AS NOTED IN CHAPTER 2, in informational interviews no particular job is at stake. They tend to be more casual than regular job interviews. You and the interviewer will be getting to know each other. You may talk about your professional goals or about the interviewer's career path and experiences. Depending on the interviewer's personality, he may be more candid about the nature of the work environment than he would be in a formal interview. You may find yourself discussing the merits and drawbacks of the particular industry or company.

But don't be misled by the apparent casualness of the meeting. There is something at stake. Many informational interviews turn into job opportunities, so you must take them seriously and present yourself as if the person you're speaking with is a potential employer. Prepare exactly the way you'd prepare for a real interview. (More on that to come.) Create the best possible impression—a job may become available in the future, and the interviewer may even be willing to pass your name along to friends in the industry.

Phone Interviews

REMEMBER WHAT I SAID ABOUT SCREENING INTERVIEWS? Anytime someone calls from a company to which you have applied, you are essentially

GREAT INFORMATIONAL INTERVIEW QUESTIONS

▶ Though an informational interview might flow like any ordinary conversation, it's possible that your "interviewer" will actually expect you to take the lead. So be prepared with some of the following questions:

- How did you get started in this field? What was your background?

- When and why did you start at this company? In this job? How has it changed since you began?

- What do you find most satisfying/challenging about your work?

- Can you tell me about the work environment and the company's values and philosophy?

- Can you describe a typical day/week?

- What are your main responsibilities? What are you working on now?

- What kinds of jobs (entry level and otherwise) exist in this industry?

- What does a typical career path look like?

- Can you tell me about general salary ranges, from entry-level to top positions?

- What personal/professional skills and talents are necessary for success in this field?

- How does the economy affect your business?

- How do you view the future of the industry?

- What advice would you give someone starting out today?

having an interview. Be polite and professional at all times. But if you have a phone interview scheduled for a specific time of day, prepare for it:

▶ If your cell phone service is likely to cut in and out, arrange access to a landline. And under no circumstances should you ever put the interviewer on hold, for call-waiting or anything else.

▶ Dress for the call. Talking in your pajamas may lull you into an overly relaxed frame of mind. If you feel professional, you'll sound it.

▶ Make sure you are in a quiet place where there will be no interruptions. You don't want your mother calling you for lunch or your dog barking in the middle of the interview. Do not multitask; focus on listening to the interviewer and preparing your answers.

▶ Sit at a desk with a pen, pad, and your résumé in front of you.

▶ Prepare a written list of questions and messages you want to impart about your candidacy.

▶ Do not be late for the call. Confirm a day ahead by phone or e-mail. "Hi, this is Stuart Little calling to confirm tomorrow's phone interview at 3:30. I understand that Mr. White will be calling me at 123-456-7891. Please let me know if anything changes."

▶ If the employer is calling you, be ready at least five minutes early.

▶ Send a thank-you note. This was an interview. See page 164.

Interviews Over Meals or in Non-Office Spaces

INTERVIEWS OVER MEALS CAN BE TRICKY. In addition to the usual stress of an interview, you'll have to deal with distractions—other diners, the waiter, your food—and show off your social skills. Interviews over meals may take place to save the interviewer time, but they're also tests in and of themselves.

That's why it's especially important that you follow the basic rules of etiquette. Your table manners should be impeccable. Check Emily Post's guidelines if you need to, especially if you're dining in a formal restaurant and aren't familiar with fancy silverware settings. (Basically, you start on the outside of the setting and work your way in, course by course.) Say please and thank you, do not reach across the table for food, do not talk with your mouth full. Do not lean on the table with your elbows, ask for a doggie bag, or exhibit aggressive or rude behavior toward the waitstaff. Never ever use a toothpick at the table after the meal. Do not make special demands—"I'll have the dressing on the side, and please substitute X for Y and P for Q"—unless you truly have special health concerns that don't allow you to eat anything on the menu as is. Even if it's your usual shtick, it will mark you as demanding and compulsive.

> Interviews over meals can be tricky. In addition to the usual stress of an interview, you'll have to deal with distractions—other diners, the waiter, your food—and show off your social skills.

DON'T TAKE THE COOKIE

▶ In the event that you're offered food (such as a cookie) in an office interview, don't take it. You don't want to end up talking with your mouth full. It's fine to take a glass of water or coffee—as long as you don't spill!

No matter what you're in the mood for, order no finger food, nothing that requires dipping, and nothing that's messy (buffalo wings, linguine, and chili-bacon cheeseburgers, for example). Don't order the most expensive thing on the menu, and don't order an appetizer and dessert if the interviewer doesn't. Follow his lead. Some other guidelines:

▶ Drinking: Don't, even if they do. If they "insist," get something light (nothing harder than a glass of wine) and nurse it. You cannot afford even mild intoxication.

▶ Smoking: Don't, even if they do.

▶ If you run into someone you know, be polite but brief—this is not the time for chatting.

▶ Don't offer to pay; if the interviewer proposed a lunch interview and suggested the place, he is taking you out. What would normally be a polite offer will in this context just create an awkward moment.

On occasion, you may be invited for a meal or drink so the employer and your prospective colleagues can "get to know you better." But in fact there is no such thing as a purely social encounter when you're applying for a job. Dress and behave appropriately. If no "interview" questions are forthcoming, don't try to force the situation—go with the flow, without letting your guard down.

Group Interviews

A GROUP INTERVIEW MAY MEAN YOU AND SEVERAL INTERVIEWERS, or one interviewer and several candidates, or several interviewers and several candidates. In a situation involving more than one candidate, you may be asked to participate in group activities, particularly if the job will involve working in teams. You will be under the microscope, so be prepared.

If you are one of several interviewees, you'll want to draw attention to yourself, but you don't want to look domineering or egocentric. Invite participation from others. "Katie, what do you think about that?" Link to what others have said and give them credit for it. "Well, I think Rob makes an interesting point. What I would add is . . ." Do not be the person always answering the question or taking control of the conversation. Acknowledge the other candidates.

If you are alone with many interviewers, try not to be intimidated. Granted, it can be difficult. Try to think of it as having five perspectives on the job—if you end up getting it, you'll already have met five people! Shake each person's hand when you enter the room. If people are entering a room you're already in, stand and shake their hands.

During the interview, vary your focus so that you spend time making eye contact with everyone. When someone asks a question, focus on that person as you begin to respond, then scan the group. As others speak, turn your attention to them. Don't zone out on a spot on the wall. And don't make the mistake of focusing only on the person with the most power; the others are clearly there because they have a say in the decision, too. At the end of the interview, try to get a card from each person in the room.

After the interview, send a thank-you note to each person who interviewed you—and of course to anyone who provided leads or links. (See pages 163–166 for more on proper thank-yous.)

> In a group interview, don't make the mistake of focusing on only the person with the most power; the others are clearly there because they have a say in the decision, too.

Job + Career Fairs

YES, INTERVIEWS DO TAKE PLACE at job and career fairs. They may be brief, but they are interviews.

Career fairs are peculiar as social circumstances go, so people tend to get nervous about them. First of all, don't blow them out of proportion. They can be useful, but they're only one small part of your networking strategy. Some tips to help make your experience successful:

▶ Don't linger at one booth, repeatedly circle the room like an animal stalking its prey, or keep coming back to the same booth.

▶ Don't be a booth hog; if there's a line of people waiting but you have more questions, it's fine to ask whether the representative has time to talk at the end, or simply reach out to her for an informational interview later on.

▶ Don't hand out your résumé at every single booth. Remember, you don't want to get called in for interviews that don't interest you.

▶ Be prepared for on-the-spot interviews, but don't assume the representatives have time for in-depth conversations. Express your interest, offer your résumé, ask pertinent questions, and move on.

▶ Be flexible. Depending on the company, a booth may be staffed by an HR person, a recruiter, a person looking to hire, or a peer in an entry-level position. Though you should always present your "best self," vary your approach based on whom you're talking to. Unlike in a regular interview, you won't be able to find out in advance. (But you can—and should—still research the company.)

Remember: Your dream job may not be open for six months. Once you've gone to the effort to make contact with people you meet at job fairs, keep in touch; thank them for their time and, if you want to learn more about the company, request a one-on-one informational interview.

PREPARING FOR THE INTERVIEW

▶ In school, you studied for written exams by trying to figure out what kinds of essay questions you might be asked and preparing stock answers, ready to be reframed on the spot. (I hope!)

Preparing for an interview is no different, but the subject matter being tested in this oral exam is you: your self-presentation and people skills, your résumé, and how your experience and skill set make you the perfect candidate for this particular job. You don't just want to ace the test, though, you also want to find out if the job is right for you. So you'll need to prepare questions of your own,

questions that will help you figure out what the job is *really* like.

Just as in school, there's homework involved. As far as possible in advance of the interview—but not so far ahead that you forget everything you prepared—you should tackle the following assignments:

■ Review your résumé. See page 129.

■ Prepare authentic questions to ask the interviewer based on your research. See pages 120 and 162.

■ Do a mock interview with a friend or acquaintance. See box, page 143.

■ Rehearse answers to tough questions. See pages 146–150.

Do Your Research

Now that you're familiar with the types of interviews you might encounter, focus on preparing for them. The most important thing you can do before an interview is research. Given a computer and access to the Internet, there is no excuse not to have done your homework on the company and the people interviewing you. Begin the process the minute you develop an interest in a company; don't wait until the day before the interview.

Start with the company's website—especially the "About Us" section and the executive biographies, if available—then move out from there, Googling any aspects you want to find out more about. Do a news search to see if the company has recently been mentioned in any major papers. The library and your network are good sources too, as are industry trade associations.

Study whatever information you can get your hands on: mission statement, annual reports, catalogs, company newsletters, or other publications.

The same goes for the individual(s) for whom you'd be working and the people interviewing you. Find out as much about them as possible before you go.

Basic information to investigate includes:

▶ How long the company has been in existence

▶ The nature of the company's work

▶ The breakdown of the company's general divisions (a good thing to ask about in more detail at the interview)

▶ The company's most recent successes.

There's no need to memorize the annual report or a person's entire career trajectory, but you want to be able to show that you are interested in the position and that you are a thorough and resourceful person. (You should do this even for an informational interview.) Exhibit tact and diplomacy: In the event that a company has received negative press, tread with care. If asked "You must have read about what's going on here," say something like "Well, I've been reading the media's version; how has the PR been affecting your department?"

If the information you've studied doesn't come up naturally during the interview, find a way to work it in at the end. You might say something like

"I'd love to ask you one more question, if you don't mind. I was studying your catalog and I noticed a shift in the way you're marketing your products. Is this part of a global, company-wide outreach toward a new audience?"

Talk Therapy

Obviously, it's not just what you say at an interview that's important, but also how you say it. Not everyone is born with the gift of gab, so here are a few tips to help with your delivery.

Maintain an even and professional tone of voice. Avoid "up-talk"—do not inflect every statement as if it were a question. Don't talk like a Valley Girl or in a baby voice, and don't giggle. Do not answer questions in a monotone or in monosyllables. Don't speak too loudly, too softly, too quickly, or too slowly. If you see the interviewer leaning in or asking you to repeat answers, speak a little more loudly. Don't touch your face or cover your mouth when you speak. (It's a habit common of shy people and people who have something to hide, according to body language experts.)

Don't say "like" or "uh" or "you know." Train these speech tics out of your lexicon by asking a friend to interrupt you every time you use them. Make sure your grammar is correct, too; refresh your understanding of pronouns. ("Me and him took a class together" and "Yes, the recommendations forms were sent to my professor and I" are both incorrect.)

> Do not say "like" or "uh" or "you know." Train these speech tics out of your lexicon by asking a friend to interrupt you every time you use them.

Here's an obvious one: Do not swear or use slang or overly casual language. Don't lapse into "shoulda," "wanna," "gonna"; say "I should have," "I would like to," "I was going to." (For the record, saying something "sucked" is equivalent to swearing.) "Freaky," "totally," "whatever," "for real," "for sure," and "awesome" are other words to avoid in an interview.

Don't interrupt. You should be doing as much listening as talking. Likewise, try not to ramble or go off on tangents. Get to the point. It's easy to lose track of your train of thought when you're nervous. If you realize you've gone off subject, wrap up your answer—better to leave something unsaid than to come across as someone who can't self-edit. On the other hand, you don't want to be too brief, offering only yes or no answers, even to what seem like yes or no questions. Find ways to work in anecdotes.

Time yourself as you rehearse your answers to likely interview questions (see page 138). Generally, you shouldn't be talking for longer than a minute at a stretch—there's a fine line between answering in depth and going into excruciating detail. If you fear you've gone on too long but you haven't finished your answer, pause and ask, "Should I continue, or would you prefer we move on?" or, "Would you like to hear more about that?" If something occurs to you after you've already answered a question, come back to it when you can. "I wanted to add one more comment about the issue of . . ."

Nobody Likes a Whiner

When you're job-hunting, the only good time to complain is in the privacy of your own home. Nobody likes a whiner, especially not a prospective employer.

Everything you say and do must project a positive vibe. The only attitude you should reveal is "can do." If you know yourself to be a chronic whiner, complainer, or "glass-half-empty" type, do some serious attitude adjustment before your interviews—no reflexive complaining about the weather or the traffic.

Do not speak negatively of a former employee or colleague. For all you know,

> When you're job-hunting, the only good time to complain is in the privacy of your own home. Nobody likes a whiner, especially not a prospective employer. The only attitude you should reveal is "can do."

it's your interviewer's relative or friend or significant other, but in any case, maligning others will make you sound bitter or like a gossip. Complaining about your boss, professors, colleagues, or even about company policies at a former workplace or college or internship is not the way to bond with an interviewer. He is only making a mental note that he might be next on your hit list, and then ruling you out. Even if you picked up the slack for a lazy colleague or unofficially took over for an incompetent boss, you must never tout your accomplishments at someone else's expense.

Never generalize about groups of people or departments, even in response to questions like, "Are there people you find it difficult to get along with?" If you catch yourself saying, "I was the only one who knew how to," "I shouldn't say this but," "I don't mean to stereotype but," stop yourself. A candidate who describes bosses or colleagues or clients as "stupid," "demanding," or "hard to get along with" sounds exactly that.

Without getting Pollyannaish, find ways to speak well of your previous bosses, colleagues, and experiences. "My boss was really smart and such a good mentor; I felt lucky to get to take on new responsibilities under his guidance."

Everything is possible and nothing is a problem. That should be your internal mantra now. A question like "You live outside of the city; won't the commute be difficult?" should not elicit an answer like "Gosh, the traffic really is terrible at rush hour." Instead, try something like, **"I've commuted for years and have never been late except in the case of major storms or train problems; I always leave extra time just in case; I like reading the newspaper on the train; this is only temporary—I'll be moving into the city as soon as I can."**

Keep Your Skeletons in the Closet

C amouflaging real or perceived problems on your résumé is one thing; dealing with them in an interview is quite another. An astute interviewer will attempt to discover your weaknesses, insecurities, and secrets. There's nothing sneaky or shady about that—it's just part of his job. Yours is to keep your skeletons in the closet. Obviously, there's no reason to volunteer information about issues that will raise red flags (addictions, illnesses, family traumas, and so on), but you should also be prepared to sidestep or diplomatically address issues that do come up.

If you've been fired, recently or in the past, don't bring it up; if you're asked about it, explain briefly, honestly, and in a calm, neutral tone of voice. Do not place blame, bad-mouth, or complain about others. Do not explain the firing in a way that could reflect negatively on you and your judgment. (One candidate unwisely confessed that she had been fired as a young waitress for serving alcohol to friends under the legal drinking age.) Use phrases like "it wasn't a good fit"; if you were laid off within your first year, explain that you were the most recent hire when the company started laying people off.

Turn Your Résumé into a Story

It bears repeating that you are responsible for everything on your résumé, so you'll want to make sure you don't say anything to contradict your stated experience. But during the interview, you also want to make your résumé come alive.

Review it alongside the job description with an eye to preparing a narrative, with "headliners" at the ready—brief statements about how each item on your résumé is relevant to the job at hand and the employer's stated needs. If the position requires working for more than one boss, you might say, **"I'm used to working for more than one person at a time; during my internship at a pharmaceutical company, I was assigned to both the communications and events departments."**

You'll want to come up with anecdotes to amplify everything on your résumé. That way if an interviewer expects you to lead the interview, you'll be able to run through your story smoothly. But don't launch into a monologue unless you really think the interviewer wants you to take charge. If he doesn't ask many or any questions and seems to be waiting for you to speak, start taking the reins. Even if you're not put in this position, you should be packaging your achievements into anecdotes—people remember stories, not bullet points. If you rewrote the staff manual at your last job or internship, offer a story about what happened the first time you instituted a new procedure and no one knew what to do—and how you solved the problem.

Choose your stories carefully. Though there's nothing wrong with introducing a little humor if appropriate, you don't want to accidentally paint yourself as the class clown or reveal something you didn't want the interviewer to know.

Every story you tell should present you as the hero or heroine. If part of a story might reflect negatively on you or someone else, omit it.

What to Wear

As in dating and mating, there is a strong "pheromonal" component to interviewing. It's not just about what you say, it's about what you look, sound, feel—see Get a Grip, page 157—and yes, smell like.

I don't want to make you paranoid, but I do want you to face the facts. The first impression you make can determine your fate. Appearance is an enormous factor in the interviewer's overall perception of you, so a professional outfit and demeanor are essential to getting hired. What you are saying when you present yourself in an interview is, "This is as good as it gets. This is the best me you will ever see. I can't look or sound more professional than this." Think first date. The little details count. If you have a stain on your clothes, an interviewer might assume that you'll smudge and spill on letters you are sending out in his name. A missing button, unironed shirt, or drooping hem might indicate sloppiness, laziness, or inattention to detail. Is this what you want someone to think about you before you've even started talking?

> If you have a stain on your clothes, an interviewer might assume that you'll smudge and spill on letters you are sending out in his name. A missing button, unironed shirt, or drooping hem might indicate sloppiness, laziness, or inattention to detail.

When I graduated from college, my mother suggested I buy a suit. I said I didn't want any job that would require me to wear a suit, but she wisely said I should get one for interviews anyway. I bought a gray pinstriped Calvin Klein number with a tight skirt and big shoulder pads. (It was 1983.) Underneath I wore a red silk blouse with cutouts in the front; a guy friend told me it could burn a barn. I didn't know what he meant. When I found out, I switched to a basic white button-down. Now I know not to wear barn burners to interviews, and I suggest you don't either. Err on the side of being conservative, unless you're applying for a job in fashion or another creative industry.

There are some job interviews to which it wouldn't be appropriate to wear a standard suit. Still, don't make the mistake of thinking that you should wear what the company's current employees wear to work every day.

While I would never claim to be fashion-forward or to dictate what should be in your closet, I can at least tell you what's appropriate to wear to an interview in general. When I work with recent graduates, I hold a volunteer "Dress 'Em Up and Dress 'Em Down" session; they wear their proposed interview outfits, and I offer forthright reactions. I suggest you set up such a session with a close friend or relative whose sense of professionalism you admire. (But this is *not* a job for a mentor or that guy you met in an informational interview—that would be a little too close for comfort.)

The key thing to remember is: You don't work there yet. Interview attire is generally more formal than everyday office-wear. That means different

MAKE SURE IT FITS

▶ There's nothing like an ill-fitting suit to give the impression that someone just doesn't have it together. Don't go to all the trouble of shopping around for new interview clothes only to ruin the effect with an awkward fit.

Men's jacket sleeves should hit at the wrist bone, with shirt cuffs extending a half-inch beyond that; trouser cuffs should break over a third of the length of the shoe in front, brushing the top of the heel in back. Jacket shoulder seams shouldn't extend too far beyond the shoulder line, but you want to make sure you have mobility; lift your arms up over your head in the dressing room to check out your range of motion.

Women, make sure your blouses aren't too tight; look out for that telltale gap between the buttons at chest level. (And it goes without saying: make sure you have adequate coverage up top—no cleavage at the interview!) If you're buying a suit as a whole, make sure both parts fit and flatter. Many women are larger on the bottom than on top or vice versa; if that's the case for you, shop for separates or have things altered to fit.

Buy your outfit far enough in advance to have things tailored if necessary. It shouldn't cost very much to have a pair of pants shortened, but know that restructuring a jacket *can* be costly, especially when work on the shoulders is involved.

One last note, more for your comfort than for your appearance: Wear new shoes around the house until they're broken in. You don't want to be limping into the interview room.

things to different companies—small nonprofits may not be as formal as law firms—but you should be dressing for business. If the company has "casual Fridays" and your interview happens to fall on one, do not dress casually. You may feel self-conscious walking around in a suit when everyone else is in khakis and polo shirts, but believe me, you won't regret it. It's always better to be too dressed-up than not dressed-up enough.

Rules of thumb: No shorts, flip-flops, sneakers, noisy clogs, or overly high heels. Make sure your look is seasonally appropriate; don't wear wool in the spring or summer, or summery clothes in fall or winter. In the summer, when air-conditioning is likely, make sure you bring a professional-looking jacket or sweater—don't ruin your professional look with a ratty cardigan.

Watch out for status-screaming high-end accessories, especially in non-profit and lower-paying industries. I find it hard to take a salary negotiation seriously when a young candidate is sporting a $500 purse and an Hermès scarf; it makes me feel that the extra $1,000 I could offer won't really matter.

In general, men should wear suits and conservative ties (no joke or "cute" ties worn as conversation starters) with brown or black shoes and kneesocks. Shoes should look new—no scuffs or tattered laces; polish the shoes if they're leather, brush them if they're suede. Under the suit, only a nice button-down shirt will do—no turtlenecks or sweater-vests.

If the interview room is hot, men shouldn't take off their jackets unless invited. If you're really dying, you may casually ask, "Do you mind if I take off my jacket?" (But keep it on if you think you may have sweat through your shirt; that's a big interview no-no.) Make sure your shirt is clean and pressed and can bear public scrutiny; no underarm stains or holes.

Same Suit Twice?

Q. May I wear the same suit or outfit to the second interview? I can only afford one until I get a job.

A. If you truly can't afford anything else, of course; but make sure everything is clean and pressed. If you've got a limited wardrobe and can't dry-clean and press clothes between interviews, you may want to invest in a personal steamer. Buy a lint brush. If possible, vary accessories: a shirt or tie for men, a blouse, scarf, or jewelry for women.

Rings and Things

Q. Can I wear whatever kind of jewelry I want?

A. I am not a fan of jewelry for men: no rings, bracelets, necklaces, or lapel pins. Discreet cuff links are fine.

For women, jewelry should be minimal. Don't wear anything too busy or noisy: reams of chains, dozens of bracelets, rings on every finger. On the other hand, an interesting piece can be a conversation starter. One woman interviewing to be my assistant had on a distinctive bracelet carved with polar bears. I asked her about it, and we were off and running. Many women tend to pull out the pearl earrings or necklaces for job interviews, but there's no need if that's not your style.

Do reexamine your everyday jewelry, especially anything on an old string, ribbon, or cord. Dirty rope bracelets do not scream "professional."

Glasses or Contacts?

Q. I'm uncomfortable wearing contacts. Is it okay to wear my glasses to the interview?

A. Of course, as long as they're clean and in good shape. (Make sure you don't fiddle with them, though.)

Oh, and if you're wearing sunglasses on the way to the interview, don't push them up onto your head or clip them to your clothes. You're at an interview, not a baseball game.

Hair-Dos . . . and Don'ts

Q. How should I wear my hair?

A. Your hair should be clean but not wet, and you should invest in a good haircut, but not too close to the interview; if you end up disliking the cut you get, you don't want to look uncomfortable and unhappy. Whether you're male or female, your hair should not hang in your face or eyes. If you have long hair and tend to chew it or play with it and haven't gotten rid of that habit in time for the interview (and you should definitely get rid of the habit), tie it back or up. If you dye your hair, make sure your roots aren't showing. If you have a dandruff problem, now is the time to try to clear it up; make sure you brush off your clothes, especially dark suits, before meeting an interviewer.

No extreme hairdos, bobby pins sticking out, hats, bandannas, or other headgear unless for religious or cultural traditions.

Men: Be clean-shaven; if you have a beard or moustache, make sure it's impeccably clean and trimmed. Excessive nose or ear hair needs to be dealt with.

Waking Up Sick

Q. It's the day of my interview and I have a bloody nose/black eye/horrible rash/fever/migraine/allergic reaction. What do I do?

A. If you really can't stop a bloody nose or cover up a rash or black eye, try to reschedule. Same goes if you're sick and can't present yourself well or risk infecting others—reschedule with as much notice as possible. Call the morning of and explain briefly, but say no more than you need to.

As for unsightly rashes: Do the best you can. The same goes for chapped lips, cuts, bruises, shaving accidents, pimples, and so on. Don't show up bleeding or oozing. Cover whatever you can with the smallest possible

THE SCENT OF SUCCESS

▶ Yes, you want an interviewer to remember you, but not because you left strong or unpleasant odors lingering in your wake. Fresh and clean is the way to go. Shower in the morning and steer clear of pungent foods like fish, garlic, onions, or beans. If you smoke, have your last cigarette before you shower, and air out your outerwear overnight. The interviewer shouldn't be able to smell smoke on you, your clothes, or your coat. If you're applying perfume, cologne, or aftershave, be sparing—some people are allergic or sensitive to scent.

bandage. Men: Don't be afraid to use concealer for acne or shaving accidents, but make sure you have the right color and blend thoroughly.

If it's something the interviewer is bound to notice—a huge bruise you can't cover—offer a brief, factual explanation and move on. I once had an interviewee show up with cotton hanging out of his nose; he said, "I am so embarrassed to tell you this, but on my way here I got a bloody nose. I've never gotten one before. I just wanted to get that out of the way!" I was so relieved he had brought it up so I didn't have to.

If the interview is scheduled for 9 A.M. and you wake up with a problem and can't reach anyone by phone, show up if you're able. Explain the situation to the receptionist and ask if the interviewer would prefer you to reschedule: "I'm terribly sorry, but I woke up with a bad case of the flu. I'm hoping to reschedule, but if that's not possible, I'm perfectly willing to go on as planned."

Is Weight an Issue?

Q. I'm quite overweight, and I'm worried that my extra pounds will affect my candidacy. Do you think that's possible?

A. The right answer is you should try to lose weight for your health. But this is not a diet book, so here goes: There is absolutely an employer bias against overweight people—you've probably read about such discrimination cases in the news.

The best thing you can do is to dress impeccably in dark colors. For men, this means well-tailored suits—the right cut can work miracles. For women, simple one-piece dresses often work better than skirts and blouses; accessories should be minimal and sophisticated. The overall goal is to look as polished as possible, drawing attention to your confidence and sense of style instead of to your extra pounds. Consider getting your hair professionally styled. Get a manicure. If you can, spend a little extra on grooming and clothing; you need a competitive edge here.

Pay attention to your body language, too—you want to look as active and energetic as possible to counter unconscious stereotypes linking excess weight and inactivity.

Don't Sweat It

Q. I sweat a lot, especially when I get nervous. Anything I can do about it?

A. Carry your jacket or sweater on the way to the interview and put it on at the last minute. Wear dark colors: They're less likely to reveal sweat stains. While we're on the subject: Make sure your antiperspirant hasn't left any white streaks on your clothing. Double-check your back and sides.

Tough as Nails

Q. It's okay to wear nail polish to an interview, right?

A. Yes, but I don't recommend a bold color. It's distracting and could be read as overly vampy. Keep it conservative—clear or natural.

For both men and women, nails should be clean and well groomed. People notice, especially when it's time for the handshake, and chewed-up cuticles send the message that you're insecure or anxiety-prone. (And you definitely want to make sure you don't bite your nails during the interview—keeping them neat should help.)

A note to women: Some people say you should never wear open-toed shoes to an interview. A little bit of toe is okay, but strappy sandals are not— your heel should be covered. Toenails should be well-groomed, with natural or classic polish.

A note to men: If your fingernails are a mess, consider getting your first-ever manicure (but no polish, not even clear!).

Suiting Up

Q. Do I really have to wear a suit to the interview?

A. For guys, the answer is yes. A good, matching suit is the way to go, even if the job itself won't require one. For some interviews, a matching blazer and pants would be appropriate, but it's probably not worth the risk of appearing too casual or mismatched. At this stage in life, you should own a suit, even a decent secondhand one if that's what you can afford right now. You can always wear it to weddings and funerals. You might as well make the investment.

Women have more options. You don't have to go out and buy a suit unless you think it fits the corporate culture (i.e., you'd wear it again once you got the job). You could also wear, say, black or neutral pants or a skirt with a complementary jacket, or an appropriate, professional-looking dress. Even the jacket is negotiable: Depending on the weather, you may be able to get away with a cardigan or just a nonfrilly, pressed blouse.

Ladies' Corner

There's a lot more leeway in women's clothes than there is in men's—and that means there's also more room for error. A rule of thumb: Lead with your competence, accomplishments, and personality, not with your outfit. Avoid dressing provocatively or eclectically. Again, in certain domains (theater, fashion, design, and so on), you may be judged on your expressiveness and creativity—but unless that's the case, I'd recommend erring on the conservative side. You don't want to be known as "the one with the miniskirt" (or the stilettos, green hair, Mohawk, or thigh-highs). Keep your accessories subtle too. No big bows or buckles, or other bells and whistles.

Even though you may be able to dress up your jeans and wear them to the office in certain industries, they're not appropriate for any job interview, anywhere, ever. Same goes for halter or tank tops; cover your shoulders. If you're going with a dress or skirt, hemlines should be modest, no shorter than just above the knee—no miniskirts or dresses with slits up the thigh. And if you are showing some leg—unless you're applying for a job in a casual industry—wear nylons. It may seem old-fashioned, but to my mind it's professional. (Bring an extra pair along with you on the day of the interview, as Murphy's Law dictates that yours *will* run.) Last, make sure your undergarments fit correctly and aren't visible. I don't want to remember you by your bra straps or visible panty lines.

Painting the Town

Q. Is wearing a red dress a good way to project confidence?

A. I don't recommend wearing anything too bright. While you will certainly be remembered, it may not be in the way you had hoped. The same goes for leather or any evening or "holiday" materials (shimmer, sequins, lace, velvet), busy patterns, or color combinations.

TAKING NOTES AT THE INTERVIEW

▶ To take notes or not to take notes? That is the question. The answer? It depends. You pack your notepad and pen (see page 153), but you don't want to pull them out and start scribbling like a student on the first day of class. A successful interview is one that feels like a conversation. Good conversations require eye contact.

But there's nothing wrong with taking notes. You can't be expected to remember everything, especially when you're applying for several jobs at a time. (And the interviewer can't remember all the applicants, which is why he may be taking notes on you.) To me, a candidate who's taking notes is taking the interview seriously. I figure that's a person who's likely to write things down and follow through on the job.

Just make sure you don't make note-taking your main focus. Don't sit down and pull out your pad right away; wait until something seems significant, then ask—"Do you mind if I jot down a few notes?" Make your writing discreet and small; you don't want the interviewer spending more time trying to see what you've written than listening to what you have to say. If you're a doodler, restrain yourself! Only write things down if they seem essential: job descriptions, any assignments you're given, books or articles you're told to look up.

I'm Serious, I Swear!

Q. People don't take me seriously in interviews; I'm petite, blonde, and blue-eyed. How can I convey that I'm a serious candidate?

A. One of my students was frequently stereotyped as a "dumb blonde" because of her looks, and she knew it. We agreed that it might help her to wear some chic but unobtrusive glasses. Her eyesight was just fine; this was about image-projection. Sometimes that's what it takes to overcome circumstances you can't control.

Another cosmetic reason to buy and wear glasses: if you have dark under-eye circles or puffiness. You won't be hired if you look unwell or sleep-deprived—it begs the question of whether you've been up all night partying. Concealer can only go so far. If you've tried the home remedies—tea bags, cucumber slices—to no avail, think about using glasses as camouflage.

Questions, Questions, Questions

N ow that we've covered what to wear and how to prepare for the interview, it's time to turn to the heart of the matter: the questions you will be asked and the questions you will ask. Remember this: If you don't understand the interviewer's question, ask a question about the question! Do not attempt to stumble through a question you don't really get. It's fine to say, "I'm sorry, could you rephrase that? I'm not sure I understand."

Though there's no preparing for every possible question, you can prepare in a global sense. When it comes down to it, interviewers only want to find out one thing: Are you qualified and willing to do the job—and will you do it better than anyone else? Every question asked is just a variation on this theme.

> Your theme is simple: I am qualified to do this job, I want to do this job, and I am the best person for this job.

Your answers should be variations on a theme as well. Your theme is simple: I am qualified to do this job, I want to do this job, and I am the best person for this job.

One caveat: Some questions are designed not to elicit information but to see how you handle tricky situations. In other words, can you remain diplomatic under stress? How you answer difficult questions reveals how you may interact with clients and colleagues.

Essentially, employers want to know:

▶ What skills you have

▶ Whether you'll fit in as a colleague in their company and office culture

▶ Whether you're professional and presentable enough to represent the company to clients and outsiders

▶ Whether you know about and truly have an interest in the company

▶ What your career goals are

▶ How you compare to other candidates

▶ What kind of attitude and level of confidence you exude—are you energetic and enthusiastic?

▶ Whether you're motivated, with a strong work ethic

▶ Whether you are honest and reliable

▶ Whether you are a good communicator and a good listener

▶ How much management and supervision you will require

▶ Whether you are a good problem-solver, with common sense and strong analytical abilities.

If an interviewer doesn't ask you questions that elicit this kind of information, you need to take the initiative, offering illustrative anecdotes at the appropriate times.

Interview questions generally fall into a few distinct categories. Read on for a breakdown with lists of questions and sample answers (the good kind and the bad kind). Study these questions and make sure you're prepared to answer them.

Skills and Qualifications Questions

▶ What experience do you have in this industry?

▶ What qualifications do you have for this job?

▶ What were your responsibilities at your last job/internship?

▶ What were your major accomplishments in your past jobs, internships, or college courses and activities?

▶ What kind of training have you had?

▶ How has your education prepared you for this job?

▶ Why should we hire you?

Q *Which items on your résumé do you think are most relevant to this job?*

Much of this answer should be prepared in advance by reading the job description and doing your research, but new thoughts will inevitably occur to you during the interview.

It seems like you're looking for someone who understands the needs of transfer students. Since I transferred from a two-year community college to a private university, I've actually been through the process. I also worked as an assistant in the Admissions office, so I think these experiences would serve me well as an assistant in the Transfers office.

Are there things you wish you hadn't left off your résumé? What are they and how are they relevant to this job?

Don't just rattle off random trivia about yourself and your past whereabouts; tie your answer back to information you've gleaned during the interview.

I didn't realize the job had a development component; I sold Girl Scout cookies for years and then organized the fund-raising efforts as a troop leader. I also was a volunteer student caller for my college alumni association. I enjoy cold-calling for donations when it's a cause that I can really believe in.

"TELL ME ABOUT YOURSELF"

▶ If an interviewer prompts you with the phrase "Tell me about yourself," beware. As with every other question, it's essentially code for "What can you do for us?" The interviewer is not asking for your favorite color or for your autobiography. He is saying, "Give me an oral summary of your qualifications as they relate to the job I need done."

So don't lead with "I was born in a small town in Nebraska." Lead with "As you can see from my résumé, I just graduated with honors from the University of Nebraska. I was an Urdu major, and while that language may not come in handy for this job, I spent three hours a day, for three years, hunkering down in the language lab. I understand that this position will require that kind of discipline and focus. I also managed the track team. It was in a college setting, but it gave me experience in managing people, working as a member of a team, and balancing a full plate. I was also in charge of purchasing uniforms for the team, pulling together our travel schedule and transportation to state meets, fund-raising for new equipment, and communicating with alumni."

Another common interview opener is "What do you know about the company?" Make sure you have something to say—and then ask to hear more. The conversation could go in any number of directions—but remember, the subtext is always the same: How will hiring you help them.

Self-Image and Personality Questions

▶ What are your strengths and weaknesses? (See page 149 for more on this interview classic.)

▶ What would friends/enemies/your last supervisor/your references say about you?

▶ Of what accomplishments are you proudest?

▶ Describe the biggest challenges/obstacles you have faced/overcome.

▶ What aspects of this job are most/least appealing?

▶ What aspects of your previous job or internship were most/least appealing?

▶ Why should we hire you?

▶ What do you do in your spare time?

▶ How do you deal with stress? What stresses you out?

What aspects of this job are least appealing to you?
Which elements are most appealing?

I'm really looking forward to learning about the industry. Of course, I realize that I will primarily be doing administrative work; I've done that kind of work in the past, and I definitely get a sense of satisfaction out of getting the job done, and doing it well.

Always lead with the positive (even if you are asked only the negative side of a question); in fact, try not to answer the negative part of the question at all. If the interviewer persists, talk about a prior job, focusing on a trivial "negative" that won't be a part of the position at stake: *At my last job, I was on my feet for hours a day; I managed, but I'm certainly looking forward to having a desk and chair!*

Manageability Questions

▶ How do you react to criticism?

▶ For what have you been criticized in the past?

▶ What kind of relationship did you have with your former colleagues or supervisors?

▶ Describe a time when your patience was tested.

▶ Are there certain people you find difficult to work with?

▶ Describe the best/worst managers you have worked with.

▶ How do you make decisions? Describe the most difficult decision you had to make and how you handled it.

What do you do when you've made a mistake or think you've made a mistake?

When I interview candidates, I like to give them a real scenario and ask them how they would respond. The formal term for this is "behavioral interviewing." "What would you do if" questions help employers gauge your problem-solving abilities. Here's my scenario: *You mistakenly hit "reply all" and send a mildly damning in-house message to a client (i.e., "We need to fudge those dates. . . ."). What do you do?*

The only good answers are: *1) Immediately tell my boss and devise a strategy to tactfully apologize to the client. 2) After consulting with my boss, I would say something like, "I apologize for the e-mail you received in error; it was obviously meant for my colleague."*

Knowledge of the Job/Field/Company Questions

▶ How did you hear about this job?

▶ What interests you about this particular industry?

▶ What interests you about this particular job? About our company?

▶ Where else are you applying?

Some people plan a career in this industry and see this job as the first in a progression; others see it as a stepping-stone to something else. What do you hope to get out of this job?

You might also be asked: Where do you see yourself in five years? Ten years? Twenty years?

I wish I could tell you that honesty is always the best policy but I can't: the only correct answer is that you're in it for the long haul. *I've always loved movies and documentaries in particular—that's the area I'm trying to make a career in, so the chance to work at PBS is really exciting to me. I hope to get a grip on the big picture: documentary funding, production, and distribution. What have people done after several years in entry-level positions here? How did you start?*

MOCK INTERVIEWS

Prior to your first interview, set up a mock interview with a friend or relative. Run through the questions in this chapter, answering them as you would in a real interview. Keep practicing any answers you stumble over. Ask for honest feedback.

Make sure your body language isn't setting you up for a fall. Have your mock interviewer watch you and alert you to any unconscious physical gestures you may have: twirling your hair, picking your ears, scratching your head, tapping or wiggling your feet, drumming your fingers or a pen on the table, averting your eyes, covering your mouth when you speak. Well in advance of your interviews, practice not doing any of those things—it's difficult to change unconscious behavior overnight.

If it's been a while since you dragged out your interview outfit, try it on. Make sure your clothes are clean and pressed.

Where else are you applying?

Don't get nervous if you're asked this question. Job-hunting is like applying to college or looking for an apartment. It only takes one, but unless you're phenomenally lucky, you can't just visit or apply for one, and employers know that. They're not interviewing only one candidate for their job, either! But employers also want to know that you're serious about their field. If theirs is the only insurance company on a list of high-profile banks, they'll suspect you're just not that into them.

Answer honestly, because the world is smaller than you think. *This is really my number-one choice, but I've also applied to similar companies, including General Mills, Kraft, and Nestlé.* Best-case scenario: The interviewer likes you and, if he can't hire you, passes your name along to a connection at one of those other companies.

Independence/Teamwork/Leadership Ability Questions

▶ Give an example of a time you took initiative.

▶ Define collaboration.

▶ Do you like to work independently or in a group?

▶ Do you work well with others?

▶ Are you self-motivated?

▶ Do you believe decisions should be made by consensus or by majority rule?

▶ How do you deal with conflict?

▶ How do you deal with people who are different from you?

What do you do when you don't understand directions?

I ask more questions. If my boss is busy, I see if the project can wait or find an experienced colleague to consult.

How do you respond to criticism?

Criticism isn't fun to hear, but it's important to have other people's perspectives. Offer an anecdote about how you grew and changed in response to criticism, making sure the instance isn't negative enough to affect your candidacy—don't say, "My previous supervisor reprimanded me for being late and working too slowly." Stay positive: *A sales presentation I did could have been stronger; I signed up for a public-speaking class to improve my delivery.*

Tell me about a time you took initiative.

This behavior-based question can be tricky to answer, because you don't want to sound like a maverick. The anecdote must demonstrate leadership while revealing maturity and respect for authority; you must show that while you always consult your boss to the extent he expects, you are a proactive, mature problem-solver.

Bad answer: *On the first day of my internship, I went in to my boss with a plan for restructuring the whole office.*

Good answer: *After several weeks at my summer internship, I began talking to people and analyzing how interns were used. I spoke to my supervisor about having interns specialize in an area and then rotate, instead of being assigned to one person for the summer. I came up with a schedule for the next summer. I thought it would be a great way for interns to learn about all aspects of the business and for the staff to get to know the interns. I knew there would be some disruption and learning curve issues, so I devised a handoff in which the interns trained one another as they rotated. I was pleased to find out that they implemented the rotations the following year, and I've heard from interns and from former colleagues that has worked well.*

Time Management/Organizational Skills Questions

▶ How do you prioritize your work? How do you plan your time?

▶ Do you work well under pressure? Meet deadlines?

▶ Do you stay late? Take work home?

▶ How do you stay organized?

▶ What systems do you use?

▶ How would you help me stay organized?

How do you communicate with your supervisors?

I check in at the beginning of the day. When I worked at a store, I would arrive a little early to check in with my boss and find out his priorities for that day. How do you like your assistants to communicate with you? What kinds of systems do you currently use?

How do you stay organized? How have you had to organize others?

I use the Outlook calendar program on my computer. I find it extremely helpful, as it automatically reminds me when a task is due. I also keep a box on my desk for loose papers; once a week, I file everything by subject.

A Case of the Nerves

Q. I get really uptight in interviews, and I feel like I can't let my personality show.

A. If you don't have a good personality, then don't reveal it. But seriously: You've got to remember that an interview is a conversation; even at its most formal, it has a human and interpersonal dimension. Don't give monosyllabic answers—be animated, radiate good energy, be enthusiastic about the job.

To help yourself relax, think of the interview as a two-way street—which it truly is. The interviewer has his questions and criteria, and you should have yours. One part of your mind should be occupied with the questions "Do I really want to work for this person? Is this the job I really want?"

Classic Interview Faux Pas

Sometimes it's better to say nothing than to advertise an unflattering truth, unless you are blatantly lying by omission. As the poet Emily Dickinson wrote: "Tell all the Truth but tell it slant/Success in Circuit lies/ ... The Truth must dazzle gradually/Or every man be blind." Following are some common instances in which interviewees tend to reveal too much:

Why do you want this job?

One candidate, asked why she wanted a job at the publishing company where I worked, said she needed health insurance for herself and her husband while she finished her novel. She might have talked about our mission or the titles or authors we published, but instead she put herself out of the running by admitting that all she cared about were the benefits.

Here's another bad answer: *I just graduated and I need a way to pay the bills.*

Based on your research and interests, you should have a compelling and real answer to this question. If you don't, you may be applying for the wrong job.

Where do you see yourself in five years?

Here are two inadvisable extremes: "In your job" or "I don't know." Say that you hope to stay in the industry and ask about the usual course of advancement. Don't reveal that you have a plan all mapped out for yourself, even if you do. (Especially if that plan involves applying to grad school or moving to another state.) Be honest but don't share too much: *I'm excited to start in this position, because I see it as a place where I can learn and grow.*

Do you have any concerns about the job?

Among the many jobs I didn't get as a young job-hunter was a position as an admissions officer at Harvard. Friends of mine were applying for similar jobs, so I decided I would go for it. I figured I had lots of experience: I had helped plenty of my friends with their entrance essays. I "researched" the job by talking to my roommate, who had worked in the admissions office as an undergraduate. She told me all about the admissions season and how at its peak you had to take home dozens of folders to read. So when the interviewer asked me if I had any questions or concerns, I more than willingly shared mine. I told him I wasn't sure I was going to have time to focus on my own writing, which was what I really wanted to do, if I had to take home work every night.

The scary thing is, I was actually proud of this concern. I felt it revealed that I had thoroughly researched the position, was being realistic about trying to balance the demands of a job with my perceived vocation, and so on. Really, what it revealed was that I was completely naive. When I told my parents about the interview, my dad said, "I guess you didn't really want that job, did you?" Needless to say, I did not get it.

Bottom line: Save concerns for *after* you've been offered the job, and run them by an outside advisor before asking about them. Try to find answers to such questions through your network or, if possible, by speaking with the person who previously held the job.

We use Access. Are you familiar with it?

If you don't know a particular program or language, don't ever lie and say you do. Your knowledge may be tested on the spot. But don't just give a resigned "no." Assuming you feel comfortable with computers and languages, you can say, "I don't know Access, but I've used Filemaker Pro and I'm sure I could learn with training," or "I don't speak French but I'm fluent in Italian; I'd be eager to take an intensive course." Be careful not to go too far—"I'm sure I could pick it up in a few hours." Even if that's the case, perhaps the interviewer has been struggling with the program for weeks! You might ask whether the company provides computer training for employees, or if you could seek it on your own. (The subtext here is whether or not the company offers or will pay for this kind of training—but you don't want to ask that outright in an interview.) Same goes for any part of the job description in which you haven't had experience—be honest, but present yourself as a quick study and motivated learner.

Will you take the job if it's offered to you?

There is only one answer to this question: Yes. If, based on the interview you've just had, you realize the job isn't for you or that you could never work for the person or company in question, then an equivocal answer is fine—"It would depend on the offer"—but if the employer gets the slightest hint that you don't really want the job, he probably won't offer it to you. Don't worry about saying yes when you're not sure; you aren't committing yourself to taking the job until terms have been discussed and an actual offer is on the table (see chapter 7 for more on that).

What really pisses you off?

Here's one of my favorite interviewing techniques. I am not an intimidating person, and I appear friendly and casual. Near the end of the interview, after a candidate is all loosened up and we're "friends," I lean over, look her in the eye, and ask, "What really pisses you off in a job? What did your last boss do that really ticked you off?" The naive interviewee misreads my casual language and lets her guard down. She may start using slang or complaining about her boss and other colleagues.

This will cost her the job.

Here's what I'm really testing: Do you understand how to behave in a professional situation? You must remain on guard at all times, even if I use language like "pissed off" and "ticked off." You do need to answer the question, but you shouldn't change your tone or register just because I changed mine.

Give an even, considered answer that does not reflect negatively on you or your boss. If possible, in fact, your answer should reflect positively on you: *Well, during our busy season, there were a few times when my boss asked me to stay late to finish a project. She would usually let me know in advance, but a few times she really couldn't; things came up at the end of the day. I try to go to a yoga class every day after work, and those days I couldn't, but at least we got the job done.* This kind of answer shows that while you're not a pushover, you understand the importance of getting the job done and are willing to make sacrifices when necessary.

The Strengths and Weaknesses Question

A classic in the "damned if you do, damned if you don't" category, this question has stymied many an interviewee. Interviewers know it, and they ask it in part to see how you handle yourself in stressful situations demanding diplomacy. Candidates who remain calm and answer with tact come out ahead.

Here's the key to this scenario: You should never reveal a real weakness. Interviewers aren't really expecting you to, either—if you do, don't be surprised if an offer isn't forthcoming. But you need to answer. ("Well, I can't really think of any weaknesses" can only sound arrogant.)

Here are some unfortunate weaknesses I've heard in interviews: "I'm always late. I'm lazy. I can't prioritize. I don't like staying late. I'm a perfectionist. I'm impatient. I have time-management issues. I'm a procrastinator. I don't tolerate stupidity well. I can't do math (it's a component of almost every job). I make snap judgments." Would you hire someone who admitted to these faults? Not only are they telling you why they'd be a poor choice for the job, they are also revealing their guilelessness.

The best strategy is to couch a weakness as a mistake made in the past. Or call on a trait that's a virtue in moderation and only becomes a flaw when exhibited in excess. Or both! **"I used to take on too much until I learned how to delegate. I've become better at managing my time, asking for help when I need it, and taking the proper measures if I feel I am in danger of missing a deadline."**

Choose a weakness unrelated to the job you're applying for: "I'm learning to be more confident in my public-speaking skills." Most people are afraid of public speaking, and most entry-level jobs don't require it. (Don't use this line if the job you're applying for has a public-speaking component.) Here's a real answer I loved: **"I used to find it more difficult to say no to people. When I was working at a homeless shelter, I found it difficult to turn away those who didn't qualify for our services, but I needed to follow city policy. I learned to steer those seeking shelter to other resources, and I've since found it easier to be clear and decisive when faced with difficult decisions."**

Show how you learned from or fixed a mistake. **"I once had an experience that became difficult when I didn't seek adequate help. I learned all I had to do was ask. Now I request clarification at the outset."**

Or choose a weakness that's really a virtue: **"I tend to be highly analytical. I was a philosophy major, so I learned to think about things deeply, but in my insurance job I saw that I needed to execute things quickly, so I've gotten much better at making sound but faster decisions." "I have very high standards for myself. I used to take forever to get certain tasks done, but I've learned to balance accuracy and time sensitivity, and am now able to get my work done much more quickly and efficiently."**

If you're asked about both strengths and weaknesses, lead with your strengths. Spend more time on those, and run through your "weaknesses" fairly quickly. (P.S. One is enough, even if they ask for several.)

Now on to the strengths. Choose qualities that relate to the job description, drawing on concrete experience to illustrate your points. Try to let the voices of others speak to your strengths: "When I did X, my supervisor told me . . ." Take it one step further by stating how you feel your strengths will be useful in the job.

Illegal, Inappropriate, and Strange-Sounding Questions

Federal Equal Employment Opportunity (EEO) laws deem certain questions and areas of probing illegal in an interview setting. Some interviewers don't know this; some know and ask anyway.

It is illegal to discriminate against candidates on the basis of age, race, color, gender, ethnicity, marital status, maiden name, country of origin, citizenship, religion, observance of religious customs and/or holidays, political views, past criminal convictions, and disabilities.

If you're asked a question you think is illegal or inappropriate, don't jump up and accuse the interviewer of wrongdoing. Act as if you didn't hear it. "I'm sorry, could you repeat the question?" If the interviewer persists, say, "I'm sorry. I don't understand how that's relevant to my candidacy here." If you want to let the interviewer off the hook, you can try reframing the question: "When you ask if I'm planning to get married, I'm guessing you're concerned about circumstances that might interfere with my ability to do the job"—then offer anecdotal evidence to allay his concerns. If that doesn't do it, say, "I'm sorry, I don't understand what this question is getting at in terms of my candidacy and I'm not comfortable answering it right now."

Note: If an interviewer does anything creepy or inappropriate, anything that makes you uncomfortable, have no qualms about excusing yourself. Seek advice and legal counsel. You won't be hired (nor should you want to be), but you might spare another unsuspecting candidate physical or verbal harassment.

Some questions aren't illegal—they're just difficult or touch on sensitive subjects: "How would your enemies describe you?" or "What's the one thing you hoped I wouldn't ask you today?" An employer may simply be out to determine how much stress you can handle, and how you handle it. So-called "stress interviews" are much less common than they used to be; they'd feature setups in which candidates might be asked to open a window that was actually nailed shut or solve other impossible problems. Frankly, I wouldn't want to work for someone who used techniques like these, but you may feel differently.

Script answers for tough questions and train yourself to respond calmly. Practice out loud in front of a mirror. If you're stumped, look the interviewer in the eye and say, "That's a tough question. I'm going to need a few moments to think about that." Take time to gather your thoughts and make notes as necessary, and take a deep breath before you answer. Don't be afraid of silence.

Below are examples of real questions candidates have been asked in an interview:

▶ Draw my dog.

▶ Are you a knee-jerk liberal?

▶ Would you have had that job if your parents didn't work for the company?

Even if you are asked inappropriate questions, there is a way to handle them professionally and matter-of-factly. Sometimes you'll want to sidestep the question altogether, and sometimes you'll want to answer it in a way that subtly indicates your awareness of its subtext. You don't want to give the interviewer the impression that you think you're smarter than he is, but you do want to convey that you're not about to be taken for a ride—an interviewer may be posing a seemingly irrelevant question to see if you've got the confidence to push back. Or—strange as it may sound—he could be testing your sense of humor.

Another category is brainteasers, questions such as, "How many screwdrivers do you think there are in America?" or "How many jelly beans would fit in a car?" These are designed to test your problem-solving skills and see how fast you can think on your feet. The point is not necessarily the answer, but the approach you'd take to get there and how well you can articulate your strategy.

> **Even if you are asked inappropriate questions, there is a way to handle them professionally and matter-of-factly. Sometimes you'll want to sidestep the question altogether, and sometimes you'll want to answer it in a way that subtly indicates your awareness of its subtext.**

Something to keep in mind: Interviews that don't go well are not necessarily your fault. Some interviewers are not good at interviewing or don't like to do it. Some may conduct a poor interview because they're tired or having a bad day. And some interviewers are just not that astute. If you get the sense that your interviewer is not doing a very good job, you need to try to take control without being overbearing. It is not solely the interviewer's responsibility to elicit information from you; it is also your responsibility to convey your message.

Q *If you were at a bar, what drink would you order?*

Bad answer: *A Tequila Sunrise.* Good answer: *I'm sorry, I don't understand how that's relevant to this job. Is there a drinking policy?* Or: *I'm sorry, I'm trying to figure out what you're trying to ascertain. I don't drink on the job, if that's what you're asking. . . .*

Q *How can you afford to live in this city on this salary? Are your parents paying for you?*

Bad answer: *My dad's buying me an apartment.* Good answer: *I've made a budget. I've made a decision to live here. I'm planning on working on the weekends at the same time.* Or: *Your question makes me wonder if we're on the same page—what's the range for entry-level positions here?*

Q *What are your politics? Who are you voting for?*

Unless your résumé already makes your position clear or you're applying for a job in the political arena, be neutral. The questioner may be less interested in your politics than in how you handle a charged question. Remain diplomatic and unflustered, and offer an innocuous comment. *It's been quite a campaign, hasn't it?* Hopefully that will guide the conversation into more neutral territory.

Bring It to the Interview

Don't shoot yourself in the foot by showing up to the interview empty-handed. You can't be too prepared, which is why you'll need a number of essential supplementary materials:

▶ Three copies of your résumé and cover letter—one for you to refer to, one for the interviewer, who may have misplaced his copy, and one in case someone else shows up for the meeting. Make the interview as easy as possible for them, and it's certain to be easier for you.

▶ The address where you're going, along with a map if you need one.

▶ The names and positions of those who will be interviewing you.

▶ A pen and small notebook. For the pros and cons of taking notes during the interview, see page 137. Whether or not you decide you want to take notes, you'll need to be prepared: The interviewer might assign you some homework or mention another job lead for you. After the interview, once you're somewhere private, you'll want to jot down your impressions and any information you want to follow up on. If you feel you didn't answer a question completely, for instance, you may want to revisit the topic in your thank-you note.

▶ A cell phone and the interviewer's contact information. If anything causes you to run late, you want to be able to call. (You should have factored in plenty of time for traffic jams and transportation breakdowns, but you never know.)

▶ Your ID. You may need it for building security or HR.

▶ Your list of references. You may be asked for them on the spot; ideally, though, you'll be able to provide your references after the interview, which will give you time to tailor them in light of what you've just learned.

▶ Your portfolio, if applicable. Depending on the industry, you may be required to present a selection of relevant professional materials you've created in the past: writing samples, press releases, or design samples.

▶ An umbrella, depending on the weather.

▶ Personal grooming items: breath mints, hairbrush, deodorant, safety pins, makeup, extra pair of nylons.

▶ A snack/protein bar. If you are prone to low blood sugar, be prepared.

▶ A small bottle of water. Nervousness can make you dry-mouthed, and you don't want your tongue sticking to the roof of your mouth during the interview.

Carry everything in a professional-looking briefcase or handbag, not a shopping bag, backpack, or fanny pack. Have papers in easy-access manila folders that you're willing to leave behind (no only-copies of anything), neatly labeled with your name and contact info. Make sure everything is well-organized. You don't want to be fumbling through your bag looking for things during the interview, or you'll create the impression that you don't have your act together.

What NOT to Bring

▶ A buddy. It should go without saying, but . . . go it alone! I've heard of people bringing along their best friends or family members, whether for moral support or because they're planning to have lunch with them afterward. Huge no-no—it's unprofessional and Mickey Mouse, and believe me, receptionists will talk.

▶ Non-interview-related stuff. Do not show up with things you need before or after the interview: shopping bags ("but the office is next to the mall!"), sports equipment (yes, it's good to exercise before an interview so you feel less tense, but not *right* before), your groceries. While you might think you're being efficient, you're simply being unprofessional. Schedule the interview so that you can appear unencumbered.

THE NIGHT BEFORE AND THE DAY OF

▶ Prepare for the interview as you would for any major event. Eat well, sleep well, double-check your alarm clock, prepare your bag/briefcase and the clothes you intend to wear.

The day of, eat enough so you don't show up with a growling stomach. Read a national news-paper like *The New York Times* or *The Wall Street Journal*. Don't be caught in the dark about major national or international events. If the newspaper has a section devoted to the industry in which you are applying, make sure you read it that week/day so you'll know what's going on.

Getting There

I t can't be overstated: You've got to allow plenty of time for inevitable public transportation snafus, construction, traffic, bad weather, and parking trouble. If you get to the interview too early—more than fifteen minutes before you're due—wait in a park or coffee shop near the office, or just walk around the block. Do arrive at least five to ten minutes in advance, though. Let the receptionist know you're there, then have a seat. Don't hover—you don't want to give the impression that you expect to be seen immediately. Settle in. In the winter, take off your coat—it will help you look and feel more composed. Don't sit there sweating, looking like you're about to bolt.

Watch yourself: From the moment you arrive, you are on display. Everyone you greet, from the security guard to the receptionist, is a potential source of information about you and your behavior. Do not be dismissive of anyone. Treat everyone politely and with respect. (I hope you do this anyway, but this is the time to go out of your way.)

You want to be friendly, to be someone others would want around day after day in the office, but not too friendly—maintain a professional interview demeanor even (or especially) when you're talking to a peer. I know of one employer who deliberately keeps interviewees waiting so his assistant can suss them out. After encouraging small talk, the assistant asks such questions as "So why are you leaving the job you have?" or "What was your last boss like?"—questions to which a candidate might respond more guardedly in a formal interview. On the other hand, under-the-radar interactions can have happy endings. . . . One candidate I worked with struck up a conversation with a receptionist; they found that they had been at college together and knew people in common. They got along so well that the receptionist ended up becoming a great source for job leads.

Remember, you are under the microscope. Do not eat, chew gum, talk on your cell phone, or pull out an iPod and start swaying to the music. Do not groom yourself in public, touch up your makeup, or lapse into nervous nail-biting. If you're anxious, do some subtle deep breathing. (The key word is subtle. You don't want to look like you're having a seizure.)

Don't let this time go to waste, either. Depending on the level of traffic through the reception area, you may be getting a valuable glimpse into your potential workplace. Observe the people around you. What are they wearing? Do they look rushed or stressed out? Are they friendly? Can you picture yourself in this environment? If there are catalogs or company newsletters around, read them. You might find material you can use in the interview. Are there displays or announcements posted on the walls? Read them as more clues to the office environment and company culture.

Take a last-minute trip to the restroom if there's time. (Let the receptionist know that you'll be right back.) Do a final hair, clothing, teeth, and breath check.

Prepare for the Worst

Q. In case of a major delay (a subway breakdown or traffic jam), what do I do? I know you're never supposed to be even five minutes late to an interview, but aren't there exceptions to the rule?

A. First of all, stop worrying! You should allow enough time to account for unexpected circumstances. But if you haven't, call the minute you're able to, apologizing and briefly explaining the situation. Be composed when you do get there. Don't rush in red-faced and out of breath. This will not create a stellar first impression. Take a few minutes to calm down and regroup.

In the Interview Room

When the interviewer appears, make eye contact and smile. If you're seated, rise gracefully. Say the interviewer's name and then yours: "Mr. Roberts? Susan Wilson, glad to meet you. Thank you for seeing me today." If he offers a hand, shake it (see box, opposite).

Maintain brief, positive eye contact and smile every once in a while. You want to appear as relaxed as possible, not as if you're about to have a tooth drilled. You are looking forward to an exciting conversation in which you have as much to judge about the interviewer as he does about you, and you have already put your best foot forward—you'll project those things if you believe them.

Musical Chairs

Q. Where should I sit?

A. If the interviewer doesn't motion you to a seat, choose one, but don't take the obvious lead chair. If for some reason the seating arrangement is unclear, ask—"Where would you like me to sit?"

Speaking of sitting: You should sit up, with good posture, legs together or crossed at the knees or ankles. Practice in your new clothes so you appear natural. Don't slump. Don't relax too far back in the chair or sit so close to the edge you fall off. (I've heard of it happening.) If you are very short or very tall and the interview chair and table don't work for you, say so! Don't suffer in silence with your knees scrunched up.

Pay attention to the interviewer's body language. Experts say that people respond better to someone whose posture mimics their own. If the interviewer leans toward you, relax and lean forward slightly; if he sits stiffly or formally, be comfortable but not too loose. No matter what your interviewer does, though, you should never fold your arms across your chest or lean back in your chair with your hands behind your head like you own the place.

GET A GRIP

Originally, the purpose of the handshake was for strangers to prove to each other that they were unarmed. I will assume that you're not packing heat at the interview, but your handshake still needs to exude appropriate self-confidence and show that you are trained in the social graces.

Practice your shake prior to the interview. A limp or dead-fish handshake or excessively hot, cold, or sweaty palms communicate nervousness or a lack of confidence. The interviewer will never say a word, but your hand will have spoken loud and clear.

When the interviewer extends his hand, meet it firmly, aiming for contact at the groove between the thumb and forefinger. Men tend to grip more firmly than women; do not be a hand-crusher or knuckle-roller. Look the interviewer in the eye as you shake. Do not pump wildly or maintain the hold too long.

Deal with calluses and chapping well in advance with creams and lotions, but make sure your hands aren't slippery at the interview. If you have a temperature issue, try rinsing with hot or cold water in the restroom. If sweating is the problem, don't go for a last-minute wipe on your pants— you'll look like a mess! Carry tissues or a handkerchief, and discreetly blot your hands in the waiting room.

The Name Game

Q. I'm terrible with names, and I'm worried that I'll get so nervous during the interview that I'll draw a blank.

A. Figure out how you learn best. If you're a visual learner, you may need to see the name written down or even to write it down yourself. Aural learners just need to hear it. Some people like to use mnemonics, but make sure you don't turn a name into a joke and then say it accidentally: If you remember Mr. McGee's name by calling him Mr. McGoo to yourself, slipping and calling him that would be bad.

Etiquette for Disabilities

Q. I have an obvious neurological condition. How should I handle it?

A. First things first: If you have a disability that requires special accommodation, you should let the employer know in advance. Do you require wheelchair accessibility? If you have a physical condition the interviewer is bound to notice, you have the option of bringing it up in advance or mentioning it just as you sit down, without making too much of a big deal about it: "I should let you know that I have a tic and can't help blinking/winking/twitching." It's better to get it out up front than have an interviewer think you're winking at him or that you're so nervous you're losing control of your limbs.

While it is illegal to discriminate on the basis of disability, the reality is that people do, perhaps inadvertently. You may want to investigate how disability-friendly the office is in advance.

Is It Snooping?

Q. If I notice personal items displayed in the office, is it okay to comment on them?

A. Sure, as long as you're not being intrusive or snooping. If you see a degree on the wall from a school you or someone in your family attended, why not try to establish the common bond? This is a professional encounter, not a social occasion, but there's nothing wrong with attempting to humanize the situation and connect with the interviewer. If you don't get much of a response, though, don't push it.

Interview Don'ts

I t's scary but true: Even the smallest mistake can throw an interview. Hiring is a big decision, one that has to be made with relatively little information. Consequently, employers scrutinize everything you do as a sign of larger patterns. Control what you can in order to create the best impression. So:

▶ Do not eat, chew gum, or pop mints.

▶ Never look at your watch or the clock as if you need to be somewhere else. You should have left adequate time before your next appointment.

▶ Do not leave your cell phone on. Do not answer a call. The interviewer shouldn't either, but if she does, wait politely, look elsewhere, and use the time to take notes or write down new questions.

▶ Do not recline in your chair, even if the interviewer does. The interviewer may be casual, but do not follow suit; remain professional at all times.

▶ Don't let your guard down if your interviewer happens to be young. Even if you're dealing with a peer, the interviewer is in a position of authority, and you must act accordingly.

▶ Do not bring up actual weaknesses if you're asked to list your strengths and weaknesses. See page 149 for more on answering this question.

▶ Don't let the interview go off track for too long. If the interviewer starts asking a zillion questions about your semester in New Zealand because he's about to go there on vacation, answer politely; but if you think you're running out of time, say "I'd love to tell you more; do we have time now?" Or ask a question about the job to shift focus.

Mistaken Identity

Q. What if I go in and I think they're interviewing me for the wrong position?

A. Take control! Stop the interviewer politely to clarify. Say that you expected a different line of questioning for the position and that you're just checking to make sure everyone is on the same page.

Résumé Confusion

Q. What if the interviewer confuses the facts on my résumé?

A. The interviewer says, "I know you spent a lot of time in England" and it was really France. Correct him politely. "I did study abroad and work for British Airways, but I was based in France, not England." Don't open yourself up to a whole line of questioning based on incorrect information.

Losing It
Q. I'm afraid I might just blank out during the interview if I get nervous enough.

A. This happens to all of us at some point. If you blank out or can't remember the interviewer's last question, simply ask her to repeat it. If you lose your train of thought in the middle of an answer, it's fine to say, "I'm sorry, I just lost my train of thought . . ." and hope that she'll prompt you. If you bungle a question you think is really important, fix it in your follow-up thank-you e-mail. Don't say, "I'm so embarrassed" or "I completely blew that question." Write: "I've thought more about your question. I wanted to let you know that I have extensive experience in . . ." But in general, unless the situation obviously requires it, do not apologize, during or after the interview; why remind the interviewer of your faults? One candidate asked me if she should write a note of apology because despite her efforts to be early, she had arrived one minute late. You can probably guess my answer to that.

When You Gotta Go
Q. What if I have to go to the bathroom during an interview?

A. Have you ever heard of an insurance pee? You should not have to pee in the middle of an interview. But if something happens and the urge strikes, excuse yourself politely. We all have bodies and bodily functions. If you feel faint or sick, excuse yourself and get out.

Interruptions
Q. What if something interrupts the interview?

A. Anything can happen in an interview. A fire alarm can go off, a company or personal crisis can interrupt. One candidate was in the middle of an interview when the interviewer's colleague ran in with a deadline emergency question that needed immediate attention. Her interview lasted all of eight minutes. If this happens, ask to reschedule.

Take-Home Assignments

For some positions and in some industries, you will be given assignments to complete at home and turn in at or after the interview. Don't balk at the work—it's your chance to stand out. Employers want to find out exactly how you respond to a real task. The way you handle the assignment will reveal a great deal about you as a potential employee, so take it very seriously.

Ask questions to make sure you understand the purpose and requirements of the assignment. Present any documents neatly, professionally (looks count), and on time. And this goes without saying: Make sure there isn't a single typo.

What kinds of assignments might you be given? For a marketing job, you may be asked to come up with a marketing plan for a product or service. This is your chance to show that you know what a marketing plan is and that you're able to research the current consumer environment. A graphics firm might ask you to design something. For a teaching position, you might be asked to come up with a sample lesson plan and execute it in a demonstration lesson observed by faculty and administrators. In publishing, editorial candidates are routinely asked to read a manuscript and write a reader's report. In business interview situations, on-the-spot problems are more common than take-home assignments—you're being tested on how you think on your feet.

No matter what the assignment, give it your all and get it in on time. Don't get so "into it" that you feel you need another week and ask for an extension.

Ending the Interview

Interviews may last anywhere from five minutes (someone simply wants to make sure you don't have two heads and run through your qualifications) to an hour or more (especially if you're meeting with more than one person).

Don't be worried if yours is short; it doesn't necessarily mean you blew it. There may have been another candidate waiting; the interviewer could have been busy; a crisis may have come up; or this could be just the beginning of a long process. Some people will be looking to hire right away, and others might take months to fill a position. One thing to keep in mind is that employers tend to procrastinate on hiring decisions. It's stressful for them: If they make a mistake, it's not easy to repair.

Near the end of the interview, you might be asked what questions you have. If you haven't demonstrated so already, this is your chance to show you've done your homework. You should have at least three questions prepared, though you may discard them in favor of ideas that come to mind over the course of the interview. Make sure your questions

> One thing to keep in mind is that employers tend to procrastinate on hiring decisions. It's stressful for them: If they make a mistake, it's not easy to repair.

aren't answered on the company website or other accessible source. Keep in mind that while you're assessing whether or not this is the right job for you, you're still the one being interviewed. This isn't your chance to turn the tables and start grilling the interviewer; the interviewer shouldn't feel as if he or his company is being judged. Keep it friendly. Rather than focusing on what the company can do for you, aim for a better understanding of the company and the job itself.

What kinds of questions should you ask? Here are a few:

▶ What is a typical day or week at the office like?

▶ What are some of the first projects I would be involved in?

▶ Can you tell me about some new company initiatives you're excited about?

▶ What have you liked best about working here?

▶ How would you describe the ideal candidate? (Take notes here—you'll use them for your closing argument and in your thank-you note.)

▶ How does this job/department fit into the work of the company overall?

Here are questions you *shouldn't* ask: "What's the salary?" or "How much vacation time do you offer?" Don't bring up salary or benefits until the second interview, or even later—see chapter 7. If you get the sense that the interviewer is looking at his watch and needs to wrap up, say, "If other questions occur to me, may I e-mail them to you?"

Before you go, offer a closing argument conveying why you are the right person for this job. Leave the interviewer with a clear message, reiterating the concrete skills and experience you would bring to the task: "You're looking for an assistant widget builder; I think my internship building widgets last summer would allow me to hit the ground running here."

Without being pushy, try to get a sense of the next step. "Do you have a sense of your hiring timeline?" If you've been asked to do an assignment, confirm the timeline you've been given to return it: "So I'll have these materials back to you by the end of next week." Thank everyone, shake hands, smile, and leave a positive, upbeat impression.

Job of My Dreams

Q. How do I convey that this is the perfect job for me, that this is the place I really, really want to work?

A. If you loved everything about the interview and feel more than ever that this is the job for you, express this enthusiastically, but don't overdo it. While it's important that the interviewer understand how excited you are about the job possibility, your candidacy hinges on your skills and personality. Reiterate your excitement in your thank-you note, but "show" rather than "tell" your enthusiasm. Go the extra mile by doing additional research on the company and incorporating what you learn into your note.

Happy Hour?

Q. The interviewer's assistant asked me to join a group for lunch or drinks. Should I go?

A. Sure, but don't let your guard down for a minute. You are still being interviewed, even if you don't think you are, and even if your potential colleagues aren't explicitly inviting you for this purpose.

"Thank You So Much!"

One of the biggest mistakes many candidates make is not following up by thanking the interviewer. To many interviewers, no thank-you note is not only disrespectful but a sign of a candidate's lack of interest in the position. After the interview, sit in a nearby coffee shop or the lobby (but not in the area where you waited for the interview; it will seem odd that you're not leaving). Take a few minutes to review any interview notes, write down questions as they occur to you, and draft your thank-you notes while the interview is still fresh in your

> Don't bombard the interviewer with e-mails—limit yourself to one thoughtful, well-written thank-you.

mind. Send the thank-you note that day to show how prompt and efficient you are.

While etiquette used to call for handwritten notes, e-mail is fine in today's professional world. If you have enough to say, you might choose to lob off a quick e-mail and follow it with a more thorough handwritten note. A caveat: If you interview with an old-world type who doesn't seem computer-savvy, a handwritten note is more appropriate. If you interviewed with several people, you should send each a personalized note. If an assistant was particularly helpful in setting up the interview or providing you with insight into the job, include her as well.

Don't bombard the interviewer with e-mails—limit yourself to one thoughtful, well-written thank-you. If you have questions, incorporate them into the note; don't send a slew as they occur to you, and don't send e-mails after midnight and before 6 A.M. You'll look like an insomniac freak.

Thank the interviewer for her time, then add in points of connection or mutual interests that came up in discussion. (If you discovered that you share

A Graceful Thank-You Note

Like all the written components of your job-search, your thank-you note should be positive, full of detail, and specific to the position at stake.

Dear Susan:

I wanted to let you know how much I enjoyed our meeting today. Thank you so much for taking the time to explain the parameters of the job in such detail. The more I learn about the job and the company, the more excited I am about the possibility of joining such a dynamic team. As you noted, in today's economy, Widget, Inc.'s success is quite remarkable, and I especially admire the company's commitment to innovation and speed in marketing. Thanks again for considering me for this position. I hope to hear from you soon.

Best, Brian Masters

ASSESSING THE INTERVIEW—YOUR TURN

The interviewer is not the only one whose opinion counts. You should be asking yourself a few questions, partly in order to figure out how interested you are in the job, but also to learn from any mistakes you may have made.

Did you achieve your goals? Do you think the interviewer achieved his? Did you connect with the interviewer? Was conversation easy or forced? Was this a function of your personality, the interviewer's personality and interview style, or some combination?

You want to impress the interviewer with your professionalism, skills, and experience as relevant to the job and offer anecdotes that reveal this. You want to demonstrate your knowledge of the company. Did you accomplish that? If not, note places where you might have inserted such information.

What was your gut feeling about the office, the people you met, your prospective boss, and the job as it was described to you? Did you get adequate answers to the questions you raised? Most likely the interview answered some concerns and raised others.

Make a list of questions for a second interview and things you want to do better next time. If you came up with great answers to questions you were asked, write them down so you don't forget them.

a passion for documentaries, you might recommend a favorite.) Repeat old or add new information about why you're right for the job. If you forgot to mention something you think is important, now is the time. Don't lead with "I forgot," though. Instead, try something like, "I thought you might also be interested to know . . ."

If you're sending a handwritten note, use a professional, neutral card with a matching envelope. The note should be brief and the handwriting neat and legible. If your handwriting is spidery, illegible, or looks like teenaged scrawl, type it up.

Before you send the note, read it out loud and proofread. If you're able, have someone else read it for you. To beat a dead horse: A single typo or mistake could ruin your chances.

Dear John?

Q. How do I address the interviewer in my thank-you note?

A. Take your cue from the interview—did you get a casual vibe, or is the office formal? If you're unsure, use Mr. or Ms. In contrast to your cover letters, you shouldn't be addressing anyone as "Dear John Smith." That greeting implies that you haven't met the addressee.

Second and Third Interviews

If your first interview was successful, you will get either an offer or a call for a second interview (and after that, maybe even for a third). Sometimes the offer will take place on the phone or by e-mail, but in some cases it takes place at the second interview. (Some interviewers don't like to extend an offer on the phone.) Still, don't go in assuming that the job is in the bag; the employer may be very far from a decision. Whatever the case, second and third interviews are opportunities for you to meet more people, ask some questions about day-to-day responsibilities, ascertain the employer's priorities, and get into more detail about working styles and personalities. The same rules apply as for first interviews, but the atmosphere might be different.

If your first interview was brief, the second interview will be more involved, possibly with new and multiple interviewers. (Sometimes the first interview is with an assistant, the second with the hiring person.) If your first interview was thorough, your second interview might be more of a casual conversation—a chance for you and the interviewer to get to know each other. You'll likely go into much more detail about what the job actually entails. Sometimes interviewers take more of a hazing tactic in the second interview, bringing up some of the less pleasant aspects of the job or company and emphasizing just how hard you're going to have to work. The message here is, Okay, you passed the first test, but do you really want to work here? (The answer, of course, being, Yes, I'm up to the challenge!)

You need to send yet another thank-you e-mail or note after a second interview, but this one can be much briefer: **"Thanks so much for taking the time to see me again. I'm more certain than ever that I would be a great match for the position, and I look forward to hearing from you."**

The Waiting Game

You've had the interview or interviews. You've sent your follow-up e-mails, thank-you notes, and references. Now you can only sit and wait to hear back. Right?

Wrong. Don't put all your eggs in one basket. Continue to schedule informational interviews, to network, and to research people and places and salary ranges and benefits. You'll multiply your options, and you'll also avoid falling prey to job-hunter's malaise, a condition characterized by a resistance to getting dressed, an unwillingness to exercise, an obsessive need to read several newspapers word for word, and a penchant for spending hours on the Internet without actually accomplishing anything.

If an employer has exceeded a self-imposed hiring timeline or just seems to be taking an awfully long time, don't automatically assume that you're out of the running—the process may take a while, sometimes months. You can't know what's going on behind the scenes. The company may be trying to fire someone or shuffle things around. The employer may not even be sure what his needs are, and whether he should hire someone senior or entry-level. Qualified candidates may have appeared at the last minute. The company may be changing its whole financial model or moving offices. Summer and major holidays often cause incredible delays—it's possible someone who needs to participate in the decision-making isn't around. It could be flu season, or there could be a major internal deadline such as a board meeting or sales conference.

Unless you've established a specific timeline, it's not unreasonable to check in by phone or e-mail if you haven't heard anything ten days to two weeks after your final interview. If over the course of the process you've become friendly with an assistant or HR person—someone other than the hiring party—you might check in with her. She may be able to give you insight into what's going on.

Good News

Q. I'm waiting to hear from a prospective employer, and I just had an article published in a well-known magazine. Is it weird for me to let him know?

A. Not at all. Send the employer an e-mail or letter. Even if the news isn't directly related to the position, it will remind him of you and let him know that you're still out there. Use your judgment, though. If your chocolate cake won first prize at the state fair, don't bother—unless you're applying for a food-related job.

Bad News

Q. What if I have news that could adversely affect my candidacy?

A. It depends. If you have become embroiled in a legal case or have been convicted of even a petty crime, my rule of thumb would be this: If you can no longer do or accept the job, you must withdraw your candidacy. You need only cite "personal" reasons. If you can do the job but the news might negatively affect the company from a PR point of view, wait until you have an offer. Explain that you've had a change in your life situation and that you hope they'll work with you to make it possible for you to take the job.

The same goes for personal issues. One candidate told me she had become engaged to someone in another city and didn't know whether to tell prospective employers, since they'd figure out that eventually she'd be moving. I advised against bringing it up unless asked. She didn't know for certain that she'd be moving very soon; frankly, not all engagements pan out; and wedding dates are often pushed back. I would give the same advice if you're pregnant or dealing with illness. If at any point it becomes clear that you would no longer be able to accept a job, that's the time to withdraw your application, explaining the situation in minimum detail and attempting to keep the door open for the future: "With much regret, I must withdraw my candidacy due to illness in the family. May I be in touch when the situation is resolved?"

Be In Touch

Q. I haven't heard anything since the interview, but I have a contact at the company I didn't use during the process—should I try now?

A. Absolutely! But make sure you provide the person with essential information: Send a copy of the cover letter and résumé you used to apply, note exactly what the position is, when you applied and interviewed, with whom you interviewed, and how you felt it went. This contact will also be useful if you get rejected; if you're lucky, you'll be able to elicit information on what went wrong or how you might improve the way you're presenting yourself.

Weighing the Offer

▶ ▶

WHAT TO SAY BEFORE "I'LL TAKE IT!"

I learned about negotiation through trial and error. For my first teaching job, the negotiation consisted of the headmistress handing me an index card on which she'd written my name and her salary offer in pencil. (Saying the number out loud wouldn't be genteel.) When she handed it to me, I laughed. I didn't mean to, but I couldn't help it. I don't recommend this as a negotiation technique, but it worked. I told her I hadn't been offered anything less than $20,000. "But that's in New York," she said. "This is Boston." We agreed that if I taught French in addition to my regular responsibilities, my salary would reach a whopping $17,000. (With two master's degrees. In 1986. But don't get me started on the issue of compensation for teachers. . . .)

Several years later, I signed a two-year contract for another job. After my first year there, everyone got a raise. Everyone, that is, except me. I kept thinking maybe it would show up in my next paycheck . . . or the next . . . but then I realized I'd better say something.

Maybe they had forgotten. I went to see the business manager.

"We didn't forget," she said. "But you signed a two-year contract and there was nothing in there about a raise." I was stunned. She offered some advice as consolation: "If I were you, I'd never sign a two-year contract . . . but if I did, I'd make sure to negotiate a raise up front."

I couldn't believe it. Why hadn't anyone told me that when I signed the contract? The answer is simple: The employer's job is to pay as little as possible, and the employee's job is to negotiate for as much as possible. I hadn't even negotiated. I was so thrilled at the offer that I had accepted it without asking any questions.

"They Want Me!"

Now it's your turn, and I hope you'll learn from my experience. You get the call, the "We'd like to offer you the job" call. This is the job you've been waiting for, hoping for, working for.

Don't say yes.

First, find out the terms of the offer.

There's a distinction between the offer of employment and the actual "offer": the salary, benefits, and terms of employment. Sometimes the person making the job offer is not the person with whom you will be discussing and negotiating its terms.

Most offers can be negotiated—something many inexperienced job-hunters don't realize. It's true that some jobs, particularly in the government sector, have little or no leeway; you may be told the exact salary and benefits at a first interview. But some things may still be open for discussion—your start date and review date, for instance.

You may be feeling uncomfortable at the thought of negotiating. Many people do, especially first-timers. But which is worse: feeling weird, or blindly accepting an offer and finding out later that you are grossly underpaid or have inferior benefits

> You may be feeling uncomfortable at the thought of negotiating. Many people do, especially first-timers. But which is worse: feeling weird, or blindly accepting an offer and finding out later that you are grossly underpaid or have inferior benefits and fewer vacation days than colleagues who negotiated?

and fewer vacation days than colleagues who negotiated? You won't get what you don't ask for. Don't think, "Oh, I'll just say yes and accept all their terms now, because once I'm there and they see how great I am, I'll be in a better position to negotiate." No, now's the time. Though you will have other negotiations during the course of your tenure, the first sets the stage for all the rest.

Prepare for negotiation discussions well in advance by researching industry salaries and benefits packages, but don't bring up terms until the employer does. (There's nothing less appealing to an employer than a candidate whose first line of questioning is about hours, vacation time, and benefits.) In any negotiation, you want to be the last to put your cards on the table. Keep in mind that you never have as much negotiating power as you do when you've been offered a job but haven't yet accepted. The employer wants you. She's gone through a long process with many candidates, and she may be willing to negotiate to get you.

Don't make decisions or accept offers on the spot. Say, **"I want to make sure I understand all the components of the offer; could you send me an e-mail outlining the proposed terms?"** Don't be afraid to ask for detail or clarification; if you're negotiating with your prospective boss, you may be referred to someone in HR for the finer points. Take the time to run the offer by experienced members of your network. One to two days of deliberation is reasonable, and some employers consider a week normal. But don't drag your feet: If you miss an agreed-upon deadline, employers are perfectly within their rights to withdraw their offer. No matter what, remain polite and professional throughout the process; be assertive, but not aggressive.

Your Salary Range

How do you find out the going rate for your position in advance of the negotiation process? Talk to people in the field. While it's rude to directly ask someone about his salary, it's perfectly fine to inquire about the range for a specific position.

There are also all kinds of websites where you can find out the average pay for your position. Many industry magazines do annual salary round-ups, and the U.S. Department of Labor publishes average salaries for a range of jobs. Remember, though, that the value of a stated salary varies greatly depending on the location—$30,000 does not go as far in Chicago as it would in a rural area of the Midwest, for example.

Keep in mind, too, that your base salary is not what you actually take home. Taxes will be taken out and health insurance and retirement contributions deducted. On the other hand, you've also got to consider benefits, which are often worth at least twenty-five percent of your base salary, sometimes as much as forty percent. One company's slightly higher salary might be outweighed by another company's superior health and dental coverage.

Create an Annual Budget

IN SOME INDUSTRIES—EVEN HIGHLY COMPETITIVE INDUSTRIES requiring advanced degrees—entry-level salaries are quite low. You don't want to take a job you can't live on, so figure out in advance what's doable for you.

First, calculate what you spend or are likely to spend annually. Include basic monthly expenses (food, rent, utilities, clothing, transportation, medical, phone, Internet connection); recurrent annual expenses from minor (haircuts) to major (insurance and taxes); and luxuries (cable television, eating out, entertainment, travel, gifts, splurges). Ideally, you should also be trying to save at least ten percent of your salary, so factor that in, too. Once you come up with a figure, you can back into a salary range. Depending on the cost of living in your town or city and the starting salary in a given industry, you may find that you need to get a roommate or cut back on entertainment unless you're willing to take on freelance or other work.

The Terms of the Offer

Whether you're dealing with a mom-and-pop shop or a huge global firm, you shouldn't accept a job without asking some questions. If possible, get the answers in writing. (If you're going to be required to sign a contract, see pages 184–185.)

Some of the following negotiation points are industry-specific—not all will apply to every job or company. Some are standard boilerplate, and some are creative takes on the negotiation process. Look them over and decide which ones you care about; only you can know what's important to you. Of course, you'll also want to consider the job itself. How desirable is it? You may be willing to take a little less cash up front if you feel the employer, colleagues, and office environment are a great fit. Consider:

▶ What your starting salary will be.

▶ What your exact title will be.

▶ How much vacation you will start with. When does that change?

▶ What health and retirement plans are available to you. Might you be eligible for a premium plan if your salary is not negotiable? Can dental or optical coverage be added? Can the deductible be lowered?

▶ Does the company offer performance bonuses?

▶ Does the company offer overtime?

▶ How often will you be reviewed? What is the review process?

▶ The start date for the position.

▶ What will your duties be?

▶ Apart from performance-based raises, are there standard annual cost-of-living adjustments?

▶ What retirement benefits does the company offer? Is there a 401(k)?

▶ Are transportation vouchers available?

Other benefits to be aware of: paid personal days, sick days, and holidays; life insurance and disability plans; worker's compensation (for on-the-job injuries); paid and unpaid leaves of absence; relocation expenses; and matching funds for charitable contributions.

Advanced Perks + Benefits

THESE NEGOTIATION POINTS ARE LESS APPLICABLE for entry-level jobs or jobs in the nonprofit or public sector, and some are perks rather than benefits:

▶ Will the company pay for your laptop/BlackBerry/cell phone/home Internet access/car/car service/parking?

▶ Is telecommuting a possibility?

▶ Are there opportunities for professional development? Will the company pay for classes, degree programs, training seminars? If the company will pay for a master's degree and you already have one, can that be translated into another benefit?

▶ Will you receive a corporate credit card and travel and entertainment budget?

▶ Are there cultural or other benefits like museum or health club discounts?

▶ Are you eligible for a wardrobe allowance?

▶ Are you eligible for more vacation time or flex hours such as half-day Fridays in the summer?

▶ Can you take on extra responsibilities for more money? Are there opportunities to do freelance work that's usually hired out?

▶ Are stock options or other profit-sharing plans available?

▶ Is there a sabbatical plan?

▶ Is there a separation agreement?

Negotiation 101

S ome people are natural negotiators; others dread the very idea. No matter what your personality, you can stack the odds in your favor by understanding five key points:

1. The salary you accept is the starting point for future raises and the salary at your next job.

2. The lowest number you state during a negotiation may be your salary. If you can't live with it or on it, don't put it out there, secretly hoping to make yourself an attractive candidate by looking inexpensive at first and then convincing the employer you're worth more.

3. The low end of your range should be higher than the lowest salary you would actually accept. That way, you leave yourself room to negotiate. (But don't overdo it at the top of your range; you don't want to appear uninformed or arrogant.)

4. The employer's job is to lowball you and pay you as little as possible; your job is to get as much as you can. This holds true especially for entry-level positions, as employers are apt to take advantage of your inexperience. It's not evil, it's just business. Companies are always looking for ways to cut costs.

5. Your lifestyle choices, debt, or financial issues are not the employer's problem. Never discuss your *needs* during negotiation; couch the discussion in terms of industry standards and what your skills and experience are worth.

NEGOTIATION DON'TS

Sometimes what you don't say is as important as the information you do volunteer. Be especially on your guard while you're negotiating the terms of an offer:

- **Don't get specific until the time is right.** Only at second interviews or when the offer is presented should you inquire about benefits, vacation, typical length of tenure for the job, and the review process.

- **Don't confuse a perk and a benefit, and don't bring up perks during the negotiations.** A perk is something like a health club membership; it's not considered a negotiable benefit, but rather an extra bonus offered to all employees. Wait until you're on the job to look into it.

- **Don't price yourself out of a job.** An employer is not going to pay an entry-level person $100,000 a year if the average base entry-level salary is $30,000. Be realistic and do your homework so you're familiar with industry and regional standards.

- **Be positive, not adversarial.** You don't want to warp a relationship with a potential employer during the negotiation.

- **Don't lie about a previous salary in the hopes of making yourself look expensive.** The information is easily verifiable. Don't volunteer your previous salary, but be honest if asked; be sure to factor in any bonuses and benefits.

- **Don't undersell yourself.** The biggest regrets I hear are from candidates who simply accept an offer on the spot without negotiating and later find out others hired at the same time and level have higher salaries or better benefits—because they negotiated.

- **Don't have anyone call to discuss benefits or salary or to negotiate on your behalf.** This is beyond unprofessional and I've heard of it happening—candidates actually having their parents call their employers. You should certainly ask mentors or parents for help and advice, but they should not be involved in your relationship with your employer.

When it comes to negotiation, mind-set is key. You need to understand and express confidence in your own worth and value. That should be easier once you've actually got an offer, because the company has shown it wants you. What could be more confidence-building than that?

Communicate that you really want the job. You *will* be able to create a win-win situation. Since some degree of compromise is likely, know exactly what *you* are willing to compromise on.

Negotiate based on concrete factors of value such as education, experience, skills, reputation, and contacts—**"As you know, I just completed a six-week training course in the field; I hope that will move me to the high end of the posted salary range."** The employer will negotiate based on how eager he is to fill the position (how long it's been open, how essential it is to the company), the company's financial state, and how sure he is about his number-two candidate.

Prior Obligations

Q. I'm currently negotiating a job offer, but I know that I'm going to need to take sick leave for a major surgery soon after the start date. Am I obliged to mention that?

A. You don't have to, but you could be skating on very thin ice. If you say nothing, start your job, and then go out of commission for weeks—courtesy of the company's health-care plan—you'll seriously and adversely affect your relationship with the boss and the company. You may not be fired, but you will be creating a difficult situation for your boss and other members of your department, and your reputation will suffer.

Fielding Other Offers

If you get an offer from one company while you're waiting to hear back from another, you have two options. If you want the job that's been offered to you, accept it. Notify the other employer that you have accepted an offer and are withdrawing your candidacy.

If you don't want the job, find out the terms before you decline. You may be able to use that information to leverage an offer for the job you want. Call or e-mail the place you haven't heard from: **"I'm taking the liberty of being in touch because I haven't heard back about an application I submitted, and I really want to work at your company. I just received** another offer, but I don't want to accept it until I'm certain there is no possibility with you. If you can't let me know now, may I have a sense of your hiring timeline?"

This may seem like playing with fire, but you have nothing to lose. What are the possibilities? Perhaps they didn't get back to you because they weren't interested in you. Now you know—and you have another job waiting. Or they haven't made a decision yet. Now you've highlighted yourself as a desirable candidate—someone else wants you—and you've flattered them by telling them they're your number-one choice.

The tricky part is that you can't keep an offer open for more than a few days, maybe a week at most. If the undecided employer can't make a choice that quickly, you are going to have to do some soul-searching. If you must have a job immediately, take the job that's been offered. If you have some time, you can choose to take the risk of declining the standing offer. But know that you *are* taking a risk. Of course, the best possible outcome would be for the company you're interested in to speed up its decision-making process and counteroffer, so you can choose between two offers. Either way, know that if you accept a job, that's it. If things don't work out, you can always move on, but don't take a job thinking you'll just keep looking and pull out if you get a better offer. That's the kind of unprofessional behavior people talk about, and it *will* damage your reputation in the field. If you want to hold out, get a temp job.

Here's one thing you definitely shouldn't do: Pretend to have an offer when you don't. It's easy enough for an employer to verify whether or not you have in fact been offered a job.

Bon Voyage

Q. I have a family trip planned for the last two weeks of August, and I was hoping for a September start-date—but it's the beginning of August and I've just been offered the job, which starts next week.

A. In theory, you should avoid taking any unnecessary days off for the first few months of your new job, so I urge you to try to push back your start-date. Offer to come in two to three days a week or on flexible hours on a volunteer basis to shadow the person who's leaving. If that's not possible and you can't change your plans, some employers may be willing to make exceptions for previously planned trips or family gatherings.

Bait and Switch

Q. I didn't like what happened during the negotiation process. I've been getting some negative vibes; the boss I thought was nice seems psycho now. What do I do? Should I pull out?

A. Don't make hasty assumptions. Try to speak with someone else at the company before you take action—I've seen many job-hunters leap to unfounded conclusions. One candidate I worked with felt he was being unfairly pressured into a quick decision. He told me, "The boss said he'd slow things down, especially after I agreed to fly back out sooner than anticipated for a second visit. A day later another guy from the company called saying that the boss wanted to know where things stood. I feel like they're going back on their word." I had to remind him that the two guys in question had not necessarily talked to each other. It could have been a busy time; signals may have gotten crossed. Who knows . . .

On the other hand, how someone handles a negotiation may be indicative of the future working relationship, so trust your gut. Better to pull out during the negotiation process than to take a job only to quit a few weeks later.

If You *Don't* Want the Job . . .

What happens when you get a job offer you don't want? First, ask yourself why you don't want it. Are there things to be negotiated that would make you want it? It might be that you didn't know you didn't want it until you went through the process, met the actual people, tested out the commute. Or you've had interviews at more exciting places. Those are reasonable considerations.

Essentially, it's your call. But here's the important thing: The moment you realize that you won't take a particular job—regardless of its pay or perks—is the moment you should withdraw your application. It's only fair to the employer and to the other candidates. While it may be tempting to wait and see if you get an offer you can leverage for a job you *do* want, you're only wasting everyone's time. And who knows—you may one day want to come back to the company that doesn't look so exciting right now. You should never burn your bridges.

Always decline offers over the phone and not by e-mail or voice mail. (If you consistently reach voice mail after trying for a day or two, leave a brief message saying you regret that you're unable to accept the offer but would like to speak with someone in person.) Thank the interviewer for his time and consideration. If you feel like you might be back one day, stress that you'd like to stay in touch and send a thank-you note.

Dealing with Rejection

The other possible outcome of a job search is rejection. When you get your first, celebrate: The worst is over! What you have feared all along has finally happened. Now you will never again suffer the agony of a first rejection.

While rejection is never ideal, you *can* make the most of it. You can't get every job you apply for—and I'm a firm believer that if you didn't get it, it wasn't the right one for you. There's a reason for everything. Perhaps you've been freed up for the right opportunity.

Sometimes, though, a rejection *is* about you. Employers may offer a reason ("We took an internal candidate"); but if they don't, and you feel you had a good rapport with the interviewer, it doesn't hurt to ask for feedback. "I'm very disappointed. I'm wondering if, at your convenience, you might be able to offer suggestions for improving my candidacy." (If you've got an ally on the inside, you may be able to get some behind-the-scenes information on who was actually hired and why.)

You might learn something useful. One candidate scheduled

> **KEEP YOUR NETWORK IN THE LOOP**
>
> ▶ No matter what the outcome—offer or rejection — remember to keep your references and mentors in the loop. Let them know that, thanks to their help, you got the job, or that you're still looking and open to leads and advice.

a feedback phone call and got some very constructive criticism: First of all, she was competing with a pool of candidates who all had MBAs; she was also told that during her interview, her "headlining" skills were weak. (They expected her to be able to offer a brief, focused summary of her résumé orally, tying her skills and experience to the stated job requirements. Good thing you've been practicing that!)

Given the legal issues surrounding employment and the proliferation of discrimination suits, don't be surprised if you can't elicit any feedback.

And remember: There are several reasons you might not get a job, even if you're perfectly qualified. There might have been an internal candidate or a candidate with more experience.

Take steps to remedy any obstacles that might be standing in your way. If you think you're lacking experience, go out and get some. Intern, volunteer, or temp in the field. Were you perceived as overqualified? Time to rethink your résumé or the jobs for which you're applying. (Of course, if you feel you've been discriminated against on the basis of age, race, gender, sexual orientation, or religion, you need to decide if you want to pursue legal recourse; U.S. Department of Labor guidelines are available online.)

If the interviews went well and you get the sense that you were a top candidate, communicate how much you enjoyed the interview process and the people; express that you're more determined than ever to find the right position at the company, and ask if they'd be willing to keep your résumé on file. Keep in touch. Another position might become available in a few months or even weeks.

Signed, Sealed, Delivered

Once you've negotiated the offer and accepted the job, ask to get the terms in writing. If the employer replies that they don't have written contracts, ask whether you might have an informal letter of agreement for your files. They might not agree to that either, but you should still ask. At the very least, send them a letter stating your understanding of the terms and keep a copy for your files.

In a large company, you will probably schedule a time to sit down with someone in the HR department to go over things like health insurance and retirement plans and to fill out a welter of forms.

Depending on the job, you may be asked to sign noncompete and nondisclosure agreements or to undergo drug, credit, and background checks. Make sure you get expert advice before signing any documents.

Finally, find out where you're supposed to be and when, and get ready to start!

You've Got the Job

▶ ▶

NOW WHAT ARE YOU GOING TO DO?

O nce you're over the excitement of getting a new job, it may sink in that you actually *have* one. Soon you will not have the time to linger in coffee shops reading the entire paper as people in suits rush in and out with their cardboard cups. You will be one of them. But you also will be the new kid on the block, the one who doesn't know the department code for the Xerox machine, the one who doesn't know where to go for lunch or with whom.

Starting a new job can be exhilarating, but it can also be difficult and confidence-shaking. Don't be too hard on yourself. If you've ever seen stress charts, starting a new job is way up there, along with getting married or divorced, having children, and dealing with death or illness.

Even if you're feeling confident or at ease in your new situation, there will be an adjustment period. Give yourself at least six weeks to begin to get a handle on what's going on. Wait and watch. A boss of mine once told me that it takes a year to know what your job actually *is,* and another year to figure out how to do it. I thought he was being kind. Now I know what he meant.

The Beginner's Mind-Set

What can you do to make starting a job as easy as possible? The first thing is to know the logistics. When and where do you actually start? To whom should you report on the first day? If no one has told you, call the HR department or one of the people who hired you; don't wait until Sunday night to figure out that you don't know when and where you're supposed to be on Monday morning.

Keep an open mind and be flexible. You may be greeted with flowers and a clean new office space, or it may appear as if no one knew you were coming—there will be no desk or working computer. You may be left to your own devices or called straight into a meeting or have a stack of folders dumped in your lap. The ideal scenario is to overlap with the person who held the job before you. Take notes and ask for advice (organizational strategies, the boss's likes and dislikes), but take that advice with a grain of salt. Someone who was unhappy or had conflicts with the boss may give you an earful. The most thoughtful employees will leave detailed job descriptions and useful information, but don't count on it.

Don't forget that you *are* a beginner. You can't be expected to know everything right off the bat, even if everyone around you forgets that. Don't let your self-confidence go down the tubes. When you're new, every task takes longer. You can't just *do* something; you have to find out what the procedures are, find people to ask, and so on. It can be exhausting. You might feel you're just spinning your wheels while your ego shrinks and you start wondering why you were hired in the first place. You might even wonder why you wanted the job anyway. This is normal. Don't give in to it—it's part of the roller coaster.

While you can't be expected to know everything, you can be expected to know how to get the information you need to do the job and how to put your best foot forward and be eager, motivated, and professional. It will get easier with time. (And if it really doesn't, see chapter 9.)

Especially in the beginning, you'll need to rely on colleagues for guidance and information. That's fine, but try not to attach yourself solely to

A PROBATIONARY PERIOD

▶ Don't be surprised if you're put on what's called a probationary period at the start of your job. It doesn't mean you've gotten in trouble, but rather that your continued employment is contingent on your review at a predetermined time (usually three to six months after you start). If you are not performing "satisfactorily," the company has the right to let you go without any of the usual red tape (and likely without severance pay and benefits).

Make sure you understand the exact terms and expectations of the probationary period. Speak to your supervisor about the measures of performance and how you will be monitored along the way.

Try to set a meeting time, at least once every two weeks, in which you generate a list of projects to be accomplished and reviewed. Not every supervisor will agree to this, but it's a great way to get regular feedback on your performance.

one person, no matter how helpful he is. You've got to get a sense of the big picture, and you also don't want to take up too much of one person's time. When you arrive, if you aren't working specifically with one person or group, find out whom to go to with questions.

Be respectful of your new colleagues' time. If possible, prepare lists of questions in advance so you're not repeatedly interrupting. Don't expect people to drop what they're doing to help you out. Nor should you take their help for granted; after you get the lay of the land, you might invite them for lunch or coffee to thank them for being so helpful. A little gesture of appreciation goes a long way.

Sick Day So Soon?

Q. I woke up really sick, but it's only my second week. Won't it look bad to stay home from work so early on?

A. It's not ideal, but don't go to work if you have a fever or something contagious. It's not good for you—the more you rest, the faster you'll get better—and it's not good for your colleagues. If you're not able to come in but can work from home and are willing to answer phone calls and e-mails, let your boss know.

NEW-EMPLOYEE PAPERWORK

▶ If you're signing a contract stipulating your terms of employment, make sure you obtain a countersigned copy. (This goes for any document you sign.) If your company doesn't offer official contracts, ask for a letter of agreement stating the agreed-upon terms of your employment: length of commitment, compensation, vacation time, benefits, review dates, scope of the job, and so on.

You may also need to fill out paperwork pertaining to your retirement benefits. If you're offered options, get advice from a knowledgeable family member or friend. You will need to provide the names of beneficiaries—the people to whom your assets will eventually be distributed.

Will you have an expense account? Company credit card? Find out about limits, but also talk to colleagues to make sure you get a sense of what's appropriate. Keep and annotate receipts, and turn in your expense reports on time. It should go without saying, but such a perk should never be abused: Do not use the company card to go out with friends, don't take office supplies home, and don't use company mail services for personal items.

There will be multiple forms relating to health insurance. You may need to procure old medical records or undergo a company

Getting the Ball Rolling

If the employer or HR department hasn't provided new-hire paperwork or guidance on logistics, start the ball rolling yourself. Is there an employee handbook? Read it, and if you have questions, schedule a time to discuss them with someone. Understand that many rules listed in an official employee handbook may be routinely broken or ignored—but don't just assume you have the right to do what longer-standing colleagues do. In the beginning, err on the side of caution.

Find out when you are expected to be at your desk (and ideally get there before that) and how you're supposed to clear vacation time, sick days, and personal days. As unassumingly as possible, ask about overtime and comp physical. Before deciding on a plan, speak with colleagues, family, and friends. When you're healthy and young, health insurance doesn't seem important, but one illness or accident will quickly change your mind. Look into what is routinely covered: annual physical, prescriptions, eye exams, dental care, one pair of glasses or lenses. What about emergency room visits, ambulance costs, visits to specialists? Figure out the deductibles—the sums you must pay out of pocket before insurance kicks in. How much will you be expected to contribute? Is that amount automatically taken out of your paycheck? Can you use your current doctors, or will you need to switch? Are you covered while traveling in the U.S. and abroad? The company may have a flexible spending plan, in which you receive a certain amount of base coverage along with a tax-exempt stipend for additional health expenses.

Speaking of health: If you have allergies or a medical condition, make sure to let someone in the office know. If you aren't asked to fill out an emergency contact form, make sure you give your details to your supervisor. (This may sound paranoid, but I'll never forget the day an intern fell writhing to the floor, clutching her gut—we were lucky she was able to tell us the name of her doctor.)

time (vacation days given as compensation if you are asked to work on a weekend—not applicable if you *choose* to come in on a weekend). Many companies don't pay overtime, yet have a culture in which staying late is the norm, especially if you want to get ahead.

Pay attention to the culture in general. Your boss may say the job is nine to five, but if you're the only one ducking out at 4:59, it doesn't look good. (In general, you don't want to leave before your boss does, especially when you're starting a job.)

Don't presume to have the privileges of long-standing staff—realize that you have to earn them. One new assistant announced she'd be out at an industry conference the following day—she'd seen a more senior assistant do this. Another assistant who felt very comfortable with me confided that she would be taking a "sick" day to accompany her boyfriend to the airport. She probably felt very responsible letting me know the day before, since she wouldn't be leaving me in the lurch. Mistake. I had no problem with her going, but now she'd put me in the awkward position of covering for her. (I told her to take the time as a personal day.)

Your Work Area

BEFORE YOU START PLASTERING PHOTOS ON YOUR CUBICLE WALLS (if you have walls) or leaving your sneakers and gym bag on the floor, take a look around. How do colleagues handle personal paraphernalia? No matter how casual the office, you need to be neat and discreet. Don't leave food on your desk or toss potentially smelly things in the garbage. Your area should always be ready for an impromptu visit from a boss or client.

If your desk isn't prestocked with Post-its, pens, notebooks, and so on, make sure you stock up—you'll want to set up your organizational systems right from the beginning. Find out the procedure for obtaining supplies. Is there a supply room? Do you order yourself? Is there a limit? Be sure to ask. Don't order the $5 pens if that's not company culture.

You may need passwords and machine codes to access computers, Xerox machines, or shared servers. If you're unfamiliar with any piece of office equipment, ask for instruction as early on as possible; if the company offers software tutorials, sign up.

Your Phone + E-mail

ONCE YOU'RE GIVEN A WORKING E-MAIL ADDRESS and phone number, make sure you're added to e-mail and phone circulation lists. Record a professional voice mail message stating your first and last name and the name of the company. Figure out how to work your phone so that you don't end up hanging up on someone you're trying to transfer.

Answer the phone professionally, whether it's yours or your boss's: "Hello, Job Inc., Morgan Smith's line. May I help you?" or "Hello, this is Emily." Keep in mind that the office phone is not your home phone. Whether anyone is listening or not, save the personal calls for before and after work, on breaks or at lunch. (Speaking of your cell phone, it should *always* be off or on vibrate during business hours. And no texting during meetings!)

A note on e-mail etiquette: I cannot overstress how absolutely vital it is that you separate your personal e-mail from your professional e-mail. There are many reasons to do this. First of all, Big Brother is watching, and the law is on his side. Any e-mail you send while at work is actually considered the employer's legal property—even if you send it from your personal account! At large companies, the IT department or a search program may regularly scan employees' e-mails for inappropriate language. The same goes for your Internet usage and personal shopping. Though some companies have more relaxed attitudes about the way their employees use the Web, it's always best to exercise caution. Restrict your browsing to reputable news sites. (You should never, for any reason, spend time on any site with inappropriate content; even the material on mainstream gossip sites may be too risqué.)

Reason number two to separate your e-mails: It's so easy to slip and send an e-mail to the wrong person. If it were to happen at work, wouldn't you rather it be an e-mail about a problem with the copy machine than a spare-no-details description of your big night out? (Or, even worse, an e-mail about your boss?) Basically, you shouldn't be writing any e-mail at work, to anyone, that you wouldn't feel comfortable showing to your boss or colleagues.

Your Boss's Communication Style

COMMUNICATION IS A KEY COMPONENT OF ANY JOB. Especially when you're new, err on the side of overinforming your supervisors and others who need updates on your projects.

Be explicit in asking your boss how she wants information. Should you copy her on all correspondence with clients? Who else in the company needs to know certain information? In the beginning, should you run e-mails and letters by her before sending to make sure you've struck the right tone and are conveying the appropriate information? Should you be preparing regular status reports? How often should you check in? At the beginning and end of every day? Before you go on breaks or to lunch? Should you keep phone logs? Notes on phone conversations? What about record-keeping? Should e-mails be printed out and archived, or stored electronically only? How should you fill out time sheets and expense forms, and who needs to sign off on them?

Different supervisors have different working styles and expectations. Check in periodically to see how you're doing. Your boss should initiate these conversations, but if not, take the lead: Ask for some time to discuss how she thinks things are going and whether there are tasks you should be doing differently. Don't be surprised or hurt if the answer is yes. Accept constructive criticism graciously. Your main priority is to get the job done as well and efficiently as possible.

CODES, CARDS, KEYS

▶ Make sure you have the necessary office keys and alarm codes and know the lockup procedures. At a small company, the system may be relatively simple, whereas at a large one you may need to have your photograph taken for an ID or electronic pass.

Your Systems

AS YOU BEGIN TO GRASP the scope of your new job, you'll need to learn existing systems and protocols and then begin to implement your own. Find out how colleagues and the previous job-holder set up their systems. I never mind receiving an e-mail or request from a new colleague asking, "Is there a standard procedure on this?"

Keep a "procedures" folder: Every time you learn how to do a new task (use the database, fill out a frequently used form or contract), save the information in this folder so you won't have to repeatedly bug colleagues for the same information. Sometimes new jobs have a fair amount of lag time; it may be a while before you have enough work to keep yourself busy. If that's the case, look into areas of the office that aren't getting enough attention. Setting up or improving departmental systems is a great way to use your spare time.

Scheduling Crisis

Q. I asked for a specific chunk of time off, and my boss said it fell during a really busy period. I'm in a bind, since I told a friend I'd go on vacation with her and we already put down a deposit. . . .

A. It may not seem fair, but your boss's needs and even his vacations come first—especially when you're new to the job. If for some reason it's really important for you to take off a particular period of time, ask as far in advance as possible. You might offer to come in early or stay late or to work from home in the weeks before or after your trip. See if that does the trick. But if the issue involves your family or your health, do what you need to do. No matter what anyone says, I believe family and health come first—but I don't mean rushing out to buy something on sale for Mother's Day or to an "urgent" midday appointment for teeth whitening. Apologetically explain the situation to your supervisor in broad terms (no need to delve too deeply if the issue is personal), and make arrangements to get your work done.

Time for Lunch!

L unchtime at a new job can be lonely at first. Office mates pair up and head out as if Noah's ark has just docked, and you're left wandering the halls like a kid on the first day of school. But don't be afraid to eat alone for a few weeks. People truly are judged by the company they keep, and when you're just starting a job, you don't know enough about that company.

While you should be friendly to everyone, don't rush to *befriend* anyone (even those who rush to befriend *you*). Form office friendships with care and discretion. Beware of outcasts and "black holes": people who strike up friendly conversations and then *just keep talking*, sucking you into a void from which there is no escape. Take time to observe colleagues and supervisors in meetings and one-on-one. Figure out the official and unofficial pecking order. Be discreet in your observations about one colleague to another: For all you know they are related, dating, married, or divorced. Beware of making comments when you think no one's listening, like in a bathroom, an elevator, or a cafeteria line. The walls have ears.

While office relationships are important, you don't need to bend over backward to connect right away if that's not your style. The most important part of your job is your work. So be as friendly as you really are. If you're the social type, great—reach out, ask people to join you for lunch or for a drink after work. If not, get to know people slowly, accept invitations, and make an effort to attend company events. Try not to hide at your desk.

A note on office etiquette: Remember in third grade when Johnny went around the room delivering valentines or invitations to his birthday party—but not to everyone? You don't have to include the whole office, but don't publicly exclude people. It's mean.

Office Romance

W hile the office may be the most likely place to meet people, workplace relationships are dangerous. If they pan out, that certainly provides motivation to show up to work! But if they don't, you're stuck seeing your ex every single day and watching him establish new relationships. (That's one form of torture not monitored by Human Rights Watch.) Worse, you could be jeopardizing your job. It all depends on the company and on the context, but in general, proceed with caution. A few tips:

▶ Check the employee handbook. Many offices actually have rules against interoffice relationships. Is it worth getting fired?

▶ Be very, very careful about dating a subordinate or a boss. In the first case, you could be opening yourself up to a sexual harassment suit; in the second, to allegations of favoritism. Are you willing to risk your job over this person?

▶ Don't allow yourself to get so distracted that your work starts slipping.

▶ Don't flaunt the relationship in public. (It should go without saying, but don't get physical at the office.) On the other hand, there's no need to go overboard in an attempt at discretion. Taking separate elevators and ducking behind potted palms will just provide more grist for the rumor mill.

▶ Don't use company phones or e-mail to conduct your relationship. Assume your private love notes will go public.

▶ Don't flirt at the office. If you're interested in someone, take it off-site.

▶ Don't use the office as your dating pool. It's one thing to meet someone at the office, and it's another to date every new hire in accounting. Reputations develop at the speed of light—protect yours.

HOLIDAY PARTIES AND OTHER SOCIAL EVENTS

▶ Oh, the infamous holiday office party! How many movies have exploited its comic potential? Office parties and other work-related social events can be great fun (or, let's face it, horrendously boring), but that fun can sometimes have consequences. Whether it's a matter of passing up the karaoke or saying no to that last glass of rum punch, it's in your best interest to keep your wits about you. Yes, you want to relax and talk to people, but you don't want to jeopardize your reputation by drinking too much, talking too much or too personally, singing or dancing with too much abandon, or engaging in public displays of affection.

Being a Good Colleague and Employee

Being a good colleague is like being a good roommate, friend, partner, or family member; an office is shared space, and you are part of a community. Being a good employee is somewhat more complicated. But keep the following rules in mind, and you'll be well on your way to becoming *both*.

Take Initiative

I ONCE TALKED TO AN EMPLOYEE ABOUT TAKING INITIATIVE, thinking ahead, and anticipating needs. I cited my boss's assistant, who did things like calling hotels to request extended checkout when she suspected he would be running late. The next day my assistant said, "I thought about everything you said about initiative, and I get it. I just have one question: How do I know when to take it?"

Though that wasn't the brightest response, I do have a few things to say on the topic. Initiative is highly valued in the workplace, but too much initiative can get you into trouble. You've got to get the lay of the land and a sense of the personalities around you before you start redesigning the company. Communicate your ideas and see what kind of response you get: "I started drafting an agenda for tomorrow's meeting based on what we discussed. Would that be helpful to you?" Don't be offended if the boss says she doesn't need it, but half the time I'm guessing she'll be delighted. Definitely ask before you embark on any time-consuming projects of your own design.

There are small ways to take initiative, too: e-mailing your boss with information you've come across that relates to projects she's working on, reminding her about a colleague's birthday. Be a team player: Take initiative in ways that benefit your whole group, not just your boss. Be helpful even when your efforts won't be recognized. Especially when you're new, volunteer to pitch in and take on those jobs nobody wants. Clean up after the breakfast meeting, take minutes, figure out how to work the projector.

Don't Be a Prima Donna

I HEARD A STORY ABOUT A YOUNG WOMAN who quit her first job on the spot when someone asked her to change a lightbulb. I was not impressed:

When I was thirty years old I was picking dead mice off the floor at a nonprofit.

While I hope you won't have to deal with rodents, I urge you to always clean up after yourself. Don't leave messes for the janitor or cleaning crew. If you break or spill something major, leave a note or tell someone—don't just run for the hills.

If you break glass or need to throw out chemicals, take precautions. Find out where the remnants should go and take the necessary steps. A custodian at a former workplace of mine sliced his arm open when someone threw broken glass in a trash barrel without wrapping it or leaving a note—an innocent mistake, but a thoughtless one with consequences.

If you eat at your desk or use the office kitchen, clean up after yourself. Be blameless when using the office bathroom. Change the toilet paper if you use up the roll, and check to make sure you've left the place clean.

When you use something up or a machine you're using breaks, don't just walk away. Refill the printers and copy machines! If they jam, try to fix them, and get help if you can't.

Be Discreet

DON'T AIR YOUR DIRTY LAUNDRY AT WORK. It's a small world. The colleague you confide in could end up being your boss one day. Does everyone need to know how you kicked your addiction or recovered from a serious eating disorder? Leave your personal problems, past and present, at home. I once had to fire an intern who not only came in late every day and mishandled every task she was assigned but tried to excuse herself by telling me how hungover she was, how late she'd been out, and how she was on a new combo of antidepressants. Another confided that he was an alcoholic as an explanation for some erratic behavior. (We recommended counseling and had to let him go.)

> Does everyone need to know how you kicked your addiction or recovered from a serious eating disorder? Leave your personal problems, past and present, at home.

If you ignore my advice because you feel you simply must have a confidante at work, don't use your boss! No matter how friendly you become, you shouldn't lose sight of the fact that your relationship is professional. There's a difference between friendly conversation and personal revelations. Know that sometimes bosses try to get intimate with their employees as a way to make them feel more comfortable, or because of what's going on in their own lives—I've heard plenty of stories about assistants becoming de facto therapists for their bosses. This isn't right. But take the high road. Keep your private life private. Disclose as much information as you feel you need to in order to satisfy your boss, but keep your emotional life and romantic crises to yourself.

Respect the Hidden Hierarchies

IF YOU WANT TO GET AHEAD AT WORK, it's not enough simply to report to your boss and do what you're told. You need to make it your goal to learn as much about the company as possible. That includes getting to know people from different departments and understanding reporting hierarchies, both formal and informal.

Obviously, the most important hierachy to understand is the one that involves you. To whom do you report? While you may have been hired by the manager of your department, it's possible that on the job you'll report to his associate. But you'll also want to determine who needs to be cc'ed on what e-mail and to whom you should bring particular issues. Is there a company directory listing titles and department heads? If not, you'll have to figure it out by watching and listening. Keep in mind that titles aren't everything: Two people with the same title may have very different jobs or levels of authority, depending on their seniority.

Listen + Learn

ESPECIALLY WHEN IT COMES TO NEW SITUATIONS, I'm a big believer in the expression "With two ears and one mouth, you should hear twice as much as you say." In meetings, listen. It's fine for you to have and express an opinion, but hang back a bit at first. Don't be the person who just loves to hear himself talk—while other people roll their eyes. As my grandfather used to say, don't be the person who states the obvious with a sense of discovery. If you do speak up, be humble: **"I may not understand the bigger picture yet, but it occurs to me that . . ."** Better to keep quiet and ask questions of or share ideas with a colleague after the meeting than make a fool of yourself in public.

A note on challenging the status quo: When you're new, you may feel you're able to bring a fresh eye to problems or situations to which others are blinded by force of habit. But do your research before proposing any changes. It could be that your big idea was thought of and nixed months ago. There may be background you're unaware of. Yes, some default routines and procedures should probably be challenged—but it could all be much more complicated than you imagine.

Be Humble + Helpful

SHOW DEFERENCE TO YOUR ELDERS and to those who have been at the company for longer than you have. I once asked an assistant to check some information in the database for me. "You should really learn how to use it," he said. I suggested a better answer would have been, "Sure, I'll get the information. If you're not familiar with the database, would you like me to give you a tutorial sometime?" His response added insult to injury: "I don't have time for that—I'm really busy!"

Who isn't busy? (Well, maybe not you, yet—but you'll soon find out how much *stuff* there is to do in the work-world.)When someone asks for help, regardless of whether it's your direct supervisor or not, you need to step up. Besides the importance of being a team player, as a junior person you are in fact "junior" to almost everyone in the company. Yes, it may be annoying to fetch a package or two for the flaky executive who can't be bothered to ask her own assistant, but just do it. In my experience, good office karma never goes to waste. If the request really seems unreasonable, make an attempt to steer the asker to someone more appropriate. If you feel someone is routinely abusing your time, talk to your boss.

> Yes, it may be annoying to fetch a package or two for the flaky executive who can't be bothered to ask her own assistant, but just do it. In my experience, good office karma never goes to waste.

Don't Play the Blame Game

REMEMBER WHAT I SAID ABOUT NEGATIVITY DURING THE JOB HUNT? It doesn't stop there. Negativity is toxic to the workplace—actually, it's contagious. One negative person can bring down the morale of an entire team. Don't be that person. Pessimism impedes your ability to get your work done: While a negative person will see situations as doomed from the start, focusing energy on diverting blame, a more productive mind-set seeks solutions.

Keep this mantra in mind: Don't place blame, offer solutions. Rather than saying, "Well, the budget for this project was insufficient to begin with, so there really wasn't much we could do," be the problem-solver: **"When I realized our budget and mission weren't in line, I reexamined the scope of the project and found we could cut costs in the following ways."**

What if there actually is a problem, and it's with a colleague who's not pulling her weight? Remember: Don't place blame, offer solutions. First try speaking directly to the colleague. Don't be accusatory. Offer guidance or a suggestion for a better division of labor, perhaps one you feel might be better suited to your colleague's talents or proclivities: **"I'm thinking we should be more organized about things the next time we tackle such a project. What if I handle the invoices and you take on the outreach?"**

If that doesn't work, seek help from a supervisor or another colleague. It's delicate, though. You want to convey the situation without looking like a tattletale or as if you're shirking responsibility. Accept ultimate accountability. "I'm sorry the project was late. I assumed Jack had gotten the figures I needed from our Dallas office, but I never checked back. When I needed them and found out he didn't have them, it was too late."

Blow Your Own Horn, but Not Too Loudly

IF YOU'RE NOT IN A PARTICULARLY HIGH-PROFILE POSITION, you're going to need to do your own PR. If you have good news about a project you've worked on, share it in an e-mail to your supervisor or team. But make sure you don't try to take all the credit for a collaborative effort— thank everyone who helped. I've seen plenty of young upstarts, but I've also seen people be too self-effacing for their own good. Don't assume your boss will remember that you were the one who closed the big deal. Slipping in a subtle reminder never hurts.

Spread the Good Word

SHARE GOOD NEWS ABOUT OTHERS AS WELL. If you hear good professional or personal news from a colleague, say congratulations and ask if it's okay to share it: "Samantha is too modest to tell you, but one of her articles has just been published. I have a copy if anyone would like to see it."

If you hear praise about an employee from a supervisor, you might repeat the compliment: **"I don't know if Andy has told you directly, but he couldn't be more pleased with the report you did and he couldn't stop talking to me about it."** Often people don't remember to offer positive feedback when things are done well; it's easier to pick on what's wrong.

What if a colleague shares negative information about another colleague? Don't repeat it. Encourage that person to speak directly to the offending party. If he won't, you might try vaguely hinting without giving away too much information: "In a meeting, I heard Bob express some concern about the project your team is working on. You might want to check in with him about the timeline." In short: Contribute to a positive office culture in any way you can.

Don't Say "I Don't Know"

INSTEAD SAY, "I'LL FIND OUT." Writer Nora Ephron has a great piece about a husband who asks "Where's the butter?" He knows perfectly well where the butter is; it's in the little part of the refrigerator marked *Butter*. What he means is, "Bring me the butter!" When your boss asks what's the cheapest way to mail a package to Australia, don't say, "I don't know"; say, **"I don't know, but I'll find out right away. What would you like mailed and when does it need to be there? Should I insure it?"** Try to figure out what your boss is really asking. Is it a question or a request for action? Even if it's a question, the correct answer usually involves "I'll find out."

Late!
Q. What do I do if I'm running late?

A. Call in right away and leave a voice mail if you can't reach your boss in person. If there was something important you needed to get to early in the morning, try to delegate. Call a colleague or intern and see if you can get someone to handle it for you. Make sure you trade home and cell numbers with your boss and close colleagues in case of emergency. At the end of the day, leave things in good enough order so that someone could find information on your desk or on your computer if necessary. (Think files, not piles.)

Pre-Vacation Duties
Q. I'm planning a vacation. How do I prepare things at work?

A. Different companies have different rules about when and how vacation requests should be made. Check your company's policy in advance. Might you be refused if others have requests in? Find out. Don't buy nonrefundable tickets and then ask. Your tickets are not your employer's problem.

Be sure to make things as easy as possible for your boss and any colleagues who may be covering for you. Leave status memos outlining any unfinished business or specific things that need to happen while you're gone, along with contact info for people you deal with regularly. Set your e-mail auto reply and change your outgoing phone messages.

When You Really Mess Up

You will make mistakes. It's a fact. Accept it. Everyone messes up, and everyone new messes up sooner or later.

So now that that's settled, what are you going to do about it? Probably the thing you least want to do. Assuming the mistake isn't easily fixable or inconsequential, go straight to your boss and explain what happened. Apologize and wait to hear what he has to say. He may offer a solution and tell you how to fix the situation, or he may offer to take care of it himself. If he does neither, offer a suggestion as to how you might fix it, and ask if he concurs. And yes, he might berate you. But generally, people are much more forgiving of mistakes than you'd think. (What bosses don't forgive is employees making the same mistakes over and over, making lots of mistakes all over the place, or making mistakes and covering them up.)

Over time, you will develop a sense of when you can dig yourself out of a hole and when you need help and from whom. Everyone makes mistakes—the best thing to learn early on is not to flagellate yourself, but to ask, "What do I need to do to fix the problem right now, to whom should I apologize, what could I have done differently to avoid this situation, and what will I do better next time?"

Taking on Too Much

Q. **I was so proactive about taking things on that I've overdone it. Now I'm afraid I'm going to miss a deadline on an important project. What do I do?**

A. The first time I had to write a grant report, I blew it. I had no idea what to do, didn't want to do it, and went into denial about it, hoping that the unpleasant and hard thing would somehow evaporate and disappear. Needless to say, it didn't go away. I didn't seek help until the end of the day before it was due, putting myself and my boss in a difficult situation. I was embarrassed, she was put on the spot—and the worst part was that it could have been easily avoided with some better communication and forethought.

Don't wait until the very last minute, when it becomes impossible to do anything about it—that's how you create a crisis. As soon as you get an inkling that you're in over your head, tell your supervisor that you're working as hard as you can but are worried about meeting the upcoming deadline: "I'm afraid I've misjudged how long this would take and I need your advice about how to manage the situation." Often things take longer than we think they will. Ask about priorities and whether other projects can wait. Sometimes a supervisor can get extra help or redistribute some of the workload, but understand that you may need to work late and come in early to finish up.

BUILD YOUR PROFESSIONAL PROFILE

▶ Once you've gotten a handle on your *job*, you need to start thinking about your *career*—there's a difference. Thinking about your career involves looking at things through a wider lens. The company you work for is part of a larger industry. As a new member of that industry, you should be taking steps to meet people and raise your profile within the field. Networking never ends. Some ideas:

■ **Join a professional organization.** You may be newly eligible for membership.

■ **Attend professional conferences.** Sign up for professional development sessions and other industry seminars. Those are great ways to meet people, and they'll help you see the way your job fits into the context of the industry as a whole.

■ **Do some alumni outreach.** Once you've been somewhere at least a year, you might offer to lead introductory classes or seminars, or to speak on professional or school alumni panels for those eager to get into the industry.

Create a Portfolio

Don't let all your good work vanish into the stratosphere. As you go along, collect a portfolio of sorts, a record of the quality of your work and the range of tasks you've performed.

Keep copies of reports, press releases, pitch letters, letters to clients, spreadsheets, catalogs and templates you've designed, ads you've created, and so on. If your job doesn't generate an extensive paper trail, get in the weekly habit of reviewing and jotting down your duties and accomplishments. Include any letters or e-mails you receive in praise of your work—if you work for a large company in which HR conducts or participates in performance reviews, have copies placed in your personnel file.

This record will come in handy no matter what your plans for the future. Should you want to move on, it will make it easier for you to update your résumé or craft your cover letter; you'll be better able to ease the way for the person taking over for you; and you'll have something to show prospective employers. If you are staying put and need to argue the case for a promotion or raise, the documentation will support your argument.

CULTIVATE IN-HOUSE MENTORS

▶ If your company has an official mentorship program, take advantage of it—mentors are even more useful on the job than they are during the search. If not, seek out an unofficial mentor. (But don't force it if it doesn't work; finding the right mentor isn't something that happens overnight.)

Another unlikely but good rationale: If your company is bought or you are fired, you may be given as little as twenty minutes to clear out your personal items and leave the premises. While the odds are slim, better to be safe than sorry.

Do be cautious about what kind of information you're taking home: Some documents and realms of information are considered proprietary to the company. Showing them to outsiders could be considered a breach of privacy. Steer clear of anything mentioning company earnings, unannounced future initiatives, or deals in the making.

Professional Development

Wouldn't it be great if we could all have jobs in which every moment of every day was filled with new challenges and exciting breakthroughs? Dream on. Every job involves a certain amount of tedium—that's why they pay you, whereas you pay for things like movies, restaurant meals, and vacations!

That's not to say that you should settle for a plateau in which you learn everything you can in the first year and then keep repeating the same tasks. At a certain point, it becomes *your* responsibility to educate yourself.

Use the resources available to you. Is there part-time education or training that's relevant to your current job or the position you might be promoted to? There are many options—business or other advanced degrees, software and database training, language courses, industry certifications, public speaking courses. Will your company pay for all or part of a program? You need to make the case for how the training would increase your productivity, and you may have to promise you'll stick around for a certain length of time—but it could be worth it.

If the company won't finance your training or if what you want to pursue isn't directly related to your current job, find out if you can enroll in a program part-time. Assuming you're managing your workload, might you be able to leave early or come in late a few days a week if you make up the time? If you're financing professional education yourself, see if you're eligible for grants or scholarships from the institution or from foundations, government agencies, or local social groups like Rotary Clubs or the YMCA.

If you're thinking of moving on from your current job, professional education might be especially relevant to you—don't just assume that you've learned everything there is to learn and it's time to bail. Consider what experience you may need for another job or to enter a new company at a higher level, and actively seek ways to get it. That way you won't move to a new job and start all over again at the bottom of the totem pole.

But most of all, seek informal ways to educate yourself. Gain as much exposure to every aspect of your company as you can. Ask your boss if you can sit in on important meetings. Go on informational interviews—on the inside. Talk to people in other departments and find out what they do. If you think you might be interested in a horizontal move into another area of the company, see if you can get a sneak peek by shadowing someone for a day. The more you know about your company and your industry, even if the information appears to lie outside your direct job, the better.

The Review

A "review" is what they call a report card at work. Though it's not the only form of feedback you'll get, it is likely the basis for raises, bonuses, promotions, and contract renewals. In other words, it should be taken very seriously.

Though you should have discussed the review process during one of your interviews, make sure you understand who's reviewing you, how, and when. Some reviews involve written evaluations, self-evaluations, and checklists;

some are informal conversations. You'll have reviews throughout your career, generally once a year, but your first review will probably occur within three to six months after your start date. If your supervisor doesn't initiate the process for the first review at the agreed-upon time, gently encourage him to schedule a meeting—though reviews may be scary at first, they're valuable.

Take notes. Accept criticism calmly, even if you feel it's off-base. If you feel you need to speak up, provide concrete evidence in your favor: **"I'm sorry you see it that way. I feel I've shown initiative in the following ways . . ."** There's nothing wrong with saying, "I agree, I could have handled that situation better." Nobody's perfect. Ask for suggestions for improvement and a timetable in which you are expected to accomplish goals or changes. If you're asked for a self-evaluation, be positive, but make sure also to note areas for improvement.

> You'll have reviews throughout your career, generally once a year, but your first review will probably occur within three to six months after your start date.

A warning: If you're asked to sign a written record of your review, never do so on the spot. Ask for time to look things over at home. Do *not* sign a negative review, particularly if you feel it's inaccurate or incomplete—you may be signing documentation in preparation for your eventual dismissal, and your signature could revoke your right to unemployment or other compensation.

If you're taken aback by a seemingly negative review, check in with a trusted colleague. Some supervisors are notoriously harsh reviewers, so it may not be as bad as you think. Follow up on any criticism or suggestions you receive. In the months after your review, periodically refer back to the notes you took. If you agreed to make certain changes or pursue certain goals, make a concerted effort to do so. Your next raise, bonus, or promotion may be contingent on the progress you make.

Asking for Raises and Promotions

Many people, young and old, are under the mistaken impression that raises and title changes are automatic—show up every day, do a decent job, and you will be promoted with a salary increase, year after year. But that's not the way it works. In most industries, it takes a lot more.

So how do people get ahead in their jobs? There's no easy answer. It all depends on the industry, the job, the situation, the timing, the person, the financial climate, and many other factors.

The first step to getting ahead is figuring out what it's going to take. What's the general advancement structure in the industry, if there is one? It's possible that you can't be considered for a promotion until a certain amount of time goes by. Do you need to achieve a specific milestone, such as bringing in a client of your own or making a sale? Sometimes people are promoted when they outgrow their jobs—they've essentially started doing the work of a higher-up. (That's why it pays to be proactive and take on new responsibilities.)

Once in a while you'll hear a story about a boss pulling someone aside and saying, "We're so pleased with your work that we've decided to promote you and give you a raise. Congratulations." But more often you hear stories in which employees didn't get raises or promotions unless they asked for them—there's actually research that says people who ask for raises regularly end up making much more money in the long run. Every situation is different. Some bosses will reward employees when the time is right; others may need prodding.

So how do you go about asking? Here's what you don't want to do: Walk into your boss's office unannounced and say, "I think I deserve a raise."

As in a job negotiation, you need to be able to speak concretely and confidently about why the work you have done and the work you can do merits the promotion and pay raise you're suggesting. Be concrete: **"The work I'm doing now and will be doing looks close to what Sarah is doing as a junior manager. I'd like to know what other duties I might take on to warrant that title and that salary."** Or, **"I understand the general raise is a four-percent cost-of-living increase; based on my successful efforts to recruit new clients, restructure the accounting system, and cut costs, I'd like to ask for five percent."** Before you ask, though, check yourself. Do you really deserve a raise? Beware of asking before an appropriate amount of time has passed or before you've proven yourself; you don't want to be perceived as an opportunistic upstart or a blatant self-promoter.

If you *are* offered a raise, find out when it will take effect and check your paycheck or direct-deposit statement to make sure the increase has gone through. (There may not have been proper communication between your boss and HR or Accounting.)

The Art of Moving On

►►►►►►►►►►►►►►►►►►►►►►►►►►►►►►►►►

(WHETHER IT'S YOUR CHOICE OR THEIRS)

I know what you're thinking. "I'm looking for a job! I don't even *have* a job, and you want to talk about moving on?" While it may seem as though I'm putting the cart before the horse, moving on from jobs is part of professional life. People outgrow their positions or find great opportunities in other fields or companies. People get fired or laid off—I hope it doesn't happen to you, but if it does, better to be prepared than panicked.

In the best-case scenario, you'll have a positive experience at your first job—and yet you *will* eventually outgrow it. You'll master the daily routines, you'll know the personalities and how to handle them. You'll no longer feel like the new kid on the block. New people will be coming to *you* to learn the ropes. Ideally, you'll be promoted just when you start to feel stuck. But if a change isn't forthcoming, it might be time to explore something else.

What if things just don't work out at all? After all the hard work you're putting into *finding* a job, it's tough to swallow the notion that your dream job can turn into a nightmare. Though you should approach your new position expecting the best, things happen: Personalities or working styles clash. The job isn't what you'd envisioned. The work you thought you'd love just doesn't do it for you. You feel you're being treated unfairly. The department is being restructured. The company is going under. After careful consideration and a reasonable amount of time, you might need to move on.

In the worst-case (but ultimately not disastrous) situation, leaving is not your choice. You are laid off or fired. This is no fun, but you will recover. Looking back, you may realize that the change—unwanted at the time—ultimately provided an important opportunity.

WHEN YOU GET THE ITCH

▶ If you feel you've learned all you can in your current position, consider whether you might be interested in another job at your current workplace. If you're a valuable enough employee (and I hope you've done all you can toward that end), it's even possible that a job might be created for you. Think about what you'd really like to be doing. If you could take on any aspect of the work you see happening around you, what would it be? With training, is it realistic to imagine yourself doing it? Could you take on these responsibilities in addition to what you're doing now, or would you need to let go of some tasks? (Understandably, you'd like to ditch the most tedious parts of your current job—can you recruit an intern to handle some of this work?)

Don't be afraid to aim high. At a trade show once, a young man approached me and said how much he admired and wanted to work for my company. As far as I knew, no one was leaving or planning to leave, and we had never hired at his level before. But he was persistent. He came in for an informational interview and ended up coming back several more times to meet more of the staff; everyone was highly impressed. Although it took a full year for the pieces to fall into place, we eventually created a position for him.

Time to Leave . . .

S tress on the job is normal, but if the situation becomes extreme, it may be time to start looking elsewhere. One new hire at a think tank found herself staying at the office until nine or ten every night while her bosses took off at five. They'd realized how competent and dedicated she was and had begun dumping all their work on her.

Soon after he started working in a public relations department, a young associate discovered that his boss was not as friendly as she'd been during the interview process. No matter what he did, he couldn't satisfy her increasingly unrealistic demands, and she began yelling at him daily in front of the rest of the staff.

Another recent graduate was hired as a personal assistant to a well-known screenwriter. She knew she'd be at his beck and call, running unglamorous errands all day long, but she would also meet all kinds of celebrities and see what fame looked like from the inside. During the interview, he encouraged her to pursue her own writing and said he'd be glad to help and offer advice. The job sounded too good to be true—and it was. After a few weeks, he told her he was moving his office to his country house, hours from the city—and he expected her to move, too.

Tolerance levels for workplace challenges like temperamental bosses or poor management may vary. Working for someone who makes your daily life miserable can be gut-wrenching—but sometimes it's worth your while to stick it out. Consider the economy. How hard did you have to work to get this job, and how likely are you to get another? I'm not saying you have to stay forever, but quitting with no opportunities in sight may not be the best idea. In any economy, you're going to run into some difficult personalities in the workplace, and in general you should try to learn to deal with them. But if you're being abused or verbally or physically harassed, it's time to go. If there's ever any question of your personal safety, get out right away. You may be concerned about "what it would look like" to leave after such a short time or before you've been promoted, but life is too short to waste your time at a job where you're clearly never going to be satisfied.

It isn't always so cut and dried, though. What happens if your responsibilities aren't what you expected? Or the great guy who hired you is leaving or the company is being sold?

If there's any kind of transition going on, give it time. Companies and their employees often go through periods of turmoil after big changes.

It can be difficult, but sometimes things work themselves out. Wait and watch—don't bail prematurely. You never know: Your job under the new boss could actually be more exciting than the job you were hired for.

If you can't put your finger on the problem but you're feeling extremely unenthusiastic about showing up for work every day, try to ride it out for a while. Every job has its ups and downs, and if you're new to the workforce, you may just need time to adjust to *having* a full-time job—any job. Try to figure out what's making you unhappy, then see if you can find ways to address the problem. If not, start looking for a new job.

> If there's any kind of transition going on, give it time. Companies and their employees often go through periods of turmoil after big changes. It can be difficult, but sometimes things work themselves out.

You might be in a great situation but realize after a year or two that the job has run its course. You know what you're supposed to do, you do it efficiently and well, and your bosses are happy. Why shouldn't they be? This is their ideal situation. Unfortunately for them, this is when an ambitious employee starts thinking about next steps. At a certain point in an entry-level position you'll have "paid your dues" and be ready for a new challenge. If you've asked for and not been granted a promotion in what seems like a reasonable time frame, it may be time to move on.

Setting the Wheels in Motion

I f you've decided to move on but you are planning on staying put while you look for a new job, you're in a good position. You can take your time, you're not as pressured, you appear less desperate, and you have access to a good pool of people and information.

Be very careful about telling people at work that you're thinking of leaving. If you're really close to a few colleagues and feel you must confide in them, go ahead, but don't say I didn't warn you. People talk. You may need to discreetly seek out a colleague or two to serve as a reference, but again, be careful: The worst possible scenario is for your boss to find out you're leaving from someone other than you.

While you're looking, you *must* continue to do your job and do it well. Who knows how long your search will take—you want to make sure you don't damage your relationship with your boss and make things hard for yourself and everyone else by dropping the ball. What if you change your mind midcourse and decide to stay? In any case, you don't want to ruin a good track record by slacking off in the last stretch of the job. Avoid using company phones and e-mail to job-hunt; use your cell phone and personal e-mail address. Don't interview for other jobs during work time. It's fine to take a long lunch or come in early or late once or twice if you give advance notice, but know that astute observers may catch on. (At a small company where I worked in which casual dress was the norm, if someone came in wearing a suit, we assumed she was either looking for a new job or going to a funeral.) If you find it too stressful to take off for an interview on your lunch hour, use personal days or vacation days. Don't call in sick or make up elaborate excuses—it's unprofessional, and people remember that kind of behavior.

Giving Notice

How much notice should you give? The absolute minimum is two weeks, but that's short. Two weeks won't necessarily allow your boss to conduct a thorough search for your replacement, and it leaves no time for you to train a new employee. (Again, not a requirement, but a nice thing if you can do it.)

If your company has an employee handbook, check to see how much notice is required—it may depend on the seniority of your position. If you signed a contract specifying a notification period, you need to honor that. If that's not possible, make sure you come to an agreement with your boss and get the decision in writing.

Some employers like a long lead time so they're able to find and train the ideal replacement.

THE VACATION QUESTION

▶ If you're quitting with unused vacation days, too bad. What I mean is, if it's important to you to use those days, do so before you give notice. If you agree to stay longer than you originally meant to as a favor to your boss, then it may be appropriate for you to take the time, but you're not going to win friends by quitting and then asking, "What about my vacation time?"

It's not unheard of for employees who have good relationships with their bosses to give notice months in advance. This wouldn't make sense if you've been at a job for only a short while, but it might if you've become so indispensable that your departure would cripple your department. Be aware, though, that some employers will assume you'll mentally check out as soon as you've given notice or that you'll infect the rest of the staff with a toxic attitude if you're unhappy. They may prefer that you wrap things up and leave quickly.

A *GOOD* PAPER TRAIL

▶ The nicest thing you can do before you go is to leave your colleagues, successors, and supervisors a good paper trail.

Get a copy of the original job description; update and annotate it with helpful hints for the new person. (Create one if it doesn't exist.) Leave status memos and neat files on all current and future projects, to-do lists, a calendar with upcoming deadlines, and contact information for people with whom you often communicate.

If you're leaving to take another job, your new employer may want you to start immediately. Don't be too quick to bail on your current employer; respectfully remind your boss-to-be that you need to honor your professional commitment. Remember: You don't have to start a job the moment you're given an offer. If you're really urgently needed at your new job, see if you can compromise by starting part-time.

When you're ready to let the cat out of the bag, set up a meeting with your boss and/or HR; don't just accost your superior without prior warning. If you're asked what the meeting is about, you can simply say, "It's about a career move" or "It's about next steps in my career." In the meeting, be direct: "I've accepted an offer as Associate Manager at Brand Co." or "I've decided to leave to pursue other interests."

Stress the positives and offer thanks for the opportunities you've had. If you're asked, "What did we do wrong?" or "What criticisms do you have?" refrain from answering right away. Talk about the new paths you are pursuing; don't let loose with a string of criticisms and don't bad-mouth colleagues. At a later date, depending on your relationship with your supervisor or with someone in HR, you might offer suggestions for things you would have liked to change if you'd stayed.

Let your direct supervisor take the reins on disseminating the news of your departure internally and to clients. Ask her when and how she'd like to go public. Employee departures can be tough on company morale—

there's a risk of a sinking-ship mentality setting in—so bosses tend to be cautious about how they're presented and framed.

Leaving on Good Terms

ONCE YOU'VE MADE THE DECISION TO LEAVE, you want to make sure you do it in the right way and on the best possible terms. It's imperative that you leave on a positive note; you don't want to give people the impression that you no longer care. Even if you were unhappy on the job, this is not the time to show it. You're leaving—you should be happy about that—and you should use this energy to be the best, most upbeat employee you can be during your last few weeks on the job. You never know when you will cross paths with your boss and colleagues again. Remain on your best behavior.

A Change of Staff

Q. I'm happy where I am but the boss I loved is leaving. What do I do now? Should I leave?

A. It depends. A shake-up can be a fast-track to a promotion: Someone who knows the ropes can be indispensable to a new employer. But a new regime could mean you're next in line for the guillotine—the new boss may decide to clean house and get rid of anyone affiliated with the old guard. Have a frank talk with your current boss before he goes. Find out as much as you can about the situation and ask for advice about its implications for you. Get a signed, written reference. If your new boss isn't restructuring the department, try to give him a chance before you decide to leave and cut your losses.

Departure Checklist

DON'T LET THE DOOR SLAM BEHIND YOU JUST YET—you've got some important business to take care of:

- ▶ Set up a meeting with your boss and/or HR. Don't just spring the news on them in passing.

- ▶ Be direct. There shouldn't be any ambiguity about your intentions. Announcing your resignation is one thing; negotiating for a raise or title change is another. Be clear about your goals.

- ▶ Find out whether the company has specific departure procedures. Do you need to write an official letter of resignation, or will verbal notification suffice? Will you have an official exit interview?

- ▶ Offer to help recruit and train your replacement.

▶ Leave your desk and files in better shape than your predecessor left them for you. Clean out your desk and organize your office supplies. Get rid of anything broken or useless. Go through your electronic and paper files and make sure they're easily accessible; throw out anything that's really outdated.

▶ Prepare an exit memo and job description, if applicable. (See box, page 208.)

▶ Gather information and materials you're entitled to take with you—samples of your work, contact information, product samples you can legitimately claim. (No raiding the stockroom or absconding with proprietary information.)

▶ Check into health insurance extensions (COBRA plans), pension plan transfers, and other paperwork.

▶ Schedule an official departure date. Turn in keys and ID.

▶ Send thank-you letters with new contact information to supervisors and close colleagues. Send around an e-mail thanking a wider group of colleagues and offering your new contact information.

▶ Let your professional network know that you've taken a new job.

When It's Not Your Choice . . .

You've seen the pictures and read the headlines. Employees are called into a conference room and told they have ten minutes—under surveillance—to pack their personal items, hand over their keys, and leave the building.

Chances are this won't happen to you. But if it does, it's a good thing you prepared by keeping your work samples. Some companies have employees leave under escort even when it's a matter of a routine layoff—it's hard to predict how a person is going to react to job loss. (Urban legend has it that a prominent financial institution in New York posted a round-the-clock guard on its rooftop terrace before a round of cuts.)

If you think you're being let go unjustly, without cause or prior notice, or that the company is in breach of contract, seek legal counsel. Do not sign agreements or accept severance offers without consulting experts.

Wallow in the anger and sadness if you need to. You might go through the first five of the seven classic "stages of grief": shock, denial, anger, bargaining, and depression. But then you'll be ready for the last two: solution-seeking and acceptance. It will be time to pick yourself up and move on. As a reintegration guide for ex-offenders so succinctly puts it—and this is advice for people likely in more dire circumstances than you— "Employers want to hire your future, not your past." Remember this.

When you job-hunt and talk to others about your situation, do your best to sound upbeat and positive. If you're asked what happened, don't tell a tale of woe and injustice; say "it wasn't a good fit" or refer to "office politics." Beware of talking about a "personality clash"—people who don't know may assume the personality problem was yours. Don't bad-mouth your former boss (even if he was truly nightmarish). If you were laid off, don't tell anyone who'll listen that the company is going under; frame things in terms of "budget cuts" and "belt-tightening."

Keep it short and sweet, and focus on the skills you acquired on the job; I'm guessing you did acquire skills, even if it didn't end the way you imagined it would.

Review your finances to see how many weeks you can afford to job-hunt without taking on temporary employment or freelance work. Try to appreciate the free time you have. Start rereading the chapters of this book you didn't think you'd need for a while. And understand that having to fire or lay someone off is no one's idea of a good time. You may have to do it yourself someday, and maybe you'll remember what it felt like to be on the other side of the desk.

Do some honest soul-searching and self-assessment. If you were fired because of performance problems, ask yourself whether you really gave it your all. Do you need a new attitude? Was the position or industry just not right for you?

You will worry about references. Reread chapter 5. If you were fired based on a claim of unsatisfactory performance, you won't want to use the boss who fired you as a reference; instead, use a colleague or supervisor who'll speak highly of you. But there's no telling who'll contact your boss on his own. Though there's not much you can do about that, your boss may be bound by company regulation to say nothing other than, "Yes, he worked here."

EARLY WARNING SIGNS

▶ Are you starting to be left out of meetings or major decisions that are normally pertinent to your work? There are several key signs that your job *may* be coming to an end. In and of themselves, none are definitive, but if they're part of a bigger picture, watch out.

If your supervisor is suddenly communicating performance feedback in writing rather than face-to-face—i.e., listing overdue or bungled tasks—pay attention: He may be in the process of creating documentation to justify a firing or layoff. (Don't be paranoid if that's been the norm, though; good supervisors are often explicit in their communication.) If you disagree with anything that's been put in writing, address it in writing, including a copy of your supervisor's original e-mail. Print and save all such communication in case it's your word against your supervisor's. Same goes for verbal feedback: Take notes during and after any conversations.

In the larger scheme of things, note the discourse in meetings: If there is talk about cutting back, belt-tightening, rising costs, or lagging sales, there may be layoffs ahead.

Collecting Unemployment

Every state has different guidelines, but in general, if you have been employed at a company for a year or longer and are fired or laid off, you are entitled to several months of unemployment benefits. The amount you'll get is based on a percentage of your salary, often fifty percent, up to a state maximum.

You are not entitled to unemployment if you quit without valid cause; leave due to illness (in which case you should investigate disability benefits); are fired for misconduct or are involved in a labor dispute; or leave for personal reasons such as getting married, going to school, or moving. You must be able to prove that you are seeking employment, sending out résumés, and accepting appropriate positions as offered. Unemployment benefits are taxable, so keep good records.

Contact your state unemployment office to find out the eligibility and reporting requirements for your area. You will be asked for your former employer's contact information and Federal ID number, your salary and dates of employment, your mother's maiden name, and your Social Security and driver's license numbers. File as soon as possible—it can be several weeks before you receive your first check. Find out if you need to go to the unemployment office once a week to collect your benefits or if can you file by dialing in or online. You should also inquire about whether you are able to work part-time, take courses, or freelance while on unemployment.

Reactivate Your Network

If you're leaving a job without a new job lined up, whether by choice or not, get back in touch with your network. Don't assume you need to start from scratch; once you've made a good connection, it should be yours for life if you've been courteous and communicative. Let your contacts know you're looking. No need to highlight the fact that you were just laid off or fired in your cover letters; when someone asks why you are leaving your job, state matter-of-factly, "I was laid off along with ten other employees." If the context of your layoff might help soften the effect, be sure to work it in: "I had just been hired and so was the first laid off" or "I left on very positive terms, and my supervisor has offered to serve as a reference."

Ideally it will be your choice to move on, but even if it isn't, you *can* control how you handle the situation and how you present it to others. You're in charge of the next step. So take charge and move on!

Good Luck!

I'll end with a joke. A man dies and goes to Heaven. He meets an angel, who asks if he has any questions. "Just one," he says. "My whole life, I was a good man. I was honest, good to my customers, good to my family, helped those in need, gave to charity . . . I prayed for only one thing in my whole life—to win the lottery—and my prayer was never answered. Why not?" The angel answers, "The least you could have done was buy a ticket."

I'm not suggesting you buy lottery tickets, but I can tell you this: You definitely won't get jobs you don't apply for. Now it's time to figure out what you want to do, and then figure out who to talk to make it happen. Help people help you. Own your nose ring, literally or figuratively. Find the right job, land it, keep it. Have some fun along the way. Good luck with your first real job.

—Ellen Gordon Reeves
caniwearmynosering@gmail.com
www.caniwearmynosering.com

Index